D0984182

Beyond Bretton Woods

Transnational Institute Series

The Transnational Institute is an independent fellowship of researchers and activists living in different parts of the world, who develop innovative analyses of world affairs.

It serves no government, political party or interest group.

Other titles in the TNI series:

Beyond Bretton Woods

Alternatives to the Global Economic Order

Edited by

**John Cavanagh, Daphne Wysham
and Marcos Arruda**

Pluto Press

LONDON • BOULDER, COLORADO

with

Institute for Policy Studies

and

Transnational Institute (TNI)

First published 1994 by Pluto Press
345 Archway Road, London N6 5AA
and 5500 Central Avenue
Boulder, Colorado 80301, USA

in association with the Transnational Institute
Paulus Potterstraat 20, 1071 DA Amsterdam
and the Institute for Policy Studies
1601 Connecticut Avenue, NW Washington,
DC 20009, USA

97   96   95   94
5   4   3   2   1

Distributed in the Netherlands by the
Transnational Institute

British Library Cataloguing in Publication Data
A catalogue record for this book is available from the British Library

ISBN 0 7453 0890 2 (hbk)

Library of Congress Cataloging in Publication Data
Beyond Bretton Woods: alternatives to the global economic order/
  edited by John Cavanagh, Daphne Wysham, and Marcos Arruda.
   229p. 22cm. — (Transnational Institute series)
   Commemorates the 50th anniversary of the Bretton Woods
agreement, which established the World Bank, the IMF, and the
international banking system.
   ISBN 0-7453-0890-2 (hbk)
   1. International finance. 2. World Bank. 3. International
Monetary Fund. 4. Sustainable development. 5. Economic
history — 1990–   I. Cavanagh, John, 1944–   . II. Wysham, Daphne,
1950–   . III. Arruda, Marcos. IV. Series.
HG3881.B49   1994
332.1'5—dc20   94–20615
                                                                          CIP

Typeset in Stone by Stanford DTP, Milton Keynes
Printed in the EC by TJ Press, Padstow

Contents

Foreword

Susan George

In the late Cretaceous Period, the lower orders held a long-awaited conference entitled 'Beyond the Mesozoic: Alternatives to the Dinosaurs'. Mammalian scholars, activists and some who were both – although all exceedingly small – turned up in large numbers. A collection of remarkably interesting papers, later published in the venerable and prestigious *Jurassic Journal*, was presented, including 'Post-Mesozoicism: Possible Paths to the Cenozoic', 'A Bill of Rodent Rights', 'Ferns Are Not Enough: Towards a Sustainable and Variegated Vegetation for All', 'Pterosaurian Accountability: What Price Prey?' and 'Coping with T. Rex'.

Pleistocene epoch mammals may not, at such a far remove, fully recognize the courage and foresight displayed by a small minority of their tiny, feeble and extremely distant ancestors in organizing such an event. The mammal mainstream had in those times always adopted the position most succinctly described as 'Eat and Let Eat'. 'Never try to interfere with a Terrible Lizard' was their watchword for every occasion. The Saurians were simply more powerful than anybody else, they said, and that had to be recognized once and for all. The best that mammals could hope for was to stay out of their way.

Once in a while, the offspring rebelled against this common parental view because the Saurian Order was so manifestly unjust for the vast majority of creatures. By the time they were off their mother's milk, however, the youngsters had generally accepted the conventional wisdom. The very notion that there could be 'Alternatives to the Dinosaurs' made most mammals snicker or sneer. Thus any endeavour looking 'Beyond the Mesozoic' was truly a landmark for the period.

The *Proceedings* of the conference make for lively reading; they also reveal a certain dissension among the phyla. Chiroptera did not take the same line as Dermoptera, who themselves disagreed with the Rodentia. Despite the conference Chair's repeated remonstrations to the effect that 'We mammals have got to stick together', participants representing a surprising number of species were at odds with each other on their analysis of the whole question of dinosaurs and thus in their strategies for dealing with them.

They quarrelled, for example, over the eternally vexed question of carnivores versus herbivores. Should mammals attempt to oppose both sorts of dinosaurs or only the carnivorous ones that actually ate them? Could herbivorous mammals ever hope to make mutually beneficial arrangements with plant-eating dinosaurs, or would the latter always revert to type, siding with their own kind, carnivores included, when the chips were down?

Even those mammals who believed that on principle they should steadfastly struggle against both the 'Meaties' and the 'Grassies', as they liked to call them in their lighter moments, debated endlessly how best to do so. Whatever their noble principles, how could a bunch of insignificant and minuscule animals possibly take on these huge beasts in practice? The balance of forces was absurdly unequal – anybody could see that.

As the conference proceeded, some shrill voices were raised. In one plenary session, the more combative shrews shrieked that talk and debate were all very well but meanwhile the existing system was crushing everyone except for – here knowing looks were directed at the bats – a tiny, privileged minority that could fly. The bats complained loudly to the organizers of discrimination – they deeply resented being singled out on grounds of anatomical difference and besides, had the shrews never heard of pterodactyls and other flying Saurians? The shrews, however, were nearly proven right when a plodding diplodocus just missed annihilating the conference site as he lumbered into a river on whose banks the delegates had assembled.

Although present at every session, some participants maintained that holding the conference at all was a complete waste of time. As one particularly pessimistic (and boring) lemur never tired of repeating, 'Dinosaurs run everything, they always have and they always will.' His view – he was not alone – was that mammals should concentrate on building larger and more evenly spaced sanctuaries. Confrontation with the Saurians was not even to be contemplated.

The more analytical and strategically minded rodents asked their fellow mammals simply to step back and think coolly about the balance of power. 'Dinosaurs,' they said, 'are big, for sure, and some of them are fast, but Holy Volcano are they dumb! Not for nothing is "Brontosaurus Brain" the worst insult you can level at a rat. We have to start analysing their vulnerabilities and our own capacities – for instance, we could maybe raid their nests, destroy their eggs, whatever. But we'd have to be unified, with well-disciplined ground, sea and air forces. Think about it.'

The majority still felt that military solutions were impractical or simply wrong and their spokesanimals tended to pontificate: 'We must either win by non-violent means or gain at best a hollow victory.' Many also asserted that the dinosaurs could gradually be brought to change their behaviour, through persuasion and counter-example, If it were made clear, really clear, to them how much damage they were causing, surely they would be converted and mend their ways. The mammals on this side of the argument presented the conference with a carefully constructed set of case studies documenting dinosaur-induced damage in detail. Naturally T. Rex and the raptors got most of the attention, but the more mild-manner stegosauri and triceratops came in for their share of criticism as well, particularly with regard to hogging the food supply.

As the conference proceeded, a disparate coalition of forward-looking mammals – a bat and a rat here, a lemur and a shrew there – began to emerge. These creatures found a bond in their common interest in a post-dinosaur world which they, alone among the conference participants, had the courage even to consider. 'Rank speculation!' 'Dangerous Utopianism!' the other animals squeaked whenever the ISC (the Inter-Species Caucus) attempted to place its motions on the floor. The ISC, however, remained convinced that planning for a world without Terrible Lizards was a rational animal activity even if most of their fellows could not even conceive of such a time or place. They looked to a future when all species could live together in harmony, without fear of being starved or trod upon.

Towards the end of the event, a single creature, who later turned out to be the ancestor of the hedgehog, timidly raised his paw. 'If it please the conference,' he said, 'could we not consider the possibility of divine intervention or of sheer ecological collapse? The dinosaurs are abusing our common home. They only care about their own power and they are taking too much from our world. They leave almost nothing for the smaller, weaker creatures and they trample us and our offspring as well. I believe that one day the Holy Volcano will refuse them their privileges and punish them. Then we shall come into our own.' The proto-hedgehog was laughed off the site, dismissed as a visionary and a fanatic.

Even in the late Cretaceous, however, history was quirky and unpredictable. Just as the mammals were dispersing, volcanoes the length and breadth of the earth began ominously to rumble. The Inter-Species Caucus immediately called an emergency all-species consultation on post-dinosaur measures. And a few turns around the sun later, the asteroid stuck.

Notes on Contributors

Marcos Arruda, an economist and educator, is the coordinator of the NGO Working Group on the World Bank, and a Fellow of the Transnational Institute.

Richard J. Barnet is a co-founder of the Institute for Policy Studies and co-author of *Global Dreams: Imperial Corporations and the New World Order* (Simon & Schuster, 1994).

Walden Bello of the Institute for Food and Development Policy in San Francisco is co-author of *Dark Victory: The United States, Structural Adjustment and Global Poverty* (1994).

Robin Broad, co-author of *Plundering Paradise: The Struggle for the Environment in the Philippines* (1993), is a professor in the School of International Service at The American University in Washington, DC.

Robert S. Browne is former staff director of the House Subcommittee on International Finance, Development, Trade and Monetary Policy, and a former executive director at the African Development Fund.

John Cavanagh, a TNI Fellow at the Institute for Policy Studies, is co-author (with Richard J. Barnet) of *Global Dreams: Imperial Corporations and the New World Order* (1994).

José Luis Coraggio, An Argentinean, is Director of the Instituto Fronesis (Ecuador). He is author of numerous articles and several books, including: *Ciudades sin Rumbo; Desarrollo Humano, Economia Popular y Educacion; Economia Popular y Politicas Sociales* (forthcoming).

Herman E. Daly was a Senior Economist in the Environment Department of the World Bank from 1988–1994, and is currently a Senior Research Scholar at the University of Maryland School of Public Affairs. He is co-author (with John Cobb) of *For the Common Good* (Beacon, 1989).

Susan George is an Associate Director of the Transnational Institute and author of several books on the World Bank and IMF, most recently (with Fabrizio Sabelli) *Faith and Credit* (Penguin, 1994).

Richard Gerster is the Director of the Swiss Coalition of Development Organizations.

Luis Carlos Delorme Prado Goncalves is a consultant of PACS-PRIES (Institute of Alternative Policies for the Southern Cone of Latin America) and Reader in Economics, at the Fluminense Federal University, Rio de Janeiro.

Reinaldo Goncalves is a member of PACS-PRIES and Full Professor of International Economics at the Federal University of Rio de Janeiro.

Alfred Gugler is a researcher for the Swiss Coalition of Development Organizations Debt-For-Development Unit.

Douglas Hellinger is the Managing Director of the Development Group for Alternative Policies and co-author (with Stephen Hellinger and Fred O'Regan) of *Aid for Just Development* (Lynne Reinner, 1988).

Stephen Hellinger is Executive Director of the Development Group for Alternative Policies and co-author (with Douglas Hellinger and Fred O'Regan) of *Aid for Just Development* (Lynne Reinner, 1988).

Smitu Kothari co-edited *Rethinking Human Rights: Challenges for Theory and Action* and *The Non-Party Political Process: Uncertain Alternatives*. He is currently working on a book on the Narmada River for Penguin Books.

Michael Shuman is the Director of the Institute for Policy Studies.

Lori Udall, formerly an attorney with the Environmental Defense Fund, is the Washington representative of the International Rivers Network.

Myriam Vander Stichele is a Fellow with the Transnational Institute.

Howard M. Wachtel is a Professor of Economics at The American University in Washington, DC, and a Fellow at the Transnational Institute.

Peter Weiss, an international lawyer, is a member of the Board of Advisers of the Transnational Institute.

Daphne Wysham is a Research Fellow at the Institute for Policy Studies and former editor of the Greenpeace magazine.

Introduction: From Bretton Woods to Chiapas

John Cavanagh, Daphne Wysham and Marcos Arruda

In this century, people have proven far more adaptable to rapid change than have institutions. People around the world celebrated the end of half a century of Cold War and the secretive, adversarial climate it had spawned. Public support for a massive shift in government priorities towards a dismantling of war systems was strong and widespread. Yet many Cold War institutions, particularly the larger bureaucracies, have proven immune to transformation. So it has been with two of the largest 'development' bureaucracies in the world, the World Bank and the International Monetary Fund.

The Bank and Fund were conceived half a century ago in July 1944 in the sleepy mountain town of Bretton Woods, New Hampshire. Two years later, they opened their doors for business in Washington, DC, just as World War Two ended and the Cold War began. They have since evolved into two of the most powerful vehicles for the ideology and development policies of the side that would eventually be declared the 'victor' in the Cold War – the capitalist nations of the North.

The pain and suffering generated by the Bretton Woods institutions are immense. They can be measured in the tens of millions of people displaced, impoverished, marginalized and sent to premature death by economic projects and policies that have subordinated human and community values to free markets and growth targets. There have been a few winners, but they are not the people and nations of the South – the ostensible targets of development. The true beneficiaries have been the several hundred large corporations and banks and the several thousand elites of the Third World. Men from the North have been the primary beneficiaries; women and children from the South have fared the worst.

Although the Bank and Fund have been largely ignored by the public in the North, they are publicly endowed institutions and hence the public can use its leverage as taxpayers to change or even to eliminate them. Lacking this public oversight, however, both institutions have allowed their agendas to be twisted by the increasingly powerful designs of large private banks and corporations that have, in the last half of the twentieth century, gone truly global.

For example, when Northern banks received notice in the early 1980s that Brazil, Mexico and other developing countries could not service external debts, the banks and Northern governments empowered the IMF to become the world's financial policeman. New credit from any source was conditional on a debtor country's agreement to an IMF austerity package. Few taxpayers were aware of the increasingly destructive power their taxes were wielding over the South's poor.

Similarly, few taxpayers would guess that the World Bank is now the primary force in restructuring (and, some would say, lowering the standards of) public education in Latin America. Or that it is now the world's foremost salesman of agrichemical products. Or that it is bankrolling massive dams and vast road and electrification projects – projects that become lucrative contracts for other transnational corporations, but that bring hardship and environmental destruction to a majority of the people they are supposed to benefit.

It was only when activists intervened in the early 1980s, linking environmentalists from the North with their partners in the South to expose the most rapacious of Bank policies that the Bank and Fund heard the cry of pain from the South over its policies.[1] At the same time, activists from churches and development organizations were forming 'debt crisis' groups in conjunction with groups in the South to demand debt reduction and fundamental change at the IMF.[2] And as structural adjustment became the universal panacea of the Bank and Fund, groups from the South and North continued to expose its flaws while pushing for alternatives.[3] New notions of 'people-centred' and 'just and sustainable' development were hammered out in hundreds of citizen declarations.[4]

Today, in addition to organized citizen resistance, there are two compelling forces pressing for change. First, almost all governments are in the grip of chronic fiscal crises. Politicians everywhere are looking for programmes to cut; since neither the Bank nor the Fund have large domestic constituencies, they are prime targets for cutting. Second, the policies and projects of the Bank and Fund have failed by almost any criteria – often even by their own.

After fifty years, the Bank and Fund have become grand rhetoricians for change, but their preferred pace of change is glacial. They have yet to indicate that they are willing to get to the roots of the crisis in the Third World.

The fiftieth anniversary of the original Bretton Woods conference offers a unique opportunity to reflect on the impact these institutions have had on the peoples of the world. This book is meant to seize upon this opportunity by offering some provocative ideas for change. The ideas in this book do not add up to a neat package that addresses all the problems; instead, they are meant to stir the debate and dialogue about new paths to the twenty-first century.

However, all the writers do arrive at the same conclusion: the process and institutions which govern the global economy must change. They must be democratized. History shows that more participatory policies and more open and democratic institutions succeed simply because more people have a stake in assuring that they do. The Bank and Fund have failed in large part because they have kept the reins of power in too few hands.

How To Think About Reform

Thousands of discussions and debates will be staged in the years to come about reforming the Bretton Woods institutions. We think it useful to start such discussions with a basic question: what kind of development do we want these institutions to serve?

If you accept the premise of recent US foreign policy that development is measured by economic growth and that the freeing up of markets should guide this growth, then only minor adjustments in the Bank and Fund are needed.

The contributors to this volume reject blind adherence to the principle of free markets. Along with tens of millions of workers, women, consumers, farmers, fisherfolk and urban poor who have organized themselves in citizens' movements across the world, we are struggling with new definitions, new strategies and new notions of development that place ecological sustainability, participation and equity at the centre.

Such new notions of development do not reject market economies. Rather they recognize that most markets are increasingly dominated by large, highly unaccountable global firms that, left to the devices of unregulated markets, play workers, communities and even nations off against one another to obtain the cheapest conditions in which to produce their wares. In this world of stateless corporations, global public institutions that are concerned with finance and with production are surely needed, but they look significantly different from the current World Bank and IMF. And, even a fundamentally reformed Bank and Fund can serve only certain functions. New global institutions and rules in other realms are also needed.

Within the ranks of the critics and advocates for fundamental change, there are a number of areas of agreement that are emerging, but there remain some fundamental debates.

Areas of Agreement

In dozens of countries around the world, citizens' organizations are commemorating the fiftieth anniversary of the Bretton Woods institutions with campaigns for change. Many have rallied around the slogan 'Fifty Years is Enough'.[5] While there are differences in the specificity of demands among some of the campaigns, there is broad agreement on six fronts:

New principles of development The starting point of most groups that pose restructuring and alternatives to the Bank and Fund is a fundamentally different definition of development.

No new funding Most citizens' groups involved in these campaigns are pressuring their governments to stop new funding for these institutions.

Spin off certain functions There is growing consensus among the campaigns and a certain number of legislators that certain functions are better done outside these institutions. These include environmental lending – like that done by the Global Environmental Facility – and the soft-loan facility of the Bank, the International Development Authority (IDA).

A narrowing of functions Most agree that the Bank and Fund should be slimmed down to perform basic economic functions.

An increase in transparency and democracy Most agree that the Bank and Fund (and other multilateral economic agencies), as public institutions, should eliminate the Cold War obsession with secrecy and make vital information public to the peoples who will be affected by their activities. Likewise, independent appeals procedures should be set up so that groups adversely affected by their activities can petition the institutions for change.

Other institutions needed Such major reform of the Bank and Fund would still leave a number of functions unattended in an increasingly privatized and deregulated global economy. New institutions are needed, along with new mechanisms to advance corporate accountability, and worker and environmental rights.

Areas of Debate

Perhaps the most fundamental area where there is still substantial debate among citizens' groups is whether the multilateral economic institutions should have their parameters expanded to include social and environmental criteria. Proponents of this linkage argue that it is precisely institutions like the Bank, the IMF and the General Agreement on Tariffs and Trade that have the clout to enforce fundamental worker and environmental rights. Therefore, this argument continues, we should fight to shift their conditionality away from narrow economic indicators and towards broader social indicators.

Opponents argue that this would simply increase the power of these institutions – to the detriment of other United Nations agencies that currently have the mandate to advance labour rights, the environment and other social issues.

Despite these creative differences at the margins of the debate, by 1994 many groups have coalesced around agendas of fundamental reform of the world economy. Many of their proposals are both more visionary and more pragmatic than those of their predecessors.

Change

Large bureaucracies backed by powerful corporate interests are unlikely to change on their own. Yet the agents of change are many. A number of environmental groups are now global organizations in their own right and their chapters from North and South are coordinating with one another and with other social and political movements to push the reform agenda. Many religious organizations have likewise woven global webs that offer witness to the impact of these institutions. Organizations of women, workers, consumers and development specialists have created a wide range of new partnerships across borders that are inventing new global economic linkages. Some of the most powerful agents of change are courageous bureaucrats who have left these institutions and dared speak truth to power.

Small but important changes have been made. Particularly destructive World Bank loans have been stopped. Bank policy directives have been revised. Public awareness has been raised on heretofore arcane issues of global trade and finance. In another, but related arena, the NAFTA fight of 1993 set an important precedent for the democratization of international economic policy. Millions of people in Canada, the United States and Mexico announced that they were no longer going to step aside and let a narrow band of government bureaucrats and corporations determine the rules under which regional and global integration would take place. So great was their strength that the Clinton Administration literally had to purchase the votes of some members of Congress to ensure NAFTA's passage.

On the day that NAFTA was to go into effect, another group that had been impoverished and marginalized by the kind of development promoted by the World Bank, the IMF and NAFTA said, 'Enough'. As several thousand Indians rose up on 1 January 1994, in Chiapas Mexico, a new kind of movement was launched that rejects deregulated global integration and reasserts that democracy and basic human dignity must be at the centre of the development process.

The fair trade activists of North America, the campaigners against World Bank projects and policies in India, and the Indians of Chiapas offer the outlines of a new breed of social movement. They are creating alternatives to deregulated global integration. They are asserting that aid, trade, investment and other forms of economic integration are not ends in themselves, but can, under the right circumstances, contribute to more just and equitable development. This book offers the wisdom of some of those who have chosen to stand up to the world's most powerful economic institutions and, like the Indians of Chiapas, say, 'Enough!'

Acknowledgements

The editors would like to thank Martin Khor, Bob Debus and Jochen Hippler for advice on this project, and Sarah Anderson and Sarah Williams for their assistance in the final stages of editing. We also thank the Samuel Rubin Foundation, the John D. and Catherine T. MacArthur Foundation, the Unified Church Board for World Ministries and the World Council of Churches for the financial support that made this book possible.

Notes

1 See Bruce Rich, *Mortgaging the Earth* (Beacon Press, 1994) and Susan George and Fabrizio Sabelli, *Faith and Credit* (Penguin, 1994).
2 See Susan George's *A Fate Worse than Debt* (Grove Weidenfeld, 1990) and *The Debt Boomerang* (Pluto Press, 1992); and a Working Group of the Debt Crisis Network, *From Debt to Development* (Institute for Policy Studies, 1986).
3 See Walden Bello *et al.*, *Development Debacle* (Institute for Food and Development Policy, 1982) and Robin Broad, *Unequal Alliance* (University of California Press, 1988).
4 See David Korten, *Getting to the 21st Century* (Kumarian Press, 1990) and Isagani Serrano, *Civil Society in the Asia-Pacific Region* (Civicus, 1994).

5   For more about this campaign in the United States, contact The Development GAP, 927 15th St, NW, Washington, DC 20005, and the Environmental Defense Fund, 1875 Connecticut Ave, NW, Washington, DC 20009. For a calendar of events around the world on the Bank and Fund, contact the Bank Information Center, 2025 I St, NW, Suite 522, Washington, DC 20006.

1

What Kind of Development Should New Global Institutions Serve?

1

Development: The Market Is Not Enough

Robin Broad, John Cavanagh and Walden Bello

As we approach the next millennium, the development debate has all but disappeared in the West. Monumental changes in Eastern Europe and Latin America are widely being interpreted as definitive proof of the superiority of private-sector-led, export-oriented development models. Free market capitalism – it is said – has prevailed because it is the only path that promises growth and democracy for the battered economies of Africa, Latin America and Asia.

Former World Bank President Barber Conable's summation of the 1980s reflects the prevailing view: 'If I were to characterize the past decade, the most remarkable thing was the generation of a global consensus that market forces and economic efficiency were the best way to achieve the kind of growth which is the best antidote to poverty.' Ample evidence exists, however, to offer caution in the face of such triumphalism. Warning signs are apparent in South Korea and Taiwan, the countries widely touted as the miracle models of capitalist development. In South Korea, we met members of a labour force who, after decades of systematic exploitation, erupted in thousands of strikes during the late 1980s, undermining the very basis of that country's export success. In Taiwan, we toured a landscape littered with poisoned soil and toxic water, the legacy of decades of uncontrolled industrial development.[1]

There is evidence that the deep popular discontent we witnessed in parts of Asia exists throughout Latin America, Africa and Asia, where privatized adjustment has been practised for more than a decade. Free-market economics, people there are discovering, invariably concentrates economic power in the hands of the few wealthy exporters, landlords and natural-resource exploiters. As a result, this privatized development path ends up being profoundly undemocratic.

Yet, the World Bank, the International Monetary Fund, and other multilateral institutions have refused to condition their loans on the basic redistribution of land, resources and wealth that would reverse growing inequalities.

The failures of structural adjustment on environment and equity grounds might appear less serious if the adjustment packages were scoring economic successes. They are not. The first World Bank structural adjustment loans were put in place in Kenya, Turkey and the Philippines nearly fifteen years ago; none can be rated a success story today. A United Nations Economic Commission for Africa study has highlighted the World Bank's own findings that fifteen African countries were worse off in a number of economic categories after structural adjustment programmes. Using nine indicators of economic performance, a 1988 World Bank study found that the debt-ridden developing countries under Bank structural adjustment programmes performed as well as non-recipients *less* than half the time.

None of these examples is meant to deny that developing countries need substantial reforms, that governments cannot consistently overspend, or that markets have a role to play. Rather, the lesson of the 1980s and early 1990s is that there are no short-cuts to development. Development strategies will not be viable unless they incorporate ecological sustainability, equity and participation, as well as effectiveness in raising material living standards.

Experience indicates that countries focusing on any of these principles to the exclusion of others will fail in the longer run. The World Bank and the IMF, either by ignoring these first three principles in their structural adjustment reforms or, at best, by treating them as afterthoughts, have adjusted economies to the short-term benefit of narrow elite interests. Their fixation on high gross national product growth rates ensures that the costs in terms of democracy and resources will mount and overwhelm an economy at a later date, much as they have in South Korea and Taiwan.

The Not-So-Silent Revolution

Out of this generalized failure of development models, there is a very different kind of consensus emerging among people with whom the development establishment seldom interacts and whose voices are not typically heard. A new wave of democratic movements across Latin America, Asia and Africa is demanding another kind of development. In citizens' organizations of workers, farmers, women and environmentalists, millions of people are saying that they want to define and control their own futures. They are beginning to lay the groundwork for a new type of development in the 1990s – one that emphasizes ecological sustainability, equity and participation, as well as improving the lives of the majority of people.[2]

All around the world, we witnessed popular organizations taking on ecological destruction, unequal control of resources and land, and the ineffectiveness of governments in advancing the quality of life. Often they were doing so in the face of government and military repression. Many citizens' groups were pushing for development strategies in which people were central, and discarding development models that measured success solely in terms of growth. At the core of almost all of these movements we found a profound respect for popular participation in initiating and implementing plans and, more generally, a greater effort to exercise control over their own lives. Hence, in a very real sense, democracy is the central theme in development as defined by these movements in the South.

A 58-year-old tenant farmer in the Philippine province of Bataan was among those who taught us about participatory and democratic development. We visited this man's small hut, in the middle of the one hectare of land he tilled – but did not own. He showed us the water buffalo that he fed each morning at 4am – but likewise did not own. He was poor. His family was poor. His children and their children lacked food, clothes, educational opportunities and land to till or alternative employment options. But this man did win election to office in the local peasants' organization. And his eyes brightened when he described his peasant organization, the demands for which it was fighting and the speeches he had given as part of it. This organization had not yet brought much to this farmer in material terms. Yet it had given him an opportunity to participate in the process of fighting for a better life for his children. According to our calculations, some five million Filipinos participate in such citizens' groups. Across the developing world, estimates Alan Durning of the Worldwatch Institute, more than 100 million people belong to as many as several hundreds of thousands of these organizations.[3] Official development organizations have difficulty taking these groups seriously and act as though they have little bearing on national development strategies. Our research suggests the opposite: it is from the programmes and experience of these grassroots groups that new development strategies of the 1990s and beyond will emerge.

Over the course of the past decade, many of the most vibrant of the organizations with visions of another kind of development have been born in battles over the destruction of natural resources. This is certainly the case in the Philippines, where the whole gamut of citizens' groups is raising ecological issues as the basis of sustainable development. This is not surprising since, by some estimates, the destruction of forests and other natural resources in the Philippines is occurring at an unparalleled rate.

Philippine villagers guided us up bald mountains that were covered with lush forests half a generation ago. Farmers showed us the path their precious topsoil had taken when rains carried it down the hills and into the river below. Fishermen paddled us out to coral reefs – dead and dying – destroyed by a combination of siltation and get-rich-quick fishing methods. As the trees and reefs fall, they explain, so do their yields, be they of fish, corn or rice.

But out of the Philippines' eroding soil and crumbling reefs, dozens of environmental groups have sprung up, many with farmers and fisherfolk at their core. One of the largest and most influential is Haribon (from the Filipino words 'king of the birds', in reference to the endangered Philippine eagle), which matured in a battle to save Palawan, an island which hosts the country's most extensive tropical rain forests. A local citizens' group in Palawan has evolved into a Haribon chapter and has taken on the wealthy logger whose forest concessions control sixty-one per cent of Palawan's productive forests. Among other things, Haribon has launched a nationwide campaign to gather a million signatures to save Palawan's forest. It has also joined with several hundred other Philippine organizations to launch a Green Forum coalition that is working towards equitable and sustainable development.

The rape of the forests has stimulated protests in other countries. In Sarawak, Malaysia, indigenous peoples have blockaded timber destined for export markets in Japan and Europe. Greenbelt movements, organized by women, are trying to reclaim parts of urban Kenya and Mozambique for vegetable gardens, while educating women about traditional, sustainable agro-forestry techniques. In Thailand, peasants in the poor Northeast region, evicted from communal forest lands by companies intent on planting industrial tree plantations, are fighting back. In the words of one observer:

> [There] has been an explosion of rural activism unprecedented in the Northeast [of Thailand] since the mid-1970s. Small farmers are standing up to assassination; ... marching; rallying; blocking roads; ripping out seedlings; chopping down eucalyptus trees; burning nurseries; planting fruit, rubber and forest trees in order to demonstrate their own conservationist awareness; explaining to newspapers the methods by which they have preserved their local forests for generations; ... Their message is simple ... They want community rights to local forests which they will conserve themselves.[4]

In numerous other countries, organizations have sprung up to battle the mega-projects that were often the centrepieces of debt-financed, export-oriented development. In 1989, 60,000 tribal people, landless labourers and peasants gathered in Harsud, India, to protest the partially World Bank-funded Narmada dam project that would inundate the town under fifty feet of water.[5] That same year, on the other side of the world, Brazilian Indians from forty tribal nations gathered to oppose construction of several hydroelectric dams planned for the Xingu River. Soon thereafter, Indians, rubber tappers, nut gatherers and river people formed a coalition to save the Amazon called the Alliance of the Peoples of the Forest.

By the onset of the 1990s, thousands of organizations across the developing world were taking on timber companies, unsustainable agriculture, industrial pollution, nuclear power plants and the giant projects that many government technocrats equated with development. Part of what has made their actions something that should capture the attention of the development community is that the focus of their battle has expanded to challenge powerful entrenched interests, inequitable structures and the national development model itself.

In many countries, movements have arisen to address inequalities in another sphere, the control of land. Most developing countries remain predominantly rural and characterized by extremely unequal distribution of land. The Philippines, in the words of land reform experts Roy Prosterman and Timothy Hanstad, 'has one of the worst land-tenure problems still found on our planet'. Successive governments have refused to implement a serious land reform.

Frustrated by government inaction on the land issue, a coalition of dozens of peasant organizations, totalling a million and a half members, gathered tens of thousands of signatures for their alternative People's Agrarian Reform Code. This code, based on peasant enforcement, would cover all lands, abolish rampant absentee landownership and offer support services to peasants acquiring land. In the face of a scandal-ridden 1988 government land reform bill, the peasants have taken steps to implement the reform on their own.

Inequities of yet another sort – of income – are at the centre of growing independent workers' movements, from Brazil to South Korea, from South Africa to the Philippines. In Brazil, the workers' movement spent part of the 1980s building the most dynamic political party in the country. As a result, in the final weeks of the 1980s, a Brazilian metalworker came within four percentage points of the presidency of the developing world's second most populous nation.

In addition to ecology and equity, many people's organizations have acted or focused on the lack of effectiveness of government programmes in addressing those most basic human needs and rights outlined in the United Nations International Covenant on Economic, Social and Cultural Rights: the rights to 'adequate food, clothing and housing'. All over the world, informal economic institutions have sprung up to fill the economic void left by cuts in government spending. Development analysts Sheldon Annis and Peter Hakim have filled a book, *Direct to the Poor*, with examples of successful worker-owned businesses, transportation collectives, peasant leagues, micro-enterprise credit associations and other citizen initiatives across Latin America.[6] Africa specialist Fantu Cheru refers to such groups in Africa as participants in a 'silent revolution':

> From Lusaka to Accra, large numbers of people are engaging in the parallel economy to satisfy their basic human needs because of the collapse of the formal economy. The need to survive has required the resuscitation of rural co-operatives, traditional caravan trade across borders, catering services and other activities that had once fallen into disuse.[7]

Other groups focus directly on pushing governments to meet people's needs. Human rights and anti-militarism groups the world over have pointed out that the only realm in which many governments are effective is repression. They stress that between 1960 and 1987, developing countries spent almost US$2.4 trillion on military expenditures, a sum greater than what they channelled into education and health combined.[8] This figure is also almost twice the total cumulative size of today's Third World debt. Calls by citizens' groups to reduce repressive activities are often coupled with publicizing government corruption, cronyism and support for special private interests. Increased accountability of corporations, multilateral institutions and governments has become central to the demands of many citizens' groups in the Philippines and elsewhere.

The point here is not simply that there is a groundswell of grassroots activity across the Third World. The point is that this activity adds up to a different kind of development.

National Development Strategies

The widespread protests by people against governments are a reflection of how few governments are accountable to their citizens – and of how much things need to change across the developing world. Yet, the 1990s hold the possibility that such citizens' coalitions will compete for government power in certain countries. During the 1970s, revolutionary movements with socialist agendas carried new governments into power in Vietnam, Cambodia, Laos, Angola, Mozambique, Guinea Bissau and Nicaragua. Might the upcoming decade see coalitions of citizens' organizations creating governments with sustainable development agendas in Brazil, South Africa, the Philippines and elsewhere – much as they ushered new governments into Eastern Europe in 1989?

Even in countries where such coalitions do not actually take over the reins of state power, their influence on governments is likely to be felt during the 1990s. It may, for instance, be through innovative citizens' groups reaching out to build links to segments of bureaucracies and even militaries that express openness to the sustainable development agenda.

However, new and more accountable governments ought not to be seen as a panacea. Governments, even popular governments, should not be looked upon as the answer to the wide array of development problems. Rather, the continued vibrancy of people's organizations will always be central to sustainable development. This said, governments do have important roles to play in transforming sustainable development initiatives into a national reality, in particular in three areas. Governments can help build up an economic infrastructure and an internal market; create a network of social services; and set the rules for a country's integration into the world economy.

We purposely reject the role of offering another universal model to replace those of free marketeers, socialists or the World Bank – the past four decades are littered with the failures of universal models. However, on the basis of respect for the principles of ecological sustainability, equity, participation and effectiveness, we can sketch the outlines of a more positive government role in development.

With respect to the ideal government role in the economy, South Korea and Taiwan offer some positive lessons. The main lesson is not that the government should be taken out of the economy, but that a strong government standing above vested interests is essential to create the social and political infrastructure for economic growth. Indeed, though this may sound paradoxical, one needs an effective government to create the market.

The problem in many developing countries is not too much government but that the government is too enmeshed in the web of interests of narrow groups in civil society. For instance, for all intents and purposes the Philippine government serves as the private property of special economic interests. In South Korea, on the other hand, the weakness of the landed and business elite allowed the government to set the direction for development in the 1960s and 1970s. Without an effective government that in many instances went against the wishes of international agencies and the hesitations of big business, the foundation of heavy and high-tech industries that enabled South Korea to become a world-class exporter of many high value-added commodities would never have been laid.

If strong, independent governments can help push economies through early stages of development, the advance to more mature economies seems to require more market signals for effective production and distribution. For market mechanisms to work, however, one must first have a market. And, for most of the developing world, the only possibility of creating a market of consumers possessing effective demand is to eliminate the severe inequalities that depress the purchasing power of workers and peasants. The 'how to' list here requires government action – through such steps as land reform, progressive taxation and advancement of workers' rights. Governments likewise must take the lead in redistributing natural resources away from the few towards community control and management of those resources.

Turning to integration in the world economy, pragmatism is essential. The choice is not an ideological one between import substitution and export-oriented growth, neither of which alone has generated anything close to sustainable development. Building development dreams on the export of prawns or minerals and the plunder of forest resources is not only unsustainable, it fails to ask the more fundamental question of whom the development is to benefit. But building an export base on top of a strong internal market does make sense. Though the long-term results varied, South Korea, Taiwan, India and China all based their early industrial development on slowly building up the real incomes of their domestic populations. Each opened up to the world market, at different speeds and to differing degrees, only after substantial domestic markets had already been developed and nurtured.

A few development specialists have offered useful advice on the logical sequence of steps that governments might follow in pursuing the various components of sustainable development. Perhaps the most relevant to the principles we have outlined is development expert David Korten's six-stage approach to sustainable development: strengthening the educational and legal systems and guaranteeing free speech and assembly; redistributing land, resources and assets;

diversifying and democratizing agriculture; pursuing rural industrialization; developing urban industries; and promoting exports.[9]

Democratic participation of people at all stages in the formulation and implementation of development plans is the central premise that will determine their viability in the medium and long term. At least one historical precedent can be cited, albeit on a subnational level: the postwar experience of Kerala, traditionally one of India's poorest states. With a population of twenty-seven million, Kerala has more people than most developing countries. A long history of large movements by people of the lower castes culminated in the election of progressive state governments beginning in 1957. Constant pressure by India's most active agricultural labour unions and other peasant organizations forced these governments to abolish tenancy in what was one of the most sweeping agrarian reforms in South and Southeast Asia and to place high priority on health and literacy.

In periods when conservative governments were voted into power in Kerala, the non-governmental citizens' organizations remained strong enough to win reforms and ensure enforcement of existing laws. Today, despite income levels below the Indian average, Kerala boasts the highest life expectancy and literacy rates among Indian states, as well as the lowest infant mortality and birth rates.

Kerala's experience suggests that perhaps South Korea and Taiwan would be more successful societies if they had combined their early land reforms and thoughtful state intervention with a prolonged commitment to ecology, equity and participation. This, however, is a controversial notion. Indeed, such a pronounced emphasis on democracy flies in the face of political scientist Samuel Huntington's claim in the 1960s that order must precede democracy in the early stages of development. Many still believe that authoritarian governments in Eastern Europe, South Korea and Taiwan served as the catalysts for industrialization that in turn created the conditions for advancing democracy.

Experiences of the last two decades suggest otherwise. Africa, home to dozens of one-party authoritarian states, remains a development disaster. Argentina, Brazil, the Philippines and other Asian and Latin American countries ruled by authoritarian governments have suffered similar fates. As political scientist Atul Kohli has documented, the economies of the relatively democratic regimes in Costa Rica, India, Malaysia, Sri Lanka and Venezuela have 'grown at moderate but steady rates' since the 1960s and income inequalities have 'either remained stable or even narrowed'.[10]

Moreover, in South Korea and Taiwan, the authoritarian characteristics of the government were not responsible for industrialization and growth. Far-reaching land reforms and each state's ability to rise above factions in civil society deserve credit for sparking growth. The only 'positive' growth impact of repression by these governments was to hold down wage levels, thereby making exports more competitive. Yet heavy dependence on exports no longer serves as an option in today's increasingly protectionist global markets. The percentage of imports into the major developed countries that were affected by non-tariff barriers to trade rose more than twenty per cent during the 1980s, a trend that is likely to continue. In this hostile global economic climate, respect for workers' rights can lead to the creation of local markets by increasing domestic buying power. Democratic development therefore implies shifting emphasis from foreign to domestic (or, for small countries, to regional) markets. This shift meets more needs of local people and takes into account the difficult world market of the 1990s.

New Opportunities

The portrait we painted at the outset – of a global development crisis masked by the triumphalism of Western development orthodoxy – was a decidedly gloomy one. Why then are we confident that citizens' movements pushing for a more equitable, sustainable and participatory development have a chance in the 1990s? Much of the answer lies in the extraordinary possibilities of the present historical moment.

For four decades, the Cold War steered almost all development discussions toward ideological arguments over capitalism versus socialism, markets versus governments. It also diverted public attention away from non-ideological global concerns (such as environment, health and economic decay) and towards the Soviet Union as the source of problems. Hence, the dramatic winding down of the Cold War opens up great opportunities for positive turns in development.

At the very minimum, it should now become possible to get beyond sharp ideological categories to discuss development in more pragmatic terms. What is the proper role of government and what is the proper role of the market? If one values both effectiveness and equity, what kinds of checks must be placed on the market? What do the experiences of South Korea, Taiwan and Japan offer to this discussion?

The 1990s provide other opportunities to cut across Cold War polarities. Paranoid Cold War governments often saw communists lurking behind the popular organizations fighting for a better society. But citizens' movements have played a central role in the transformation of Eastern Europe. From this should emerge a greater openness to not only treat such non-governmental organizations with the respect they deserve but to realize that they have vital roles to play that are out of the reach of governments and individuals.

Finally, the eclipse of the Cold War has opened up the front pages of newspapers – and the public agenda itself – to basic societal problems. Ecological issues are at the forefront. All over the world, new environmental organizations are springing up; their scope is increasingly global. Maximizing this opportunity in effective international action requires sensitivity to the different brands of environmentalism evolving in developed and developing countries. In the Philippines and other developing countries, the abusive exploitation of forest and fishing resources by a few large concerns has directed the attention of environmental groups onto issues of equity and ownership. Developed country environmental groups have largely bypassed these issues as they have focused their efforts on changing consumer behaviour, planting new trees or passing new regulations that limit pollution. Successful international action requires close attention to these different priorities.

Beyond the Cold War, shifts in the global economic line up also offer new possibilities for the sustainable development agenda. While much attention has been focused on the United States' relative decline, there are potentially positive openings in this shift. A decade of unprecedented military overspending by the US government, for example, has bequeathed fiscal deficits that preclude significant increases in foreign aid. This adds impetus to proposals that the United States should give less but better aid by slashing the military aid that is often used to suppress citizens' movements in the developing world, and by redirecting economic and development assistance away from unaccountable governments towards citizens' organizations.

Likewise, persistent trade deficits are pushing the US government to restrict imports that enter US markets with the assistance of unfair trade practices. Again, the US government could assist developing country movements for equity and workers' rights by implementing more consistently existing legislation that classifies systematic repression of workers' rights as an unfair trading practice. Finally, the failure of the Baker and Brady Plans to staunch the debt haemorrhage should reopen the debate for substantial debt reduction plans, plans that shift payments towards sustainable development initiatives.[11] Perhaps the more intriguing questions about the international context of development efforts in the next decade have to do with the displacement of the United States by Japan as the world's most powerful economy and its biggest aid-giver. Already twenty per cent of all non-military aid from the industrial world now comes from Japan, which surpassed $10 billion in 1989.

This is a juncture fraught with both danger and opportunity. Japan can take the easy road and mimic what the United States did when it was number one: ally with local elites and subordinate development policy to its security policy. Or Japan could take leadership, divorce the two, and open up the possibility for a qualitative change in North–South ties. Will Japan seize the opportunities?

Further, will Japan follow the US example of using the World Bank and IMF as extensions of its commercial, trade and aid policies, thus further eroding the credibility of these institutions in the Third World? Or will Japan's ascension encourage these institutions to delve more objectively into the development lessons of South Korea, Taiwan and Japan and thus add realism to their prescriptions?

And, finally, can the Japanese and US governments respect the emerging citizens' movements as they reach out internationally to work with one another? The realization that governments have severe limits on what they can do in the development field should not be seen as negative. Rather, it opens up a variety of possibilities for new forms of joint government–citizen initiatives.

In the face of such opportunity, it is an enormous travesty that the development debate is all but dead in the industrial world. Rekindling that debate, however, is predicated on listening to new approaches in the rest of the world. Exciting alternatives to the dominant development paradigms of the last decades are emerging in the hundreds of thousands of citizens' groups that flourish amid adversity and repression in Latin America, Africa and Asia. These voices must be spread into the development establishments of Washington, Tokyo and Bonn.

We all must seize the new opportunities for attacking the problems of today freed from the ideological blinkers of yesterday. From the ruins of the Cold War can emerge new experiments of peace and sustainable development.

Acknowledgements

An earlier version of this chapter appeared in *Foreign Policy*, No. 81 (Winter 1990–1).

Notes

1 Walden Bello and Stephanie Rosenfeld, *Dragons in Distress: Asia's Miracle Economies in Crisis* (San Francisco: Institute for Food and Development Policy, 1990).

2   Interviews for this chapter were conducted by John Cavanagh and Robin Broad in the Philippines during 1988–9 and 1991, and by Walden Bello and Stephanie Rosenfeld in South Korea and Taiwan in 1988 and 1989.

3   Alan Durning, 'People Power and Development', *Foreign Policy*, no. 76 (Fall 1989), p. 66.

4   Larry Lohmann, 'Commercial Tree Plantations in Thailand: Deforestation by Any Other Name', *The Ecologist*, vol. 20, no. 1. (January/February 1990), p. 10

5   Claude Alvarez, 'India's Gigantic Harsud Rally Says "No" to Destructive Projects', *Third World Network Features*, No. 532, 1989.

6   Sheldon Annis and Peter Hakim, eds, *Direct to the Poor: Grassroots Development in Latin America* (Boulder: Lynne Rienner, 1988).

7   Fantu Cheru, *The Silent Revolution in Africa* (London: Zed Press, 1989), p. 19.

8   Calculations based on figures in Ruth Leger Sivard, *World Military and Social Expenditure 1989* (Washington, DC: World Priorities, 1989), p. 6. Over this period, developing country expenditures on education totalled around US$1.65 trillion; health added another US$0.6 trillion.

9   David C. Korten, *Getting to the 21st Century* (West Hartford, Connecticut: Kumarian Press, 1990).

10 Atul Kohli, 'Democracy and Development', in *Development Strategies Reconsidered*, ed. John P. Lewis and Valeriana Kallab (New Brunswick, Transaction Books, 1986), pp. 153–4.

11 See Susan George, *A Fate Worse than Debt* (New York: Grove Press, 1990).

2

Equitable and Sustainable Growth in the Philippines in the 1990s

Walden Bello

Breaking out of economic stagnation is the universal preoccupation in the Philippines today, and the fact that the Philippines is not a NIC or 'newly industrializing country' is something that is frequently deplored. The frustration is understandable, since many Filipinos – and not just the middle and upper classes – are aware that while the Philippine economy has been stagnant in the last few years, neighbouring countries in East Asia have been claiming 7 to 10 per cent growth rates per annum. And indeed, when Vietnam, once Asia's sick economy, registers a growth rate of 8.5 per cent, as it did in 1992, while the Philippines is stuck at 1.5 per cent (an optimistic estimate at that), then there is truly cause for alarm.

Close to 60 per cent of the population continues to live below the poverty line, according to UN statistics. Inequality and corruption continue to be major causes of poverty, but there appears to be a widespread feeling that the absence of economic growth is the main problem. The fact that middle and lower-class Filipinos continue to leave the country at record levels and accept work as seamen and domestics under conditions that can only be described as dismal reminds one of Joan Robinson's saying that in many capital-short and stagnant Third World countries, 'People would prefer to be exploited by capital than not to be exploited at all.'

The point of the foregoing remarks is that a credible development programme cannot focus simply on demands for redistribution to be able to win over people, but must be able to present a credible programme of economic growth. Or more appropriately, it must reframe its demands for redistribution so that these are seen not only as desirable from the perspective of economic and social justice but also as necessary and central elements of a strategy for economic growth and development.

At the same time, such a strategy of growth cum redistribution must internalize and incorporate the sensitivity to nature and the environment that was absent in both traditional capitalist-oriented and socialist-oriented development strategies. Such a strategy must, in short, be ecologically sustainable.

This proposal for a progressive agenda of sustainable growth cum redistribution begins by discussing those obstacles that must be eliminated before the Philippines can even begin to pursue a serious development effort. Then it moves to a discussion of the key preconditions of development. Finally, it presents what ought to be the key thrusts of a development strategy.

Removing the Obstacles

A serious development strategy cannot be put in place unless two serious barriers to growth are removed: the massive net outflow of capital in the form of debt service payments and the stranglehold that the World Bank and the IMF have on economic policy.

Stopping the Haemorrhage of Financial Resources
One of the most serious obstacles to development is the constant haemorrhage of financial resources represented by debt service payments. The Philippines' external debt rose from 54 per cent of GNP in 1980 to 70 per cent by 1990. And over the last few years, from 5 to 10 per cent of our GNP each year has left the country in debt service payments. This simply cannot go on. As Lester Thurow put it, indebted countries like the Philippines 'cannot grow if they must service international debts as large as those that now exist. Too many resources have to be taken out to pay interest on those debts; too few are left for reinvestment.' Whether by putting a cap on debt service payments or by a selective debt repayment scheme or by a coordinated debt repayment strategy with other indebted countries, the Philippines has no choice but to radically stem the haemorrhage of financial resources if it is to even think about developing.

Ending the IMF–World Bank Stranglehold
Another major barrier to economic growth that must be lifted before we can even begin to think about development is the hold that the IMF and the World Bank have over macroeconomic policy. This control has been exercised through the Bretton Woods institutions' long-time pervasive influence at the Department of Finance, the

dominant agency of the Philippine government in matters of economic policy.

Since 1979, the Philippines has been almost continuously under a structural adjustment programme, the main elements of which are export-oriented industrialization (EOI), liberalization of external trade and investment, and deregulation and privatization. All three elements have been extrapolated from the experience of the Asian NICs as 'necessary conditions' for economic growth. All three, however, have either been rendered obsolete by global economic trends or revealed to be false lessons from the NIC experience.

Export-oriented industrialization It is certainly true that export markets played a key role in the development of the NICs. But this must be qualified: the domestic market was just as important as a source of growth. Moreover, the international market conditions that prevailed when the NICs embarked on their industrialization are very different from those that now exists. Export-oriented growth depends on the maintenance or expansion of an international regime of free trade. Protectionism in the main developed countries of the North, however, has been the main trend in the last decade, and this development has impacted most on those developing countries that have followed export-oriented strategies. From being the guardian of the world liberal trading order, the United States, for instance, has in the last few years transformed itself into an aggressively protectionist power which has limited imports from the Third World through quotas, 'voluntary' export restraints, or forced currency appreciation.

The closing of the US market has been paralleled by escalating protectionism in the European Community and Japan's resistance to dismantling its formal and informal barriers to manufactured imports from the NICs, the 'would-be NICs', and other Third World countries.

Export markets are a valuable stimulus to economic growth, but to make them the main engine of economic development, as the World Bank and the IMF continue to advocate, would be nothing short of suicidal in the Brave New Protectionist World Economy.

Liberalization The prescription of export-oriented industrialization is accompanied by the demand for the World Bank–IMF prescription of liberalization or abolition of protective tariffs for the domestic market and loosening of rules for foreign investment. The rationale is that the exposure to international competition will make local firms more 'efficient'. The problem with liberalization is that, contrary to the IMF–World Bank analysis, it was not in the NIC 'formula' for growth. If it had been, we would not have seen the emergence of world-class Korean corporations like Samsung and Hyundai, which would have been strangled in their infancy by unrestricted competition in their home market from Japanese and US multi-nationals.

In fact, high growth rates in both Taiwan and Korea were registered by trade and investment regimes that were among the most restrictive in the world. In these two NICs, aggressive trade protectionism and highly discriminatory foreign investment laws ensured that the domestic market would be 'reserved' for local players, whether private or state-owned.

Privatization and deregulation The third pillar of the IMF–World Bank orthodoxy is privatization and deregulation, or reducing the role of the state in the economy and expanding the scope of the free market. Again, the watchword is 'efficiency'. Again, this prescription flies in the face of the NIC experience, where the state played a prominent role in the development process by picking industries to develop, channelling private investments to 'difficult' areas by a combination of carrot and stick methods, protecting local corporations from foreign competition and regulating domestic competition. Compared to the NIC state, the Philippine state is really quite weak relative to local and foreign private interests, and the result of applying the doctrine of privatization and deregulation would only be to destroy its capacity to intervene in and channel the development process towards the goal of equitable and sustainable growth.

The Real Aims of Structural Adjustment

But if these elements of structural adjustment programmes have been either rendered obsolete or shown to be fallacious as prescriptions for growth, why do the World Bank and IMF continue to insist on them? The reality is that whatever their original intent in the early 1980s or the subjective beliefs of the neoclassical technocrats and economists who implement them, structural adjustment programmes have long ceased to have anything to do with achieving growth.

Export-oriented growth is mainly a strategy imposed on the Philippines to make sure that it earns enough foreign exchange to be able to service its US$30 billion debt to western banks. Liberalization of external trade and investment is principally geared to integrate and subordinate the Philippine domestic market more tightly to the North-dominated world economy. And deregulation and privatization are meant to emasculate the Philippine state – the only institution capable of resisting the onslaught of the North's transnational corporations, transnational banks and international financial institutions on the domestic economy and serving as the motor of an alternative nationalist development strategy.

The imposition of structural adjustment on the Philippines must, in fact, be seen as part of the larger global economic counterrevolution launched by the Reagan–Bush administrations to roll back the gains that the Third World had made in the 1960s and 1970s. The universal instrument of this rollback strategy became the SAP – or structural adjustment programme – the common aim of which, in the more than seventy Third World countries where it was applied, was the dismantling of the state-led economic structures and the freeing of market forces that would inevitably favour more competitive Northern interests. By the end of the 1980s, the Philippine situation was replicated throughout most of the South, where growth was nonexistent, per capita income in some areas was down to early 1960s levels, and the state as an agent of economic growth, redistribution and Southern sovereignty had been severely weakened.

Like the rest of the South, the Philippines must reverse this descent to permanent stagnation by decisively putting an end to the reign of structural adjustment.

Preconditions for Development

Moving from the obstacles to the preconditions for development, a comparison with the NICs reveals that the real lessons to be learned from them are not export-oriented growth, liberalization and privatization but the decisive importance of two preconditions for development: a dynamic internal market and the strong directive role of the state in development.

A dynamic internal market Why did the domestic market sustain its dynamism in Korea and Taiwan but fail to do so in the Philippines? Here we come up against a factor that goes unmentioned in the standard analysis: the social origins of economic dynamism. In the early 1950s, Taiwan and Korea carried out what the Philippines was never able to do: land reform. By breaking up the concentration of income in the landlord class and spreading it through the rural population, the market for industry was dramatically expanded beyond the limited circle of the landed elite and the small urban middle class. Moreover, not only did land reform and agricultural credit policies stimulate industry by creating rural demand, but the prospering countryside became the source of capital that was extracted through taxation and invested in the physical and social infrastructure that served as the springboard for Korea's and Taiwan's leaps to higher stages of industrial growth.

True, the rural sector in both countries became less important as a source of demand and capital by the early 1970s, owing to population decline and to the fact that it had been milked by the state to provide the surplus for industrial take-off. But the lack of sharp income disparities in Korean and Taiwanese societies as a whole (in comparison to the Philippines and other Third World countries), a legacy of land reform, was one of the key factors accounting for the continuing dynamism of the domestic market well into the 1990s. In fact, the internal market in both Taiwan and Korea was just as important as an engine of growth and development as export markets.

In the Philippines, by contrast, the absence of land reform and other social reforms limited the size of the effective market mainly to a tiny elite and a small middle class that came to no more than 15 to 20 per cent of the population. With the stagnant economic situation of the last few years, the market has probably shrunk further below 1980s levels owing to the deteriorating living standards of the fragile middle class.

With a small, stagnant market, investment has been channelled to such activities as land speculation, lending and trade, which add little or no real value, not to value-adding economic activity like agricultural and industrial production. Moreover, with a limited demand for consumer goods in general and durable goods in particular, there is little stimulus for the development of medium and basic industries that would supply the inputs for finished products.

Clearly, no economies demonstrate the essential role of redistribution in growth better than the NICs, and no economy underlines the economic irrationality of inequality more clearly than the Philippines.

The need for a strong developmental state The ability of the NICs to carry out major redistributive efforts and the inability of the Philippines to do so underlines another major precondition for economic development absent in the Philippines: a state that provides leadership for the economic development effort.

In the Philippines, during the latter part of Marcos' rule and throughout the Corazon Aquino era, the Philippine state became increasingly immobilized as an agent of economic growth as it was converted into a battleground among cronies of Marcos or relatives of Aquino who used state mechanisms for private accumulation, inefficient local capitalists who perverted protectionism to protect monopoly rents, and World Bank and finance department technocrats who sought to emasculate its capability to protect national interests and direct the economy. Moreover, Aquino devoted her six years of rule to devolving much of the political and economic power that Marcos had centralized to regional and local elites – a perverse process that was marketed to the masses by equating centralized state leadership with 'authoritarianism' and adopting the attractive western political rhetoric of decentralization.

It is essential to reverse this process and forge a strong state that can discipline private interests in the service of the national interest.

Only a strong developmental state will be able to ram through land reform and other redistributive measures necessary to create a dynamic domestic market. Only a strong state can effectively undertake the urgent task of protecting our national resources against the pillage of private interests, like the 400 timber concessionaires who, by legal and illegal means, have reduced the country's forests to less than fifteen per cent of the national territory. The full coercive authority of the Philippine state – not to mention its firepower – must be deployed against the powerful resource rapists if we are to avoid ecological collapse from deforestation and erosion as well as having natural resources left for a rational, sustainable development strategy.

Several additional considerations on a strong, activist state are in order here:

An activist state and capital accumulation First, such a state, while extracting resources to support development from the whole citizenry, must place the burden of capital accumulation on the economic elite. While growing demand brought about by land and income redistribution stimulates agricultural and industrial production, a large part of the investment for infrastructure, capital equipment, and research and development necessary to meet growing demand could come from the firm imposition of a progressive income tax regime – a measure that will bite mainly into the incomes of the elite and upper middle class. Additional domestic capital could be realized by combining stringent measures to prevent capital flight with attractive incentives for investment in technology-incentive industries.

The public/private question Second, an activist state leadership must approach the question of the institutional agents of development with pragmatism and flexibility, rather than with doctrinaire assumptions, aiming at the optimal combination of private, cooperative and state firms to carry out the development strategy. Certainly, the private sector – especially small and medium entrepreneurs – should be the driving force of the economy. But public interest considerations may determine that certain areas of the economy, like telecommunications and electricity distribution, are reserved for state corporations, while others may be managed best by having private, state and cooperative firms compete, with the government ensuring a level playing field.

Democracy and the developmental state Finally, an activist developmental state does not mean an authoritarian state. Indeed, if there is any lesson that came out of the Marcos experience, it is that there are no authoritarian short-cuts to development. Democratic accountability, in fact, upgrades the capability of a state for economic leadership since it endows it with legitimacy. What it lacks in speed, democratic economic management makes up for in terms of solidity. This is one of the negative lessons that we can learn from the Korean experience: because they imposed a high-growth strategy on the working class rather than building a democratic consensus around it, Korea's state and corporate elites are now finding out that they have created a vast mass of people who are alienated from the economic strategy in spite of the rise in living standards that it sparked – a social force whose lack of cooperation, if not outright hostility, is making it difficult to forge the social consensus for a new stage of development under more democratic political conditions.

In any event, countervailing forces in civil society must be insti-tutionalized to prevent abuse by the state leadership, make it accountable to the people, and guarantee that feedback is consistently provided to ensure that development initiatives do not stray from the national interest. In this system, however, balance would be provided not by elite vested interests – which must be regarded mainly as forces to be disciplined and harnessed for the development process rather than as partners – but by people's organizations (POs) and non-governmental organizations (NGOs).

POs and NGOs, however, must not be seen only as countervail-ing forces, but as partners of an activist government. This relationship of NGOs and POs to the state can be best summed up as a critical partnership: on the one hand, they have to fiscalize government ini-tiatives, including progressive ones, to ensure that the rights of individuals and communities are not trampled in the course of devel-opment; on the other hand, without becoming absorbed by government but remaining part of 'civil society', they have to work actively with progressive elements in state agencies to bring to fruition initiatives that serve the national interest.

Can such a government be brought to power?

It is not at all impossible that owing to the current sense of a seemingly irreversible economic free-fall that affects most sectors of the population, a populist strategy that paints the landed and business elites as forces intent on derailing economic growth and national devel-opment to preserve vested interests may now have greater popular appeal and may contribute decisively to their electoral isolation. Such an electoral strategy should, of course, be coordinated with non-electoral pressures such as already ongoing local struggles for land redistribution, cancellation of timber concessions, defence of ancestral domains and a halt to open-pit mining.

Key Elements of an Alternative Development Strategy

Moving now to the key thrusts of an alternative development strategy, we see these to be:

- the priority of rural development;
- a synergistic relationship between agriculture and industry;
- sustainable industrialization; and
- a strong orientation towards the Asia–Pacific region.

The Priority of Rural Development

With over sixty per cent of the Philippine population living in rural areas, the countryside must be the centrepiece of an alternative development strategy. Rather than moving people from the countryside, as previous strategies like export-oriented industrialization sought to do, a development strategy must focus on improving their rural living standards.

This means, above all, transforming agriculture, and in this process land reform would be central. Land redistribution must not, however, be narrowly conceived as a process of subdividing big estates into smaller farming units. In areas where too many farmers compete for too little land available for redistribution, a small-farm emphasis might fragment farming units into tiny uneconomic plots. In such cases, both ecological and economic rationality might favour banding land reform beneficiaries into cooperatives or worker-owned and run enterprises.

Transforming Philippine agriculture into a landscape dominated by small farming units or small and medium cooperative enterprises would, first of all, be essential to the urgent task of making the transition from the ecologically destructive chemical-intensive agricultural technology of the Green Revolution to more environmentally friendly technology. Chemical-intensive technology is hostile to small farms, since it relies on economies of scale achieved through industrial monocropping to achieve greater profitability. Organic and biodynamic farming, on the other hand, encourages decentralized production by small farms owing to the close attention necessitated by the process of adapting to the micro-diversity of soil, plant and environmental conditions to achieve sustainable production.

Sustainable agriculture under a small farm regime is terribly labour intensive, not in a backbreaking sense but in the sense of 'tender, loving care'. Thus it is also the key to solving one of the countryside's greatest problems: the existence of a large number of people whose labour has been made redundant by the combination of chemical-intensive agriculture and semi-feudal and capitalist tenure systems. Alternative agriculture under a reformed system of land ownership, in short, absorbs labour rather than expels it.

The other thrust of rural development must be to devise a natural resource policy that would serve the national development effort, enhance the environment, and ensure survival of upland and coastal communities that are threatened by the pillage of our forests, fish and natural resources. Here the main obstacles to both development and community wellbeing are the 60 to 70 timber concessionaires, big local and foreign mining corporations, and large Taiwanese, Japanese and Philippine fishing enterprises.

Thus, in tandem with agrarian reform, we need policies that would recognize the communal ownership rights of minority and other upland communities to land they have lived on for centuries; replace the corrupt timber-licensing system with community-based systems of resource management; and ban big commercial fishing within a defined distance from the shoreline.

Synergy Between Agriculture and Industry

A prosperous agriculture is the key to a dynamic industrial sector. But this should not be interpreted in the traditional sense of dynamic rural demand sparking urban industrialization. A key thrust of an alternative development strategy must be to hitch industrial growth to rural demand by 'ruralizing' industry so that it directly serves agriculture and absorbs part of the rural surplus population, thus ending the fifty-year-old pattern of heavily urban-focused industrialization that served as a magnet for the labour surplus in the countryside and subordinated agriculture to its disruptive logic.

A decentralized system of labour-intensive small- and medium-sized enterprises could emerge to provide power-tillers and other electronically controlled farm implements designed for small-scale agriculture, user-friendly computer systems for uses ranging from weather tracking to accounting, and components for decentralized energy generation and rural electrification systems.

Needless to say, in the critical area of providing inputs to sustainable agricultural technologies that will replace the obsolete and destructive chemical-intensive agriculture, rural-based industries would be better placed to receive community input in the complex but challenging task of adapting biotechnology for small-scale, ecologically friendly production.

Sustainable Industrialization

Rural industrialization is central to balanced growth between the city and the countryside, but unless it takes place within a strong environmental regime, the Philippines could end up like Taiwan, which pioneered rural industrialization with shattering ecological consequences.

While there are positive lessons to be absorbed from the NIC industrialization experience, there are also negative ones, and among the latter is the high-speed industrialization strategy pursued by the NICs. This was abnormally focused on achieving high growth rates, which could only be possible without meaningful environmental controls.

What this underlines is that an equitable distribution of income allowing equitable consumption is more than ever an ecological necessity, since the environmental limits to growth allow much less room for the elite to corner a large chunk of the surplus while still allowing a substantial portion to trickle down and raise living standards.

The ecological limits to growth also necessitate that equity be accompanied by an effective programme of family planning to ensure that the limited additions to the national wealth each year are channelled into steadily rising living standards and are not simply consumed by the added population.

An ecologically sensitive industrialization programme must not only be characterized by moderate growth rates but also by tight regulation of pollution-intensive industries, like petrochemicals, leather tanning and semi-conductor manufacturing. Industrial projects must be subject to full-cost accounting, to reflect the environmental costs that do not appear in orthodox cost-benefit analysis.

Environmental control, however, can itself be a source of economic and employment growth. Restricting the growth of the environmentally destructive petrochemical industry, for instance, can be counterbalanced by investing in the development of a techno-manufacturing sector devoted to the production of anti-pollution devices, waste-treatment facilities and other environmental-protection systems. Developing cheap and appropriate environmental clean-up technologies for a Third World context could not only create a vibrant domestic industry but also produce a valuable, high-value-added export activity directed at the Asia–Pacific region and other parts of the Third World.

Of course, developing such an environmental protection industry would entail a more activist technology policy, in which the government would set strategic guidelines for the uses of the Philippines' limited but not insubstantial pool of scientists and technical personnel. This would include government-initiated revision of the focus of technical education in this country, which will have to de-emphasize the production of scientists in such specialties as nuclear physics and nuclear engineering and stress the training of ecologists and environmental engineers.

A Strategy Oriented Towards the Asia–Pacific Region

Active external trade must be a key part of an alternative development strategy, to supplement the demand emanating from the domestic market. But in view of the strong winds of protectionism sweeping the world economy, especially the traditional target markets of the United States, Europe and Japan, Philippine external trade must be decisively reoriented towards our Asia–Pacific neighbours.

Liberalization thus has a role in this development strategy, but it is not the indiscriminate liberalization advocated by the IMF and the World Bank. It is, instead, discriminatory liberalization, that extends preferential trading privileges to members of an Asia–Pacific trading bloc while maintaining protective tariffs on products from powerful economies.

But the Philippines' regional strategy must go beyond participating in the formation of trading blocs like the AFTA (the ASEAN Free Trade Area). Expanded regional trade must be seen as a part of a broader process of regional economic coordination, particularly in the area of technology-intensive and skill-intensive industries. Owing to their tremendous capital and R&D requirements and the country's still limited technical personnel pool, the development of strategic high-tech industries such as transportation equipment, machine tools, computers and semi-conductors must be pursued by the Philippines in the context of a regional, Asia–Pacific-wide industrialization strategy that deliberately excludes not only the United States but Japan.

'Industrial complementation' is a vision that has, in fact, long floated about in ASEAN circles. That vision is now reality. Unfortunately, however, industrial integration is taking place under the auspices and in response to the needs of Japanese transnationals. This is most advanced in the automobile industry: Mitsubishi, Nissan and Toyota have located the different phases of car production in different Southeast Asian countries. For instance, in the Toyota scheme, the Philippines makes the transmission system; Thailand the stamped parts, diesel engines and electrical equipment; Indonesia, gasoline engines and stamped parts; and Malaysia, steering links and electrical equipment. Toyota assembles the whole car together in Thailand and ships it to Japan or the United States. Through a rapid process of horizontal and backwards integration during the 1980s, Japanese corporations have, in fact, rapidly integrated the East and Southeast Asian region around the needs of the Japanese economy.

This trend must be reversed, and soon, if the Asian and Pacific economies are to avoid the unenviable condition in which Taiwan and Korea now find themselves – despite their tremendous industrialization efforts – of being technological dependencies or colonies of Japan. Only through a coordinated regional effort to develop and upgrade high-tech capabilities would this be possible.

Acknowledgements

This chapter is adapted from a paper prepared for the 1993 Forum on Philippine Alternatives International Conference by Walden Bello, with contributions from Josie Atienza, John Cavanagh and Lyuba Zarsky. Other members of the Equity, Environment, and Development Cluster Group are Elsie Castrence, Rommel Simon and Roberto Castrence. The full paper is reprinted in John Gersham and Walden Bello, eds, *Re-examining and Reviewing the Philippine Progressive Vision* (Forum for Philippine Alternatives, 1993).

3

The Human Rights of the Underclass

Peter Weiss

It is always best to begin with definitions. What are human rights? According to Edmund Burke, who, although a valiant fighter against the excesses of the British Crown in Ireland, the American colonies and India, never recovered from the shock of the French Revolution, they are mere pretexts behind which hide 'pride, ambition, avarice, revenge, lust, sedition, hypocrisy, ungoverned zeal, and all the train of disorderly appetites'.

But according to Antigone, determined to bury her brother Polyneices despite Creon's prohibition, they are 'the unwritten and unfailing laws of heaven, for their life is not of today or yesterday, but from all time'. More than two millennia later, Alexander Hamilton expressed the same view, in words bordering on plagiarism: 'The sacred rights of mankind,' he said, 'are not to be rummaged for among old parchments or musty records. They are written, as with a sunbeam, in the whole volume of human nature, by the hand of divinity itself, and can never be erased or obscured by mortal power.'

For myself, I am not convinced that the hand of divinity ever bothered itself with the drafting of a code of human conduct or that, if it did, the results have been reliably reported to us, although Moses on Mount Sinai and Saint Thomas Aquinas in the *Summa Theologica* seem to have made a pretty good job of it. But, while I would agree with Edmund Burke that the language of rights can be a mask for hypocrisy, self-interest and disorderly appetites – as in 'I have a right to be a racist, or a sweatshop operator, or an imperialist' – I am firmly on the side of those who regard human rights as overarching precepts of universal validity. And it does not matter a great deal whether one views human rights as given by God or deduced by reason from the nature of human beings and human society, because, while the starting points of the inquiry are different, the goal is essentially the same. Thus Thomas Jefferson, good politician that he was, based the right of the American colonists to assume their separate and equal station among the powers of the earth on 'the laws of nature *and* of nature's god'.

Moreover, the half century since the founding of the United Nations in 1945 has witnessed the validation and expansion of classic human rights doctrine in the form of countless international, regional and national treaties, declarations, conventions, constitutions and laws defining and refining the rights of virtually every conceivable constituent group of society, from human beings as such – what used to be called 'the rights of man', before women were discovered – to children, the disabled, refugees, workers, minorities, war victims, prisoners, stateless persons, you name it. It is as if, for thousands of years, poets, dramatists, philosophers and various others in the thick of or on the fringes of statecraft had been taking snapshots of the landscape of human rights and finally, starting about the middle of this century, all that exposed film had been developed, yielding a series of pictures so stark and dramatic in their clarity that they are impossible to ignore. Taken together, they constitute what has been dubbed the international bill of rights and what I prefer to call the emerging constitution of the world.

One result of this extraordinary development is that it has virtually swept away the centuries-old conflict between human rights idealists and human rights positivists, between those seeking to persuade others what human rights ought to be and those who maintain that a human right is whatever is defined as such by a lawmaker; nothing more, nothing less. If you don't believe me take a look at a United Nations Publication entitled *Human Rights: A Compilation of International Instruments*. It contains the texts of some 70 such instruments, from the Universal Declaration of Human Rights (1948) to the Convention on the Rights of the Child (1989).

If you still don't believe me, go to Section 701 of the Restatement (Third) of the Foreign Relations Law of the United States, the authoritative text on international law, published in 1986 and representing the consensus of the leading scholars in the field. Section 701 is headed 'Obligation to Respect Human Rights' and reads as follows:

A state is obligated to respect the human rights of persons subject to its jurisdiction
(a) that it has undertaken to respect by international agreement;
(b) that states generally are bound to respect as a matter of customary international law; and
(c) that it is required to respect under general principles of law common to the major legal systems of the world.

But, I hear you saying, if that is the case, why are billions of the world's people hungry and millions homeless when Article 11 of the International Covenant on Economic, Social and Cultural Rights, which has been ratified by ninety-two countries, provides that: 'The States Parties to the present Covenant recognize the right of everyone to an adequate standard of living for himself and his family, including adequate food, clothing and housing'? Good question. For the answer, you must look to Article 2, which states that

Each State party to the present Covenant undertakes to take steps, individually and through international assistance and cooperation, especially economic and technical, to the maximum of its available resources, with a view to achieving progressively the full realization of the rights recognized in the present Covenant.

There's the rub, or rather, the two rubs: one, the word 'progressively'; two, the phrase 'to the maximum of its available resources'. No such word, no such phrase, appears in the International Covenant on Civil and Political Rights, which deals with such 'classic' rights as the right to life, freedom from torture and slavery, liberty and security of the person, freedom of movement, equality before the law and freedom of speech, religion and association. On the contrary, Article 2 of the Civil and Political Covenant provides that: 'Each State Party to the present Covenant undertakes to respect and to ensure to all individuals within its territory and subject to its jurisdiction the rights recognized in the present Covenant' and Article 4(2) provides that most of these rights may not be abrogated even 'in time of public emergency which threatens the life of the nation'.

In other words, political and civil rights, so the conventional wisdom would have it, are real; economic and social rights are to be implemented only to the extent that states, meaning the rulers of states, decide that it is feasible, in their opinion, to take them seriously. One way that lawyers have of expressing this difference is to refer to political and civil rights, at least those which may not be derogated under any circumstances, as peremptory norms, which sounds like something closely related to categorical imperatives, while calling economic and social rights 'aspirational', or, worse yet, 'merely aspirational'. Another semantic distinction sometimes made is between 'first generation rights' and 'second generation rights', thereby taking all the bite out of the latter, not to mention such 'third generation rights' as the right to development, to peace or to a safe environment. However, in what may be a sign of things to come, the UN General Assembly, in its Resolution 48/141, adopted on 22

December 1993 without a vote, said the following about the newly created post of High Commissioner for Human Rights:

> [He/she should] be guided by the recognition that all human rights – civil, cultural, economic, political, and social – are universal, indivisible, interdependent, and interrelated [and should] recognize the importance of promoting a balanced and sustainable development for all people and of ensuring realization of the right to development, as established in the Declaration on the Right to Development.

What is the Underclass?

Let us now put human rights aside for a while and turn to the underclass. I am not sure where that term originated. While I disagree with William Safire about almost everything – except that Henry Kissinger sold out the Kurds – I am an avid reader of his 'On Language' column in *The New York Times Magazine* and, to the best of my knowledge, he has not yet gotten around to dealing with this particular neologism. Nor is it to be found in any dictionary or encyclopedia at my disposal.

My intuition tells me that the underclass is situated somewhere between what used to be called the proletariat and the lumpenproletariat, before Marx was excommunicated. My intuition also tells me that 'underclass' is one of those terms coined by an establishment semanticist charged with defanging militant words; probably the same person who substituted 'preventive defensive action' for 'nuclear strike', 'user fee' for 'tax', and 'underprivileged' for 'poor'.

'Proletariat', after all, evokes images of underpaid workers storming factory gates and 'lumpenproletariat' suggests the great, smelly unwashed. 'The underclass', on the other hand, has about it an aura of resignation and docility, like the poor who – don't we know it? – will always be with us anyway and therefore have little to gain by making trouble. (What, by the way, is the underclass under? Under the horizon? Under the middle class? Under the volcano?)

As good a definition as any probably comes from a cartoon by Rob Rogers. It shows a census taker consoling a homeless person with the following words: 'You'll no longer be the invisible sufferers, the forgotten people, the uncounted Americans ... Now you'll be a statistic.'

But then, we all know what the underclass is. It's the 50 per cent of all Americans over 65 who, according to the Congressional

Committee on Aging, lack money for food at some time; it's the millions of homeless (no one knows just how many) and the additional millions living on the edge of homelessness; it's what Senator Daniel Moynihan calls the feminization of poverty and what Dr Jean Mayer of Tufts University called the infantization of poverty; it's the 32.5 million of our people who live in poverty and the 23 million who are functionally illiterate; it's the 12 per cent loss in household income for the poorest fifth of the population since 1973; it's the 63 per cent cut in education block grants to states during the Reagan years and the 81 per cent slash in federal funding for subsidized housing; it's America's number 21 rating in infant mortality among 140 countries, with black infant mortality twice that of white, and black prenatal care one half that of white; it's the racism and the sexism still endemic in our society, which keeps millions down while a few rise up.

Let us say that, in the United States, the ignored, the forgotten, the stepped over, the ones who have fallen off the train, amount to roughly 20 per cent of the total population and 40 to 50 per cent of the population of colour. For the world at large, the situation is reversed: probably no more than one billion, roughly 20 per cent of the total – shall we call them the overclass? – can be said to enjoy that quality of life which the aforementioned human rights instruments purport to guarantee to all.

Here are some statistics taken from the 1993 edition of Ruth Leger Sivard's masterly *World and Social Expenditures*:

- One adult in four in the world is unable to read and write.
- Over two billion people in the world suffer from real or hidden hunger.
- The proportion of people living in poverty was 49 per cent in South Asia in 1990 and is expected to reach 50 per cent in sub-Saharan Africa in 2000.
- Infant mortality in Africa in 1990 was 100 per 1000 live births.
- In 1991, 2.5 million unvaccinated children died from measles, tetanus and whooping cough.

And, needless to say, the unchecked population explosion – from 1.6 billion in 1950 to a projected 6.25 billion in 2000 – will only aggravate all of these 'statistics'.

The Next Stage of History

Does the underclass have human rights? In one sense, this is a silly question. The underclass, being made up of human beings, has the same rights as all other human beings. In another sense, it may turn out to be the most relevant question of the next stage of history (and there will be a next stage of history, Francis Fukuyama to the contrary). So far, the only definition of that stage on which there is consensus is that it is post-World War, which doesn't tell us very much about its content. But some shadowy contours are beginning to emerge. Let's list some of them:

- With no significant visible enemies on the horizon, an annual expenditure of US$600 billion on defence is not only the height of folly, but a veritable crime against humanity.
- The debate over whether political and civil rights are a western luxury or a universal norm is over. The pro-democracy movement has carried the day. While torture, censorship, preventive detention and other forms of societal brutalization are still practiced in too many countries, hardly anyone defends them any more on theoretical grounds.
- 'Quality of life', the demand for the satisfaction of basic human needs, is emerging as one of the dominant themes of the last decade of this century and will certainly carry over into the next one.
- But, as the Russian experience demonstrates, the formula for achieving social and economic progress remains elusive. Shouting 'market economy' from the rooftops does not put a chicken in every pot.
- And, paradoxically, while the developed world gloats over the triumph of its 'system', the system is beginning to crumble within the developed world: witness the increasing pauperization of ever larger sectors of its population.
- From Bensonhurst to Baku, from Sarajevo to the Sudan, racism and tribalism are flourishing. Pluralism releases all sides of human nature, including the darker ones.
- Concern with the environment is no longer the exclusive province of the privileged, 'liberal' few. While Europeans are building the common house of Europe, millions throughout the world fear the collapse of the common house of humankind, from climate change, air and water pollution and the exhaustion of life-sustaining resources.

What, then, are the chances of the underclass climbing out from under, of achieving the *egalité* which, along with *liberté* and *fraternité*, was one of the triple goals of the French Revolution; the freedom from want which was one of FDR's four freedoms; the right to a 'standard of living adequate for ... health and well being' guaranteed to it by Article 25 of the Universal Declaration of Human Rights?

At the moment, not very good. In the United States, a spineless Congress and a well-intentioned but counterproductively 'realist' President seem intent on moving the country forward at the price of leaving the underclass behind. In Eastern Europe, it looks as if consumerism will have to have a field day before some kind of synthesis is forged between the gentler aspects of socialism – universal health care, social security, education for the masses, minimal unemployment, affordable culture – and the productive forces being unleashed by the wild swing toward the market as *deus ex machina*. And the poor Third World, no longer able even to get a pittance from playing off one superpower against the other – no longer entitled to call itself nonaligned! – is left swinging in the wind of change, its terms of trade steadily worsening, its raw materials less and less necessary to the developed economies, its burden of debt sitting on its back like a huge, grinning, unshakable monster.

True, Western Europe, the Pacific Rim and parts of Latin America seem set on a slightly upward course, but, as John Major's stupendous unpopularity and the recent events in Chiapas demonstrate, what progress there is highly compartmentalized.

In fact, while the world's attention has been focused on the abominable phenomenon of ethnic cleansing, an equally abhorrent process of vastly greater proportions but less visibility has been taking place: class cleansing.

A New Vision of Human Rights

Is there some hope for 'taking seriously', to use Ronald Dworkin's phrase, the rights of the one-third of a nation and two-thirds of a world ill-clothed, ill-housed and ill-fed? Let me be bold and suggest that there is. If what we are looking for is an ideology, or, more modestly, a motivating and ordering principle, it is, in the words of the Bard, 'invisible as a nose on a man's face, or a weathercock on a steeple'. It is, in fact, right there, under our collective noses. It is called, as I have said before, the international bill of rights, or the constitution of the world.

Now the trouble with constitutions, as we know only too well from our own experience, not to mention those of countries which lock people up for demanding their constitutional rights, is that they are far easier to commit to paper than to translate into meaningful action. I am fully aware of the difficulties which beset even the most high-minded legislators and administrators in the face of contending interest groups, growing deficits and shrinking budgets. But I submit that the outline of a decent world order has, for the first time, been formulated on the basis of a very broad, to some extent universal, consensus and that this constitutes both a mandate for governors and a powerful tool in the hands of the governed.

How is this to be done? Here are some suggestions, from a lawyer's perspective:

1. The first step in human rights enforcement is to expose the violations and the violators, who are as dedicated to covering up their misdeeds as to committing them. Non-governmental organizations like Human Rights Watch and Amnesty International are playing an increasingly important role as observers of and reporters on violations of political and civil rights. There is no comparable, systematic non-governmental operation in the field of economic and social rights, producing periodic reports and organizing country missions. There should be.

2. A massive effort needs to be made to overcome the invidious distinction between 'real' and 'aspirational' rights, to which I have referred earlier; to convince judges, government officials and the public at large that the growl of the stomach is as offensive to human dignity as the midnight knock on the door. This must have a political action component to it, like the comprehensive welfare rights movement of the 1960s or the various issue-specific, currently functioning organizations concerned with homelessness, hunger, inadequate health care and other deprivations of human needs. It also requires serious theoretical work, to get beyond such conversation-stoppers as 'How are you going to feed everyone when there isn't enough food to go around?' and move on to such questions as 'Why isn't there enough food to go around?' and 'Do the underfed have an enforceable right to some of the nourishment of the overfed?'

3. When it comes to the United States, it is a sad fact that no economic or social rights are specifically guaranteed by the federal constitution. We need, therefore, to go on a great scavenger hunt for other morally, politically and, to some extent even legally significant sources of such rights, such as:

- 'The pursuit of happiness' in the Declaration of Independence;
- the general welfare clause of and the mysterious 9th Amendment to the Constitution of the United States ('The enumeration in the Constitution of certain rights shall not be construed to deny or disparage others retained by the People');

- various provisions in state constitutions and legislative enactments, e.g. the right to health in the constitution of New York, the right of the disabled and elderly to equal access to public transportation in the Mass Transportation Act of 1968;
- the common law;
- the various international human rights instruments, both as independent sources of rights and as aides to the interpretation of domestic legislation.

4) Judges must be educated to move to higher ground in the area of human rights, in the only way that ever moves judges, which is a combination of persuasive legal argument and forceful expression of public opinion, including, if necessary, in the streets. The Indian Supreme Court is a model for other courts to follow in its recognition of economic and social rights, although it has not always been successful in enforcing its writ.

5) I have referred to the 9th Amendment to the US Constitution as a sleeper. Here is another: Article 28 of the Universal Declaration of Human Rights reads: 'Everyone is entitled to a social *and international order* in which the rights and freedoms set forth in this Declaration can be fully realized.' These rights include the right to social security (Art. 22), work (Art. 23), rest and leisure (Art. 24), a standard of living adequate for health and wellbeing (Art. 25) and education (Art. 26). Does this mean that the starving children of the Sudan have a call on the treasury of the United States? Yes. Am I talking about a system of international taxation? Yes. Is this crazy talk? Yes, but no more so than was talk of a US tax based on income prior to the adoption of the 16th Amendment in 1913, after a nearly four year ratification process.

Words alone will not solve the problems of the underclass. But, as Jimmy Carter once said during his Presidency, 'It is a mistake to undervalue the power of words and of the ideas that words embody ... In the life of the human spirit, words are action.'

Conclusion

Perhaps we should think of this strange, heady, unnerving time through which we are living as time out. Time to lick wounds, to catch a little breath, to think about past mistakes, to plan for the next bout. And perhaps, when the gong sounds, there will be no opponent in the other corner. Except war and famine, global warming and AIDS, illiteracy and poverty, sexism and racism. Perhaps the referee, a tattered copy of the Universal Declaration of Human Rights in hand, will admonish the fighters:

> WHEREAS disregard and contempt for human rights have resulted in barbarous acts which have outraged the conscience of mankind, and the advent of a world in which human beings shall enjoy freedom of speech and belief and freedom from fear and want – I repeat that, *and freedom from fear and want* – has been proclaimed as the highest aspiration of the common people, THEREFORE go to it! Fight clean, and fight hard!

Acknowledgement

This is an update of a speech delivered at the University of Denver on 4 April 1989 and first published in *Global Justice*, Vol.1, No. 1.

4

Global Economic Institutions and Democracy: A View from India

Smitu Kothari

India is one of the newest entrants into the fold of the IMF–World Bank dictated structural adjustment programmes. Within a brief period of three years, far-reaching and what members of the ruling Congress party call 'positive, irreversible changes' have taken place. A sizeable proportion of the elites has been unequivocally celebrating not only the fastest pace of foreign deals since Independence but the virtual explosion of consumer choices – from a wider range of new goods to MTV and CNN.

Are there no options but to accept and, at best, soften the adverse social and ecological impact of these developments? In fact, the forces of resistance that have surfaced in the past few years (that draw their inspiration and support from the wide range of democratic struggles in different parts of the country) are already taking the first tentative steps towards challenging the brash economic arrogance of the alliance of national and global capital. One such initiative was the decision to initiate a Campaign Against the World Bank and Destructive International Aid (CAWBADIA). This decision was taken by the participants of a convention on Development, Planning and Mega-Projects organized by the Narmada Bachao Andolan (Movement to Save the Narmada) in August 1992 in New Delhi. CAWBADIA then organized a second national meeting comprised of victims of World Bank funded projects.

A majority of participants at the second meeting were working in areas which had been adversely affected by international economic aid. In the general context of the growing controls over the domestic economy being exerted by international capital and by international institutions such as the World Bank, it was decided to improve coordination of the widespread opposition and resistance as well as to work towards strengthening alternative efforts to the slow recolonization of the country. It was the general consensus that the practice of these institutions and their structural adjustment programmes had compounded ecological disruption, social destabilization and economic dependency.

The two national meetings of CAWBADIA empowered a smaller group, primarily in Delhi, to take the campaign forward with a particular focus on the World Bank. It was recognized that similar efforts to hold these institutions accountable were underway elsewhere in the world and that some global coordination, particularly around specific projects and policies and around the NGO meetings that coincide with the annual World Bank–IMF meeting, had already taken place. In fact, many members from the Indian initiatives were already active in a global Multilateral Development Bank (MDB) campaign. All these initiatives had underscored the need for a more sustained and coordinated national, regional and global campaign.

The two CAWBADIA events and the global campaigns made three facts clear:

1. The adverse impacts of the new economic policies could not be countered and reversed without the active involvement of social and political movements;

2. Political parties had to play an important role, and their radicalization was the responsibility of both internal processes within parties as well as pressure from movement groups and other concerned citizens; and

3. Efforts had to be made – both within the country and across national boundaries – to link with as many initiatives as possible that were working to challenge the adverse impacts of the current patterns of economic development and to define alternatives to them. It is with this understanding that a major national convention was organized in the central Indian town of Badwani in January 1994 to take the process further and bring together representatives from the wide variety of initiatives[1] in the country that were not only opposing the World Bank–IMF–GATT policies but working on alternatives to them. Leading social scientists and activists from all over the country attended the event, which led to understanding the emerging situation and to preparing for future plans, including an Asia-wide meeting.

The opposition draws its legacy from the widespread community mobilization around predominantly ecological issues which is centuries old.[2] For instance, in numerous parts of India, by the beginning of the nineteenth century, communities had mobilized to oppose colonial intrusion which attempted to transform local ecosystems. This opposition was significant in tribal areas where communities did not acquiesce quietly in the face of external intervention.[3] There were protests and rebellions against colonial laws such as the Forest Act of 1876. While the newly emergent colonial science of forestry had begun to blame the agrarian system of forest dwellers for decline in forest coverage, tribal peasants in India were waging struggles against state intervention in forest resources, based on their own moral economy. In many ways, the contemporary interests of international banks and transnational corporations in collaboration with domestic capital represent a similar neocolonial onslaught on India.

The Indian Context

India is now pursuing a developmental path that even at the level of rhetoric has abandoned the commitment to national self-sufficiency and social justice. Global capital and multilateral institutions in collaboration with Indian capital and the present regime are increasingly controlling the Indian economy.

Most of the key decision-making positions in the country's economic policy establishment have now passed into the hands of ex-World Bank or ex-IMF employees. These include Dr Montek Singh Ahluwalia (secretary, Ministry of Finance), Dr Bimal Jalan (until recently the head of the Prime Minister's Economic Advisory Council and now executive director of the World Bank), Arvind Virmani (economic adviser, Ministry of Finance) and Dr Rakesh Mohan (economic adviser, Ministry of Commerce). Since 1991, these senior governmental officials, including the Finance Minister, have essentially been implementing a series of policy measures dictated by the World Bank and the IMF. One of the main texts that influences these measures is the World Bank report entitled 'India: Strategy for Trade Reforms' (November 1990). Interestingly, this report was withheld from the then Prime Minister, Finance Minister and other cabinet ministers and senior officials. Even the budget for 1992–3 was first sent to the World Bank, whose changes were almost entirely incorporated *before* it was tabled in Parliament. In league with select politicians, bureaucrats and members of India's industrial elite, the country is slowly being strait-jacketed by global elite control.

Of equal concern has been the manner in which governments and institutions like the World Bank are increasingly employing more sophisticated strategies to coopt (or manipulate) dissent and to seek legitimacy for themselves by 'seeking partnerships' with NGOs. Towards this end, the Bank has commissioned comprehensive studies of NGOs and of social and political movements and drawn up strategies to reduce the possibility of opposition to Bank policies. For instance, witness the recent steps by the Bank to provide direct grants to NGOs for various 'poverty alleviation' projects (i.e. catchment area development and programmes for poor women) and its commissioning NGO activists as consultants. This is a matter of serious concern not only since the Bank remains one of the most undemocratic institutions in the world but also since its primary purpose continues to be the facilitation of neocolonial economic and political forces. The programmes through which they are attempting to generate wider social credibility are being constantly undermined by their macroeconomic policies which cause widespread social and ecological disruption. The Bank has made almost no effort at the country level to become more transparent and accountable, and structurally to alter its overall policies in the direction of greater social and ecological justice. Yet, 'sustainable development' is what they widely proclaim they are doing.

How Sustainable Is Sustainable Development?

The rhetoric of sustainability pervades development literature. It is only a matter of time (if we haven't arrived there already) before the concept of sustainability becomes so misused as to become meaningless. There was a time when, for countries like India, who were coming out of a long history of colonization, sustainability had another meaning – it was a powerful socio-political concept. It meant self-sustaining growth and self-reliance. In that sense it was a far more potent concept and motivating force than the term today, which has become like putty in the hands of the user – the form and content being dependent on who is sculpting it.

Despite the multiple interpretations associated with the term, it is the belief of this author that the notion of sustainability applies not only to the replenishable use of renewable resources (a process of natural resource use where the rate of take is equal to the rate of renewal or regeneration), but to a much broader concept which embraces ethical norms pertaining to the survival of the diversity of living matter, to the rights of future generations and to the definition of institutions responsible for ensuring that such rights are integrated into policies and actions. It is not therefore an attempt to reconcile current strategies of economic growth with environmentalism, what one might call 'the greening of growth'.[4] Rather, true sustainable development would challenge capitalist industrialization and restore primacy to those who seek ecological sustainability and social justice.

It is in this overall context that this essay looks at two major questions:

1. Are the patterns of economic development which are legitimated by the Bretton Woods institutions compatible with the protection and nurturance of the diversity of ecosystems on the planet, ecosystems which in an immediate sense are the life and culture-supporting basis for a majority of the earth's human habitants? and,

2. are these patterns compatible with a process of strengthening the ongoing struggle for equity, justice, and democracy?

Threats to Ecology and Justice: The Changing Configuration of Economic Power

Global capital has become increasingly mobile. While India has been recently entrapped into the IMF–World Bank restructuring process, the other countries of the South Asian region have already become critically dependent on the western-dominated financial and economic system. In that sense, it can be said that the global economy continues to be heavily dominated by the industrial countries, with selective and tactical alliances with elites in the industrializing world. It is no coincidence that during the recent political changes in Pakistan, the transition Prime Minister was none other than Moeen Quereshi, until recently a senior vice-president of the World Bank. Similarly in India, the appointment of the new finance secretary, arguably the most powerful bureaucrat in the economic domain, was not only allegedly subject to approval by the Bank but was an individual who had worked as a senior Bank economist for a substantial part of his professional career.

Loss of Control

The resulting policy prescriptions and structural changes that have been implemented (or suggested) legitimate an extractive economy which is geared primarily to the elites who control world trade and which provides fiscal incentives to invest in export-oriented extraction. In fact, for most parts of the region, local producers are slowly losing control over what they produce, how they produce it, and at what price they can sell it in the market.

In India, most obviously over the past two years, this control has even started to slip from the hands of national elites. This economic process is significantly dependent on the intensive and extensive extraction of natural resources. Given that the majority of people in the region are still critically dependent on the sustainability of the natural resource base, this extractive economy generates large-scale impoverishment and immiseration.

However, it is not just a consensus among elites that is of concern but the emerging realignment of global institutions to shape and sustain this control. These institutions, despite their rhetoric to the contrary, are also perpetuating a dynamic that sustains national and global centralization. This is a major shift from the past when the Third World was attempting to define a more autonomous identity and independent economic priorities in keeping with their own needs.

Multilaterals, Transnationals, Trading Regimes and Elites

The Indian experience, particularly from an ecological and social per-spective, indicates that it would be naive to assume that institutions like the World Bank are 'developmental institutions'. There is now overwhelming evidence that there is an emerging nexus between four actors: Transnational Corporations (TNCs), multilateral banks, trading regimes like GATT and NAFTA, and economic elites in the so-called North and South to control the global and national economies. For countries all over the less industrialized world, this nexus is very powerful. The only exceptions where this control is not being freely exerted are where there are strong governments or where civil strife has significantly disrupted the local economy (several countries in the Middle East and in Africa) or where religious fundamentalism is acting as a bulwark against imperialist forces. Fundamental changes in the global political economy in the past two decades have helped bring this nexus about:

- Fifteen of the world's largest TNCs now have gross incomes larger than the GDP of 120 countries. Over the past decade, these TNCs have succeeded in exerting enormous power over global and national economic policy, aggressively pushing for deregulation and privatization not only in national economies but in the world economy as a whole. The Indian government's former chief economic adviser, Deepak Nayyar, stated last year that TNCs are emerging as the new global government, a World Inc, Ltd, with the G-7 as the board of directors.

- The implications of these trends transcend notions of national sovereignty. The emerging thinking among a sizeable cross-section of those who are currently shaping the global economy is that there should be a restructuring of the United Nations system itself. Specifically, it is being proposed that the UN should confine itself to the social and cultural terrain, with global economic issues being controlled by an institution like the World Trade Organization recently agreed upon in the conclusion of the Uruguay Round of the GATT negotiations.

- A careful study of the GATT proposals and the process that led to their drafting demonstrates the almost total exclusion of most governments of the Third World, with no participation of independent citizens' groups or other non-governmental agencies. In fact the only non-governmental actors that were permitted access in most of the deliberations were senior representatives of TNCs. Undoubtedly GATT legitimizes a fundamentally undemocratic trading regime that will lead to the acceptance of a lowering of environmental standards[5] and an inevitable escalation in the violation of human rights, as governments are coerced into accepting the terms of the new global regime.

- The Third World debt has reached staggering proportions. Current estimates are US$1,400 billion. Annually, the South pays the North $150 billion. If we were to compute the capital value of additional losses due to brain drain and the reverse transfer of technology, this negative outflow would amount to about $750 billion, which is equivalent to a *quarter* of the GDP of the Third World as a whole.

Threats to Federalism and Sovereignty

For countries like India these proposals and the emergence of the more coordinated nexus poses a direct threat to their federal structures since they would increasingly be brought under one homogeneous economic regime, whose terms would primarily be set by global and national economic elites in collaboration with global economic institutions.

This critique should not be misunderstood as an argument against globalization, per se. It is nevertheless the contention here that globalization only helps when trade, labour and capital flows are between equals and, even here, there can be tremendous problems as the current differences between the US and Japan indicate. It is indeed a pernicious philosophy that with globalization the market becomes available to all parties. In a differentiated heterogeneous world – both within and between countries – globalization can only be equated with the slow subjugation of weaker actors and the annihilation of cultural and ecological diversity.

The current agendas for liberalization in the absence of social and economic restructuring to a more democratic and accountable system are then just a means to the ends outlined above. These homogenizing macro-policies are inevitably leading to a closure of the spaces for sustaining the struggles for ecological sustainability and democracy. Clearly proposals like GATT, as well as the directions of the new alignment of economic power, are part of an agenda for the recolonization of most of the world.[6] Any honest assessment would make it abundantly clear that this neocolonizing end is embedded in the dominant strategies of achieving economic development.

Marginalization, Militancy and Militarization

Internally, the social and environmental impacts of export-led industrialization are far-reaching and grim. Of course, these impacts are differentially felt, both at the level of the national economy as well as at the individual level. Yet, since India is now implementing significant internal restructuring, liberalization impels a maximization of the export of primary goods and natural resources. Gandhi had predicted the dangers of adopting the colonial and capitalist mode of resource extraction when he said,

> God forbid that India should ever take to industrialization after the manner of the west. The economic imperialism of a single island kingdom is today keeping the world in chains. If an entire nation of 300 million took to similar economic exploitation it would strip the world bare like locusts.[7]

The continued expansion of export-led development, which is dependent upon the extraction of natural resources, leads to a perpetuation and strengthening of processes of internal colonization. The resultant escalation of the loss of control over productive resources and the consequent increase in economic and social insecurity contributes to the growth of social polarization and the escalation of social conflict. The case of Punjab is an example of how declining surpluses from Green Revolution agriculture (caused primarily by unsustainable agricultural practices), ecological degradation and the low availability of employment outside the land can cause disaffection, part of which gets channelled into militancy and terrorism.[8]

The government has been militarizing itself not just as a check to threats from other national aggressors but also as a means to contain internal unrest and militancy. Regional movements, dissent and other social conflicts are used as pretexts for strengthening the coercive arm of the state. This in turn absorbs key resources and disrupts the possibilities of long-term culturally and socially sensitive sustainable development. The government is increasingly becoming unresponsive to democratic and peaceful movements and their concerns. This reality continues to push many of these movements towards militant struggle, setting in motion a vicious cycle of repression, militarization of the state and popular militancy.

The Other Costs of Economic Development

The ecological impacts of export-led industrialization and of the dominant patterns of economic growth which have been furthered by IMF–World Bank-imposed policies are no longer 'externalities' that can be neglected or 'managed'. In India, there is mounting evidence that more and more areas are becoming unsustainable and unliveable. Mini-Bhopals are taking place everyday. Despite a virtual explosion of awareness, legislation and action, the root causes have hardly been touched.

Even though our current foreign exchange reserves are now considered 'comfortable', we are still getting deeper into a debt crisis[9] that is in turn increasing the pressure to export more primary products, including raw materials. Consequently, India may continue to be locked into a spiral of pollution, degradation and conflict. The resource crunch would also severely limit expenditures on clean-up and preventive initiatives.

The Indian experience suggests that current patterns of achieving economic growth are incompatible with social justice and with sustainable ecological principles. In fact, most strategies of economic growth have left the basic systemic and structural issues untouched. Despite overwhelming evidence in the post-World War period, there continues to be a belief that this growth will not only percolate downwards and 'lift' the poor from their poverty but will generate enough surpluses to provide governments the incentives and resources to 'protect the environment'.

However, India's reality tells another story. Under the new regime of economic liberalization, almost across the board, there have been cutbacks in social service spending ranging from 20 per cent to 80 per cent. Several crucial programmes have been withdrawn altogether.[10] Some efforts have been made in the 1994 Budget to increase expenditure on rural development and to define 'safety nets', but, considering the scale and pace of environmental decline and increase in impoverishment, these are little more than temporary palliatives.

The sharpening of resistance has come in the wake of the preceding reality and a realization that if the issues of equity, democracy and sustainability are to be seriously raised, they have to confront hegemonic economic and political power. Although this is not the place to present the diversity of such movements which are struggling to define an ecological politics,[11] a growing number of such movements are asserting greater autonomy from centralized governance, arguing that their livelihood is critically dependent on the productivity of the local resource base and that they must have primary control over those resources. A significant debate has been initiated around issues of equity and governance.

In places across the country, areas as diverse as the valleys of the Narmada River and the banks of the Ganga, the missile sites of Baliapal and the Chilika Lake, the forests and lands of northern Karnataka and the hills of Tehri-Garhwal, an unprecedented range of collective assertions and grassroots mobilization – stimulated in part by the continuing conflicts over natural resources – is growing stronger. Within the past two years alone, in addition to numerous actions at the local level, there have been several significant events at the national level – events which have not only challenged the 'destructive development' that generates social and economic inse-curities but also the threats that this poses to social cohesion and identity. Both tribal and non-tribal groups have participated in these collective assertions, and have been seeking not only greater political autonomy but also control over productive natural resources that are the basis of their lives.[12]

Conflicts of Interest and Conscience

As we move into the next century, we will increasingly be confronted with two conflicts, those of interests which I have alluded to above and those of conscience, the latter broadly encompassing struggles for social and ecological justice. There are five (among numerous) important responsibilities that flow from the preceding arguments:

1. It is imperative that we transcend reductionist economics and the technocratic managerial ethic and self-consciously and politically align

ourselves with those peoples, ecosystems and nations that have been rendered impoverished and destitute by the current patterns of economic development and ecological imperialism. Development is less about financial flows that need to be programmed and targeted and more about empowering people and about social and ecological justice within and between nations. Social equity is not a long-term project that can wait and ecological sustainability is not feasible without social justice. At the level of policy planning, the obvious further challenge is to integrate an ecological worldview into developmental processes.

For India, many are also arguing that the strategies of achieving relative self-reliance must be restored and that even within a conventional economic alternative, domestic savings should be made to finance investments and exports should meet all our import needs. Of course this has to be pursued while halting large borrowing from international institutions, converting short-term borrowing to longer-term (with lower interest rates), reducing and ending nonessential imports (like microwave ovens and two-door refrigerators as well as technologies that are resource-intensive and degrading), and increasing investments that strengthen local self-sufficiency.

2. While in the interim, efforts to improve the accountability of states, national governments and global institutions must continue,[13] it is imperative that greater recognition, support and legitimacy be accorded those institutions and mechanisms that empower and facilitate the relative self-sufficiency of local communities, nations and the planet itself. One immediate and urgent task is the recovery and regeneration of degraded ecosystems. It is estimated that recovering, regenerating and redistributing half of India's degraded lands that are capable of biotic production could support 400 million people!

3. Social justice and ecological sustainability are not feasible without centrally confronting modes of consumption. Current rates of consumption of the industrialized world and of Third World elites are incompatible with the realization of sustainability and democratic goals. Increase supply, yes; decrease waste, yes; locate and use 'greener' substitutes, yes. But what of the appetite itself?

The Indian case is even more complex because historically the Brahminical caste system had sanctions preventing ex-untouchable and peasant castes from consuming and wearing what the upper castes consumed or wore. In the post-Independence democratic milieu, emulating the destructive and wasteful consumerist ways of our Brahminic-capitalist elite is a natural but misconceived way to assert the dignity of the 'bahujan samaj'.[14] This emulation of consumerist lifestyles can be tackled only by counter-cultural lifestyles and anti-caste movements where Brahmins and other high-caste progressives participate along with the bahujan samaj communities and where austerity becomes a social value, particularly among progressive sectors of society.

4. Multilateral institutions like the World Bank which are undemocratic and lack the basic structures of transparency and accountability are incapable of reform beyond certain limits. One basic test of their ability to become more democratic would be to ask them to institutionalize a one-country, one-vote principle, with office-bearers chosen through an open, democratic process. (There are obvious limitations in this process including the fact that nation-states are often not representative of the people living within them.)

Another proof of greater democracy would be a citizens' appeals commission. For a number of years, citizens' groups from around the world have been seeking the establishment of an independent appeals commission which would oversee global and regional economic institutions, particularly the World Bank. The commission would investigate violations of policies, procedures and agreements as well as human rights as defined in UN covenants and declarations. Additionally, the commission would be competent to recommend suspension and cancellation of funding for specific programmes or projects. The recent setting up of an inspection panel meets some of these requirements but falls far short of democratizing the Bank's basic structure and priorities. The response to these three basic democratic demands – a truly representative board, democratic elections and an appeals commission – would be indicative of how much these institutions are committed to deepening democracy.

5. The struggle is a massive one. It is nothing short of reversing the conquest of society by the economy; of restoring the ethic of self-limitation; of recognizing that positive values are not just material acquisitions but dignity, an integration of an ecological politics, and a respect for deepening democracy. Development is not feasible without listening to our conscience, without restoring an ethics to economics and development, without restoring a symbiotic relationship with nature, without being relevant in what we do to the last person in this country and to mother earth.

Some Additional Challenges

There are a few other challenges that any process which attempts to reverse the control of global economic institutions and redefine the dominant paradigm of development must face.

1. What has been undoubtedly significant about the past decade has been the growing initiatives outside political parties to link together not only for specific collective actions but to begin a process of evolving new political perspectives. On the issue of individual corporations like Cargill and Union Carbide or on issues like GATT, forest rights, or displacement, there have also been significant collective processes. However, much of this has been reactive and difficult to sustain, though some of the energies generated in the process are now concentrated in building more broad-based movements (within countries and those that transcend national boundaries) – movements which respect the distinctiveness of individual efforts yet assert the need for continuous struggle and reflection. All this is not, as yet, translating into a sustained political alternative, though the continuing politicization as well as participation in the wider political process is creating conditions for this.

2. Most NGOs, political parties and even movements are built around charismatic individuals and the participation of average citizens is becoming increasingly difficult. Without the institutionalization of democratic mechanisms and strengthening of democratic traditions in civic and political institutions we will not be able to pave the ground for a decisive struggle against the centralizing–homogenizing aggression of the global market economy. The pervasive fragmentation of the entire democratic spectrum has to be replaced by coalescing our dispersed efforts.

3. Directly arising out of this is a related issue of a differentiated participation by movement groups in the formal political process. Despite a history of internal divisions wrought by a confusing mix of political parties, many independent movements have felt the need to participate in the electoral process. This has inevitably led to compromise and to dispersal. Yet, many feel that despite this reality, a more focused, more coordinated movement can be forged. Options vary from creating direct linkages or support for existing political parties to the formation of new parties.

The other political institutions of the system have also created enormous confusion. For instance, repressive and regressive legislation or non-implementation and repressive administration has undermined the capacity to use progressive legislation to gain democratic space. In fact, in many areas there is a growing alienation from the judicial system and from the 'democratic institutions' of the state.

4. This highlights another issue. Even where dissent has been sustained, the state and the formal political process have found numerous and more sophisticated ways of absorbing, manipulating or coopting this

and, where strategies of cooption have failed, they have used outright repression. Political activists have complained of 'battle-fatigue', of an inability to remain perpetual dissenters – others continue to be incarcerated and even killed. For still others, the lure of consumerism and other avenues of economic security have wreaked havoc with movements attempting to sustain independent political struggle.

5. Increasingly, those who have been historically marginalized are being pitched in conflict with one another and with communities who are being impoverished by 'development'. Many of these communities recognize that, often, this is a conscious strategy of the state and of the ruling classes to divide 'victim groups' along ethnic or class lines and create disaffection and competition between them. Increasingly, these communities believe that democratic movements will have to resist these divisive forces and seek alliances that cut across different 'conflicting' identities.

6. There is the need to increase the proportion of community resources of ideas, activists and finances rather than being dependent on external and international donors. Many liberal economists have, in the light of failed social experiments, often advocated pragmatism in dealing with these institutions. However, this is obviously inadequate since we continue to react to the prescriptions of 'efficiency' of the global economic institutions which, 'are likely to be inappropriate at best, and self-serving at worst. Ultimately, each nation, each people, each society [will have] to face and solve its own problems, and set its own agenda.'[15]

7. Similarly, taking up the lifestyle issue seriously and launching a movement for ecologically sensitive lifestyles is imperative. A growing number of people realize that it is not desirable or feasible to replicate the values and lifestyles of national and global elites. Barring a few honorable exceptions, movements and individuals, particularly in the industrialized world, who are committed to economic and social justice, have not been adequately introspective and vigilant about these issues. Confronting the lifestyle issue is one of the most serious challenges in the long road ahead.

Notes

1   Among those represented were initiatives working on a critique and alternatives to the new economic policies, including the Movement to Protect Independence (Azhadi Bachao Andolan), the Working Groups on Alternative Economic Policies and Alter-

native Economic Survey, the local and national campaigns against GATT, etc.

2 For a representative analysis of social movements in Latin America see two recent books: Susan Eckstein (ed.), *Power and Popular Protest: Latin American Social Movements* (University of California Press, 1989) and Sonia Alvares and Arturo Escobar, *Latin American Social Movements* (Westview Press, 1992).

3 Surajit Kumar Saha, 'Historical Premises of India's Tribal Problem', *Journal of Contemporary Asia,* 16:3, (1986), pp. 294–321.

4 Edward Barbier, 'The Concept of Sustainable Development,' *Environmental Conservation,* 14:2, pp. 101–10.

5 Several leading environmental organizations in the United States argue that regional trading regimes like NAFTA will lead to a strengthening of standards in Mexico and an increased environmental awareness generally. While there may be some truth in this, the trends that will get reinforced when the current GATT proposals become international enforceable norms point to the conclusions that I have outlined. There is no indication from the interests behind GATT that they are indeed willing to make global trade democratic, equitable and ecologically sane with an emphasis on empowering local production as well as relative national self-sufficiency. The recent Forest Ministers Conference in Delhi is also an indication of this. The commercial value of forests took precedence over the rights of local communities and the long-term sustainability of the biodiversity of the forest.

6 Chakravarti Raghavan, *Recolonization: GATT and the Third World* (London: Zed Books, 1991). Also see Robert Weissman, 'Prelude to a New Colonialism,' *The Nation,* 18 March 1991.

7 Mahatma Gandhi as quoted in Pyarelal, *Towards New Horizons* (Ahmedabad, India: Navjivan Publishing House, 1959).

8 For one of the best documented studies on the Punjab see Vandana Shiva, *The Violence of the Green Revolution* (London: Zed Books, 1992). Also see Mark Tully, *Amritsar* (New Delhi/London: Penguin Books, 1988).

9 December 1993 estimates place India's external debt at around US$ 85 billion (up from US$62 billion in 1989).

10 Praful Bidwai, 'Budget Slashes Social Sector Spending', *The Times of India,* 5 March 1992.

11 I have consciously not called these movements ecological or environmental, as this is not their self-definition of themselves. While they are attempting to integrate and address fundamental ecological issues, they are basically social and political movements. For a recent article that discusses the range and sig-

nificance of the present movement scene in India in a historical perspective, see my 'Social Movements and the Redefinition of Democracy', *India Briefing*, ed. Philip Oldenburg (Westview Press, 1993).

12   For a comprehensive article on the history of social and political movements including Jharkhand and Narmada, see Smitu Kothari and Pramod Parajuli, 'No Nature Without Social Justice: A Plea for Ecological and Cultural Pluralism in India', in Wolfgang Sachs, *Global Ecology* (London: Zed Books, 1993).

13   For a recent statement on recasting the corporations and exerting citizen accountability on them, see Richard L. Grossman and Frank T. Adams, *Taking Care of Business: Citizenship and the Charter of Incorporation* (Cambridge: Charter, Ink, 1993).

14   The society of those who have been historically discriminated and oppressed.

15   Kari Polanyi-Levitt, 'IMF Structural Adjustment: Short-Term Gain for Long-Term Pain?,' *Economic and Political Weekly*, 18 January 1992.

II

Alternatives to the International Monetary Fund

5

Alternatives to the International Monetary Fund

Robert S. Browne

The monetary mechanisms which underpin the international economic system tend to be taken for granted except in time of crisis. Because the functioning of these mechanisms is arcane and inconspicuous, they are not generally a topic of popular interest and the mystique which envelopes them often leads to an underestimation of the very powerful role which they play in determining the economic profile of our global society.

At the conclusion of World War Two, the allied leadership, recognizing that a sound and reliable monetary system was essential to the creation of a stable and prosperous global economy, created the International Monetary Fund and entrusted to it the responsibility of harmonizing the myriad, often conflicting, monetary policies and aspirations of national societies into a format which presumably would benefit all participants. Specifically, the IMF was charged with maintaining stable exchange rates, although some flexibility was to be permitted for countries whose economies had been subjected to severe shock of one sort or another. Exchange rate stability was felt to be a vital prerequisite for the expansion of international trade and a vigorous expansion of international trade was viewed as the key to a sound and prosperous international economy.

During its first thirty years, the IMF's direct involvements were primarily with the developed countries, to whom it made short-term loans on an 'as needed' basis to prevent countries which were experiencing temporary imbalances in their current accounts from being obliged to alter their exchange rates and risk destabilizing the global monetary structure. The IMF managed to achieve a remarkable degree of monetary stability during its first twenty-five years, and as a result little popular notice was taken of it.

In the early 1970s, however, a vastly changed global environment resulted in a gradual shifting of the focus of IMF lending from the developed countries to the developing countries. The IMF was not well equipped for servicing this new, Third World clientele, and the fallout from this bold but ill-advised shift plucked the IMF from its previous obscurity and made it a household word (usually pejorative) in scores of countries around the world.

The First Twenty-five Years

The basic ingredients necessary for the proper functioning of any international monetary system are:

(a) a basis for the determination of realistic currency values; and
(b) an adequate source of internationally accepted money (or 'global liquidity', as it is called by economists). At the Bretton Woods conference, full responsibility for the former requirement was assigned to the IMF, and the latter was to be jointly provided by the IMF, the World Bank and the United States.

Exchange Rates

A mechanism for the determination and maintenance of exchange rates is the foundation block of any international monetary system. If a number of countries with differing currencies are to have monetary relations, it is essential that there be agreement on the relative values of their several currencies and on how any changes in these relative values are to be determined. The IMF managed this quite well during its first quarter century of operations. During this period, the dollar was installed as the international reserve currency and its value set as equivalent to 1/35th of an ounce of gold. The values of all other currencies were set at some mutually agreed rate of exchange with the dollar. Once agreed upon, these rates could be altered only with the IMF's permission, which was contingent upon a determination that a permanent change had occurred in the underlying relative strength of the two currencies. Temporary deviations from these official exchange rates, which were usually attributable to short-term imbalances that had arisen in a country's balance of payments, were corrected by the IMF extending a short-term loan to the country having difficulty, thus enabling it to make whatever adjustments were necessary to move its currency back to its agreed parity with the dollar. In the early years, when the borrowers were mainly the industrialized countries, these adjustments were often carried out by the borrower with little or no pressure from the IMF. In later years, however, when the borrowers were principally the developing countries, these adjustments, or 'conditionalities' as they were called, became substantially more explicit and more encompassing.

Liquidity

The second requirement for a stable yet dynamic international monetary system is an expanding supply of money (liquidity) to handle the growing number of international transactions. Under the original Bretton Woods arrangements, by tacit agreement, this liquidity was to be supplied by the United States, which would (principally via the Marshall Plan and the World Bank) accede to maintaining an ongoing deficit in its balance of payments. This deficit would generate a supply of dollars for the war-ravaged and developing countries, thus enabling them to buy the goods and services necessary for their reconstruction or development. Like the fixed exchange rate, this arrangement also worked well for twenty-five or thirty years, and as a result of it Europe and Japan rebuilt their societies and a number of undeveloped countries began their journey towards development.

By the 1970s, so many changes were occurring in the international economic picture that the system of fixed exchange rates could no longer be held together. The dollar was delinked from gold in 1971, and shortly thereafter it was severely devalued. The system of fixed exchange rates was replaced by a system of floating rates, with the major developed countries, the G-7, coordinating their monetary activities around exchange rates loosely agreed to among themselves. Most other countries pegged their currencies to one or the other of the G-7 currencies, or to a basket of several currencies.

As for liquidity, the growing instability of the post-1970 dollar, and the decline of the United States' hegemonic status within the family of nations, encouraged the view that the dollar's reserve currency role in the international monetary mechanism should be reduced and perhaps terminated. There was also a growing realization that the utilization of any single member country's currency as the international reserve currency conferred severe and inequitable burdens (and advantages) on the economies of the reserve and the non-reserve currency countries alike. After extensive debate, the IMF Board of Governors agreed, in 1968, to issue an artificial reserve currency unit, the Special Drawing Right (SDR), which could be used for international transactions among nations, and between nations and a number of official multilateral financial institutions.

Paradoxically, however, just as the consensus for creation of SDRs was coming together, the need for additional global liquidity was beginning to decline as a result of the rise of the Eurodollar market, new communications technology which substantially enhanced the velocity of international transactions, and the surge of petro-dollars and other sources of commercial bank credit. Two modest issuances of SDRs were authorized, in 1969 and 1979, but thereafter the United States, and perhaps other major powers, blocked any further issuance of them, on grounds that the system now had adequate liquidity.

The Second Twenty-five Years

It is safe to say that by the mid-1970s, the IMF's status as an international monetary institution had been greatly diminished. It no longer played a significant role in the determination of currency values, nor was it a major player in the creation of global liquidity. It continued to make short-term loans to meet crisis situations, but the loan terms were not especially attractive so the demand for them was somewhat desultory. Thus, largely precluded from pursuing its original mandates, the IMF was largely reduced to the pursuit of its surveillance activities, which consisted of the periodic examination of the economies of its member countries and the making of recommendations based thereon. It was becoming increasingly apparent that the IMF was a large and well-paid bureaucracy with very little to do.

When the debt crisis burst upon the world in 1982, it was hardly surprising that the IMF was quick to see an opportunity for making itself relevant again. The debt crisis first manifested itself as a series of balance of payments disequilibria, and the IMF promptly placed its resources at the disposition of a number of those countries which found themselves unable to service their debt burdens. It made its traditional short-term loans on the assumption that borrowers could soon regain equilibrium in their balance of payments, and thus be in a position to resume the full servicing of their international debt as well as repaying the IMF. 'Conditionalities' were attached which were supposed to assist the borrower country in reining in its balance of payments deficit and putting its economy on a sounder basis.

It did not take long, however, for the IMF to discover that the heavily indebted countries were often not suffering from temporary payments imbalances – the type of which it had been used to addressing – but rather from longer-term structural deficiencies which were bringing the countries close to insolvency. The inappropriateness of the IMF stabilization programmes rather quickly became apparent, as country after country failed to meet the IMF's loan criteria and saw their IMF loans cancelled, and as the public took to the streets to protest against the negative social effects which these loans were inflicting. The IMF's response was to lengthen its loan maturities and to lower the interest rates on its loans, while retaining, and sometimes even enhancing, the severity of its loan conditionalities. Meanwhile, it turned a deaf ear to critics who dared to question the appropriateness of some of the economic policies which it was imposing on its borrowers.

During this period, the efforts of both the IMF and the World Bank to nudge their borrowing members towards more complete adoption of the market system became overt. Such a bias had characterized the Bretton Woods institutions from the time of their creation, although the official position was that their policies were ideologically neutral. Both institutions did indeed lend both to market economies and to those centrally planned economies which chose to be members, although the latter were obviously the stepchildren of the Bretton Woods family. In the 1990s, however, the pretence of ideological neutrality was dropped and access to much of the Bretton Woods institutions' resources became conditional on the borrower's adherence to market principles.

An International Monetary System for the Twenty-first Century

We have noted that the IMF has lost much of its *raison d'être* as a result of the demise of the fixed exchange rate system. The reasons go far beyond the technical activity of exchange rate management, however. The explosive expansion of the global economy, the quadrupling in the numbers of independent countries, the rise of a plethora of new global economic actors such as the transnational corporation and the Eurodollar market, the breathtaking advances in communications technology, and the pressure of an enormous and intransigent Third World debt, are only a few of the new factors whose impact on the global economy have created pressure for reconceptualization of the type of global monetary institution most appropriate for today's world.

There is also a crescendo of criticism regarding how the IMF pursues its operations under its existing mandate. During the many years when the Fund's lending was directed principally towards the developed countries, complaints about the Fund's structure and operations were muted. Perhaps the disproportionate power wielded by the United States was resented, but inasmuch as the IMF was basically a club of the rich nations, disagreements among peers were handled discreetly and rarely became the focus of popular national discontent. As the Fund's clientele shifted from the developed countries to the developing ones, however, complaints about the IMF's operations escalated *pari passu*.

These complaints against the IMF can be grouped into two categories:

1. those arising from the intrinsic inadequacy of the mandate which has been given to the IMF, and

2. those focusing on the flaws in the ways the IMF carries out the mandate which it does have.

Listed below are the IMF's principal conceptual inadequacies, followed by the structural flaws which prevent it from fulfilling its currently limited role as the monetary steward for the international community:

Conceptual inadequacies:
• Absence of an independent (country-neutral) reserve currency;
• Absence of a mechanism to stabilize exchange rates;
• Absence of a mechanism to provide macroeconomic direction to the global economy; and
• Absence of a lender of last resort.

Structural and operational deficiencies:
• Undemocratic voting structure;
• Absence of public participation and excessive confidentiality;
• Asymmetry;
• Medium-term loans used for long-term needs;
• Duplication of development work of World Bank;
• Freeze on issuance of SDRs; and
• Irrational allocation of SDRs.

The structural and operational deficiencies represent items which lend themselves to modification within the framework of the IMF as it is now conceived. Although some of these modifications, especially the introduction of a more democratic voting policy, would certainly entail some reshaping of the institution, they would leave intact the IMF's present conceptualization as an institution seeking to coordinate and harmonize the interests of its sovereign member states. Regardless of how the voting structure was modified, however, the IMF's policies would continue to be merely the reflection of the policies demanded by the dominant voting bloc within the governing body.

The conceptual inadequacies can be addressed only via the replacement of the IMF with a new supranational entity which would be empowered to influence global economic policy without the constraints imposed by conflicting national interests – much as a strong central bank operates independently of its nation's executive branch. The achievement of a global consensus necessary to create such an entity probably lies in the distant future, although the urgency for moving forward with some sort of supranational economic entity may arrive sooner than one would expect.

A Visionary Alternative to the IMF

Before proceeding to an examination of the flaws in the IMF's present structure and operations, let us first examine some of its conceptual inadequacies and reflect on what a vision of an appropriate global monetary entity might entail. The last twenty-five years of experience of the IMF, as it has wrestled with the host of new, and newly identified, factors exerting an impact on international affairs, have served to demonstrate the inadequacy of the IMF as a monetary instrument for bringing economic stability and growth to today's global community. This inadequacy was prefigured at Bretton Woods, where the birth of the IMF was marked by controversy as to whether the tasks which were being assigned to it were sufficiently comprehensive to meet the world's monetary needs. The English economist, John Maynard Keynes, had argued that the global community needed a more far-reaching monetary institution than the IMF, an institution which would have the ability to issue its own currency and to function much as a global central bank. Keynes seems to have foreseen that the attempt to use the currency of a particular country as the reserve currency for the world would prove to be non-viable over the long term.[1]

Not surprisingly, as the United States lost its position of unrivaled economic strength *vis-à-vis* other major countries, it progressively lost its claim to unchallenged global monetary leadership, a weakness became ever more apparent as the United States' acquiescence in on-going balance of payments deficits (as implicitly agreed to at Bretton Woods) gradually transformed it from a creditor to a debtor nation. Furthermore, the use of the dollar as the international reserve currency imposed awkward strictures on the United States' ability to manage its domestic economy, a handicap which was, to be sure, balanced by the tremendous advantage which the United States derived from its unique entitlement to issue unlimited amounts of its currency and oblige other countries to hold it.

A number of events suggest that the time is long overdue for replacing the remnants of this clumsy, largely defunct, system by the creation of a global central bank, authorized to issue currency in its own name. Although this would be a radical change from present monetary arrangements, it would offer a high potential for addressing some of the ills which plague the current international monetary system. Replacing the dollar with a neutral reserve currency could, by itself, introduce a greater measure of equity into the relations between the poorer and the richer countries. Utilizing the dollar as the reserve currency unavoidably links the fate of virtually all countries, and especially the poorer ones, to the economic policies pursued by the United States. For example, when the United States delinked the dollar from gold and devalued it, the countries holding their reserves in dollars sustained serious losses, whereas those which could afford to hold their reserves in gold experienced tremendous windfalls. Although this was a unique event, other examples can be cited of negative consequences for other countries arising from the system's use of a country-based reserve currency. The reserve currency tends to become the principal monetary medium for conducting international trade, thereby enhancing the economic strength of the issuing country *vis-à-vis* other countries, but especially *vis-à-vis* the poorer ones. Poor countries are also less able than the rich ones to hedge their own monetary transactions against fluctuations in the value of the reserve currency.

The vulnerability of the existing system was never in greater evidence than in September 1992, when a private American financial institution, engaging in currency speculation for private gain, managed to inflict several billion dollars in losses on the powerful Bank of England, precipitating a stiff devaluation of the British pound and forcing that once proud currency out of the incipient European currency union. The American speculator is reported to have made one billion dollars in profit, and the European exchange markets were thrown into total disarray by the incident. If the existing monetary arrangements cannot protect strong national currencies from such private speculation, it is unlikely that any type of entity of less than supranational status can do so. A global central bank could certainly devise tools to counter such destabilizing activities. Similarly, the phenomenon of the transnational corporation, a rootless profit-seeking entity which knows no nationality but which is capable of moving vast amounts of investment capital around the globe in an endless search for maximum profits, constitutes another supranational threat to the maintenance of global economic stability which can only be countered by another supranational entity such as a global central bank.

The mere thought of so powerful an institution as a global central bank is, of course, cause for considerable concern. It must be pointed out, however, that a mild, if unpredictable, form of global macro-economic policy is already being practiced by the G-7 nations, who periodically attempt to implement coordinated monetary policies with a view to achieving macroeconomic outcomes on which they have mutually agreed. In the Bretton Woods conceptualization, this was to be the task of the IMF. If the IMF finds that it can no longer carry out this task, then a more appropriate institution is needed. Abdicating this responsibility to the G-7 not only introduces an element of unaccountability to the process; it undermines the very concept of a global democratic order.

An international central bank practising global macroeconomics could function only if its member countries were prepared to yield to it some degree of sovereignty in the exercise of economic policy. For instance, countries enjoying payments surpluses or experiencing unusually high growth rates would on occasion be obliged to restrain their economies so as to bring about greater stability in the global economy. This could entail such politically sensitive trade-offs as dampening the economic activity of country A so as to stimulate the economy of country B. Do countries exist which are today prepared to accede to such a surrender of sovereignty?

Another important question is whether it is really possible to impose a distribution of power within a global financial institution which is contradictory to the distribution of wealth and power in the external world. Theoretically, the new bank could distribute liquidity in ways which would help to achieve whatever policy results it wished. In practice, of course, the central bank would be only a tool of its members, and the policies it chose to follow would reflect the wishes of those members. There is, therefore, no guarantee that the global central bank would not mimic the IMF and become the tool of the rich nations.

The imperatives of the human condition may call for the creation of a global central bank, but the likelihood that any significant number of the industrialized nations would, in the foreseeable future, be prepared to yield the sovereignty necessary for its operation is very slim indeed. The ever increasing evidence that the present system is badly in need of repair or replacement is so overwhelming, however, that it is almost certain that within the next few years we will see some sort of change in the collective management of global affairs, including monetary affairs. In this perspective, some visionary thinking is probably not inappropriate.

A Pragmatic Alternative to the IMF

If a global central bank is at present little more than a visionary hope, then we are left with the more immediate task of refashioning the IMF with a view to making it a more effective vehicle for providing international monetary stewardship in the near term.

There is perhaps no better way to approach this topic than by examining the distribution of power within the IMF. Voting is based upon each country's 'quota'. An IMF quota is primarily an indicator of how much money a country antes up to the IMF's treasury, so the richer the country, the larger its quota is likely to be. There is a certain logic to this linkage between contributions and votes inasmuch as the IMF is a lending institution, and lenders are expected to demand some degree of control over the use of their funds. On the other hand, much lip service is paid these days to the concept of democracy, which, if it is to have any meaning whatsoever, can hardly be reconciled with a situation where the vast majority of countries are denied any real influence over so vital an economic instrument as monetary policy.

The IMF's undemocratic nature is even more sharply exposed by the fact that, for the approval of certain 'important' issues, a majority vote of as much as eighty-five per cent is required for passage.[2] While it may be unrealistic to expect the industrialized countries to place their funds into a 'one country, one vote' structure, it is not unreasonable to expect a more democratic arrangement than that which exists at present. (See Chapter Eight.) Nor is it unreasonable to demand that the inner deliberations of the IMF be more open to public scrutiny and participation than is now the case. A valid case can be made for a certain amount of confidentiality surrounding high-level negotiations at the international level, and for preventing speculators from having premature knowledge of pending changes in policy. These considerations can be respected without resort to the high degree of secrecy which characterizes much of the IMF's operations.

Another egregious example of the inequitable treatment of the poor and the rich countries in the IMF relates to the degree of compliance which is exacted for IMF directives, what IMF critics refer to as the 'asymmetry' problem. Although considerable publicity is given to the often highly controversial conditionalities which the IMF imposes upon its borrowers, it is less well known that the economies of the non-borrowing countries are also subjected to regular 'surveillance' by the IMF staff. Following each such surveillance, the IMF makes strong recommendations to countries whose economic policies are perceived as being harmful to the global economy. Countries with persistent payment surpluses are urged to reduce them; countries with persistent budget deficits are urged to eliminate them.

The asymmetry comes from the fact that, where borrowing countries are concerned, the IMF insists that the policies which it recommends be carried out, or the erring borrower will face the loss of his loan. With the non-borrowers, however, the IMF can do little more than urge that the policies that it is recommending be followed. It lacks any mechanism for insuring that its policy recommendations will be implemented by non-borrowers, and it is common for the non-borrowers to ignore them entirely. The United States is a prime example of this phenomenon. For years the IMF has highlighted various nefarious global effects arising from the persistent US budget deficit, and has publicly urged Washington to reduce it, all to no effect. If a poor, famine-stricken country in Africa is expected to slash its budget deficit when its people are already at the brink of disaster, why shouldn't the United States be expected to do the same, especially if its deficit is hurting other, less fortunate countries?

Actually, this asymmetry is doubly objectionable, because bad policies pursued by the industrialized countries frequently have strongly negative effects on the poorer countries whereas the bad policies pursued by the poor countries generally damage only themselves. Asymmetry undermines the credibility of the Fund, and is a manifestation of the sovereignty problem cited earlier as the principal obstacle to the establishment of a global central bank. It could, of course, be resolved were the will there to do so.

We have noted how the emergence of the debt crisis afforded the IMF an opportunity to again become a major player on the international economic scene, after it had lost its mandate to maintain fixed exchange rates. The fact that it disposed of only short-term funds did not seem to daunt it. Not surprisingly, it rapidly became the focus of considerable protest because the short-term nature of its funds led it to demand that policy reforms be implemented within unrealistic time frames, thereby producing serious negative effects within the borrowing countries. Eventually, however, the IMF managed to win authorization from its members to provide medium-term loans. Faced with the prospect of serious defaults from insolvent countries, it created the Structural Adjustment Facility and later the Enhanced Structural Adjustment Facility, both of which served as vehicles for rolling over the IMF's shorter-term, near market rate loans, into medium-term maturities at very modest rates of interest.

By this time, however, the World Bank, which is a development agency well supplied with long-term loan funds, had also entered the debt amelioration business, extending what were known as 'structural adjustment' loans to the debt-strapped countries. Unlike the Bank's normal 'project' loans, which were designated for such identifiable items as roads and bridges, the structural adjustment loans could be used for reducing balance of payments deficits, for debt servicing and for the purchase of imports. Qualification for these loans required the adoption of strong policy reforms, however, reminiscent of the 'conditionalities' earlier imposed by the IMF's stabilization loans.

Indeed, it was not long before the work of the two institutions had converged to the point where much of their work had become virtually indistinguishable, and questions began to be raised as to why two bureaucracies were needed to plough the same ground.

Meanwhile, environmental groups and other interested NGOs, who had for many years been demanding that the World Bank take human rights, environmental impact, poverty and other social criteria into consideration in approving its project loans, soon realized that such demands also needed to be directed toward the IMF. The IMF, however, has a narrowly specialized professional staff, virtually all of whom are economists, and hiring specialists from other disciplines to handle these additional issues would create an expensive bureaucracy parallel to that of the World Bank.

Inasmuch as the Bank is the agency designated to do development lending, there is little justification for the Fund to duplicate that task. This is not to suggest that the two institutions should merge, although there is a growing chorus calling for such an action. The monetary issues are quite distinct from the development issues and the Fund has proved itself to be well equipped to deal with the former but ill equipped to deal with the latter. What the Fund needs to do is to find a means to reinsert itself into monetary policy. The need for an international monetary institution has certainly not disappeared. Despite the prevalence of floating exchange rates, countries continue to find themselves in temporary need of funds to carry them through short-term payments imbalances. An IMF-like institution is vitally needed to assist in such circumstances.

Perhaps even more vital, however, is the role which the Fund could play in facilitating the widespread use of a country-neutral reserve currency. Unfortunately, the IMF's failure to continue to expand the usage of the SDR and to introduce it more visibly into the public consciousness has rendered it virtually stillborn, at least for the moment. The need for such a currency instrument has not disappeared, however, and the IMF is derelict in not pushing its usage more vigorously. The IMF is, of course, the instrument of its wealthy members, and it can be paralyzed by the opposition of these members, and especially by the veto power of the United States. The solution lies with mobilizing Congressional support to push the Treasury Department towards new monetary initiatives such as the SDR. However, most members of Congress have probably never heard of an SDR, so that struggle could be long and arduous.

In any case, the struggle should not be simply for more SDRs to be issued, but for a more relevant SDR. When SDRs were first created it was mandated that they would be distributed to countries on the basis of their quotas within the IMF. If one believes that it is in the best interest of the 'haves' to lend a helping hand to the 'have-nots', then a splendid opportunity was thereby missed for helping to close the intractable gap between the richer and the poorer countries. It was the influential IMF members' own arbitrary action which decided that quotas should be used as the basis for SDR distribution. A needs-determined basis could just as well have been chosen and, indeed, was requested by the Third World countries. The response of the rich countries was that the SDR was intended solely as a mechanism for providing liquidity and should not be linked to welfare considerations of any sort. Later, when the big powers decided to block further issuance of SDRs despite the pleas of the poor countries that they were experiencing severe liquidity shortages, the rationale offered was that the SDR was intended solely as a means of preventing global liquidity shortages, and as there was no longer a *global* shortage, no further SDRs were needed. The fact that many of the member countries were suffering from enormous national liquidity shortages was treated as irrelevant.

In 1987 a bill was offered in the US House of Representatives instructing the Treasury Department to raise with the IMF the idea of making a one-time issuance of 'special purpose' SDRs,[3] which would be allocated among the poorest of the debt-burdened countries on a needs-determined basis, with the proviso that they could only be used for the repayment of official debt. It promised to be an innovative and relatively burdenless way of effectively writing down a significant portion of the Third World debt. Unfortunately, the bill was emasculated in sub-committee, and as finally passed,[4] merely mandated the Treasury Department to prepare a 'study' of the proposal. This effectively killed it, because the Treasury Department was adamantly opposed to the further issuance of any SDRs whatsoever, even of the orthodox type. None the less, this proposal continues to offer a concrete method for engaging in some serious

debt reduction and deserves to be revived, although there is as yet
no indication that President Clinton's Treasury Department is any
more adventurous than was President Bush's. Nor is it entirely clear
why the United States, after having initially supported the creation
of the SDR, has been so opposed to any expansion of its usage.
Alarm in Washington at the prospect of a gradual usurpation of the
role of the dollar by the SDR may provide a partial explanation,
although the decline in the dollar's hegemony is so inevitable that
United States interests would probably be best served in the long run
if the dollar were to be replaced by an international currency unit
rather than by one or more national currencies.

Conclusions

It has become fashionable to demonize the IMF, a practice which is
not particularly helpful in understanding what the IMF is, what it
is meant to achieve, and what its future direction should be. It is most
frequently criticized for the harsh policies it imposes on poor countries
seeking to borrow from it. Considerable criticism is indeed warranted
in this regard, because the IMF has taken an excessively economistic
approach to the problems of the poor countries, often demonstrating a total insensitivity to the social and political realities within these
countries. The time frame within which it has expected policy
reforms to be implemented has generally been unrealistic, and too
frequently the IMF has found itself to be a net recipient of capital
from the Third World rather than a net exporter of capital to it.
Happily, the IMF has taken some limited steps to respond to these
criticisms, by softening its lending terms and extending its payback
period. Many of these criticisms arise from the fact that the IMF's
reserves and its structure were not designed for the type of medium-
term, development-focused lending in which it now finds itself
immersed. It would be well advised to leave these activities to the
World Bank and other institutions.

To relinquish its development lending activities to other institutions would not leave the Fund with nothing to do. Rather, it would
free it up to refocus its attention on global monetary affairs. The demise
of fixed exchange rates did indeed eliminate the main role which
the IMF had been playing in the international monetary system. It
did not, however, leave it powerless to play some role, if its major
members would permit it to do so. Whether by design or by chance,
the existing global economic system favours the rich countries over
the poor ones. After three so-called United Nations 'development
decades', the gap between per capita incomes in the poor countries

and the rich ones is even larger than at the outset. This is an immoral as well as a dangerous situation, which the world has been much too slow in addressing effectively.

The monetary system by itself cannot solve this problem but it can be structured to assist in its solution. It should definitely not be an obstacle to its resolution. The IMF recently demonstrated its willingness to break with orthodoxy when it introduced a new method of calculating country GDP figures, utilizing as a basis the purchasing power of country currencies rather than their official exchange rates with the dollar. This is a significant move towards reality. Only an entity with the stature of the IMF could have institutionalized so novel an idea, despite the fact that the concept has been under discussion in academic circles for many years. A logical next step might be for the IMF to test the feasibility of an entirely new type of international currency, one which would maintain a constant purchasing power, based perhaps on a basket of commodities.[5]

More democratic voting arrangements and less secretiveness about its inner workings would enhance the IMF's credibility in most of the world, and would be in keeping with the current shift towards more democracy at the national level in many countries. The asymmetry problem, which is just another form of discriminatory treatment favouring the richer countries, is not likely to be ended soon. The rich countries will probably continue to ignore the IMF's strictures until a new, more effective supranational structure is imposed or agreed to.

These suggested adjustments in the way the IMF operates, although offering prospects for genuine improvement in the IMF's effectiveness and usefulness to the global community, will not be sufficient to meet the fast changing needs of the global society of the twenty-first century. For this, an entirely new mindset must be nurtured, one which accepts the inescapable interconnectedness of the human condition everywhere in the world. This realization will ultimately drive society towards the fashioning of global, rather than exclusively national, approaches to problem solving. The need will then become apparent for the nation state to sacrifice some of its sovereignty in the interest of achieving a greater good. The achievement of consensus on the fashioning of a supranational monetary institution would be a necessary component of building such a global community. One aspect of preparing the public for such a step would be for the IMF to move the SDR out of the closet and accustom people to the concept of a global currency. Americans and others were gradually brought to accept a paper dollar whose value rests solely on its public acceptance rather than on any intrinsic physical backing. The same can be done for the concept of an internationally issued currency, but it will require considerable time. The sooner we begin, the better.

Space does not allow for a detailed discussion of the myriad facets of a supranational financial institution, or global central bank. It may, however, be helpful to anticipate some of the concerns likely to be expressed by those seeking to evaluate the merits of such an institution: sovereignty; allocation of power; and funding. There is little which can be predicted with regard to the yielding of national sovereignty to an international body. It is likely to be agreed to by a significant number of nations only when the global monetary system finds itself in a prolonged crisis from which there appears to be no alternative means of escape.

The other two concerns can be addressed simultaneously. Because most international institutions are financed by their member states, they are usually structured so that the allocation of power within the institution roughly parallels the financial contributions of its member states. The United Nations General Assembly is the major exception to this pattern. This is not a very democratic outcome, of course, and the best way around it is to find another way of funding the institution. One possible source for funding a supranational monetary institution would be from the imposition of a small tax on international monetary transfers of all types.[6] Because such transfers now run into the trillions of dollars annually, a very tiny tax would yield a very large revenue. Such a tax would not be a serious burden for international trade, inasmuch as in excess of eighty-five per cent of contemporary international financial monetary transfers arise not from trade but from speculative movements of capital, some of which may be useful but many of which may be actually harmful to the international monetary system. Other possible sources of financing could be from the revenues yielded from the sustainable management of some of the 'international commons', such as the oceans and the poles. Such non-nation-based funding would go far to counter the pressure for control of the global central bank by the richer countries.

The ways in which we have approached international monetary arrangements in the past must give way to creative new thinking about how mankind can best organize itself for survival in the twenty-first century. We must prepare ourselves for bold new initiatives, just as we did in 1944.

Notes

1   *The Collected Writings of John Maynard Keynes* (Cambridge University Press), vols. 25 and 26, 1980.

2 The United States has 17 per cent of the votes in the IMF's governing board, and is thus able to exercise a veto over major policy issues coming before the IMF.

3 The 'special purpose' SDR would be interest-free for the first user.

4 US Congress, *Trade and International Economic Policy Reform Act of 1987*, Title IV, Subtitle A, chapter 2, sec. 421.

5 See for example, R. Browne and A. Makhijani, 'The World's Monetary Arrangements', *World Policy Journal*, vol. III, no.1, Winter 1985–6, pp. 59–80.

6 See for example, J. Tobin, 'A Proposal for International Monetary Reform', *Eastern Economic Journal*, vol. 4, July/Oct. 1978, pp. 158–9.

6

Taming Global Money

Howard M. Wachtel

Of all the changes in the global economy over the past generation, none have occurred with such alacrity as those in the realm of money and finance. And nowhere else have governments lagged further behind in putting in place effective checks and regulations. Walter Wriston, who as chairman of Citicorp was in on the creation of this new global financial order, has written that this was a

> new system ... not built by politicians or economists ... which in turn has allowed [the] creation of a new international monetary system. This state of affairs does not sit too well with many sovereign governments because they correctly perceive [it] as an attack on the very nature of sovereign power.[1]

As political sovereignty is challenged by privatized global finance, economic performance in the industrial economies suffers: unemployment grows as wealth forsakes capital formation for financial speculation; trade volumes fall as firms cover the higher cost of foreign exchange risk; and real rates of interest rise as countries competitively position their interest rates to stablize foreign exchange values.

The Federal Reserve Board of New York estimates that each day some one trillion dollars of foreign exchange transactions are completed on a twenty-four hour clock in New York, Tokyo and London. Only about eighteen per cent support either international trade or investment – the ostensible reason for a foreign exchange market. The other eighty-two per cent is speculation, where speculation means simply that the purpose is to buy enormous volumes low and sell high in order to make a small unit profit (but a large overall profit) on the activity of buying and selling what appear as ephemeral jottings on a computer screen.

A globalized money system that recognizes no geographic boundaries threatens the most fundamental economic *raison d'être* of the nation state: the ability to control its money supply and influence the value of its money. Using telecommunications technology that nests in satellites far above internationally recognized national boundaries and the marvel of modern computer power, this foreign exchange system comprises the essence of a supranational economy. This is an economy governed by the fundamental tension between the unbounded economic geography of a private global money system and the bounded political geography of nation states. While recognizing that this technological and institutional genie cannot be put back in the bottle, it is essential, nevertheless, that boundaries be placed on its operations for two reasons: its potential for vast financial instability and its undermining of the twentieth century's governing project of social democracy.

The proposals and policies for dealing with this problem are motivated by several principles:

- the simpler the better;
- existing national policies should be extended where feasible;
- existing venues and organizations for international collaboration should be used and no new ones created;
- no new international treaty arrangements.

With these principles in mind, I would begin by extending all existing national monetary controls, regulations and supervision to this global money system which presently escapes all such government policies. Much of this unregulated money flows through what has come to be called the Eurodollar System, and it comes under no national regulatory authority. The system takes its name and is defined by the phenomenon of currencies used outside the borders of a country and, therefore, outside the jurisdiction of their nation of origin. The birth of this system goes back to the late 1940s when the Soviet Union placed their dollar holdings in a French bank to avoid the possibility of having these accounts frozen should the United States choose this strategy. They grew slowly and their potential was not realized until the United States imposed exchange controls in the 1960s. Banks and their multinational customers then found ways around the exchange controls by using the Eurodollar system. The system reached maturity in the 1970s by being the principal receptacle for some US$350 billion in surpluses earned by oil-exporting countries.

Some eighty-five per cent of Eurodollars accounts are made up of dollars, with German marks and Japanese yen the two other principal currencies. Technically, these currencies should be regulated in the jurisdiction in which they are used. But this is not done for fear that the operations would be moved to an unregulated venue if a government began to regulate their activities. We do not even have a good counting of the dollars in the Eurodollar markets. A rough estimate is that it is nearly US$2 trillion, but no agency of the United States government regulates or monitors its movements.

Effectively the Federal Reserve Board has abdicated its central function of control over the portion of the money supply that is influenced by the Eurodollar System. The Fed's principal control instrument is the power to set reserve requirements: set-asides against deposits that banks are required to sequester. For the dollars that circulate inside the US, banks are required to set aside such reserves and this is what limits the expansion of the money supply, affords the Federal Reserve control over this crucial monetary function and allows it to influence interest rates. But for Eurodollars, no such reserve controls exist and the growth of this money supply lies solely in private bank hands. In Eurodollar accounts, banks can theoretically lend out all of their deposits (though they tend to hold small reserves but less than required on domestic accounts). The ability to hold less idle and unused reserves is what makes the Eurodollar System so attractive to banks. They can make all of their deposits work for them, receive larger profits, while charging lower interest rates than on domestic activity. The policy of extending reserve requirements to Eurodollars, therefore, would place Eurodollars on an equal footing with domestic dollars and eliminate what is now an incentive for banks to hold and invest dollars outside the United States where they can earn higher profits, charge lower rates of interest and escape regulatory and tax obligations.

Such a measure, combined with others, could encourage investment inside the United States and reduce the incentive to invest outside the United States. The Eurodollar System presents the classic supranational dilemma for public policy. If banks are offered an unregulated and lower-taxed arena outside of their nation of origin, while giving up no domestic supports, they will opt to do business there rather than in the regulated and higher-taxed domestic economy. Without precluding banks from operating in the Eurodollar System, it is the job of government to equalize the domestic and international structures in which banks do business. Otherwise the outcome is readily predicted: banks will protect their Eurodollar environment by investing outside of the tax and regulatory scope of the US government. The increasingly aggressive flight of capital from the United States in the past two decades is in no small measure induced by the skewed incentives provided by this abdication of public policy responsibility.

This is one outcome of the privatized and unregulated global financial system: lower volumes of investment inside the United States and more investment outside. A second represents the higher costs placed on international trade and the resulting lower volume of world trade than would be the case if public boundaries were placed around foreign exchange speculation. With speculation in foreign exchange comes risk for anyone dealing in transactions that require conversion of currencies. This is true for the lone tourist as it is for a large international trade enterprise. The higher the volatility of exchange rates, the greater the risk and the higher the cost of covering the risk. The volatility in exchange rate fluctuations in the 1980s and 1990s is far greater than anyone anticipated after the end of the Bretton Woods fixed-rate regime between 1971 and 1973 and the introduction of market-determined exchange rates. And with this volatility comes risk, higher costs of internationally traded goods and a lower volume of world trade.

Unfortunately for consumers, risk is a cost that is added to the price of products exchanged internationally. The cost occurs when firms have to enter the futures markets to hedge against possible losses in their future foreign exchange transactions. While this adds a little to the employment and income generated in the peripheral financial sectors of the economy, the goods-production economy suffers as these higher costs are passed on as higher prices in internationally traded products. And higher prices mean less goods and services produced and sold, lowering employment in the goods-producing sector. There is, consequently, a distributional shift in employment that arises from foreign exchange speculation. Employment in the financial sectors that engage in speculation increases – foreign exchange and futures markets – but employment in the goods-producing segments of the economy suffers. The most fervent advocates of free trade are also the ones that resist most aggressively any efforts to place public policy boundaries around the present foreign exchange markets. But they fail to realize that these arrangements increase the cost of internationally traded goods and, therefore, lower the volume of international trade. Public policy that addresses foreign exchange volatility and speculation is also trade policy in the best tradition of an open trading system shorn of the ideologically driven mantra of 'free trade'.

How can this volatility be brought under control? Foreign exchange speculation feeds off interest rate differentials among the industrial countries. Even small differences in interest rates, after adjusting for inflation and the risk associated with future exchange rate changes, can trigger large movements of foreign exchange. Such a development can then take on a life of its own, magnify whatever differentials started the process and end up destabilizing the structure of interest rates in the currencies that are in play. For example, interest rates are lower in Great Britain than in Germany after taking account of risk and inflation. Under ordinary circumstances relatively small movements of currencies out of sterling and into marks would be of no consequence. But if the movement becomes a stampede, then both the mark and sterling face destabilization. A large rush out of sterling will lower the pound's exchange rate *vis-à-vis* the mark. If it cannot be contained by intervention, then pressure will be placed on British interest rates. First the market will signal a drift upward of British interest rates to attract and retain capital and eventually it will have to be ratified by the central bank, thereby forcing a change in policy inside the British domestic economy. This scenario is not fiction. It happened to Great Britain in the summer of 1993, exaggerated somewhat by the adherence to fixed exchange-rate boundaries within the European Monetary System.

The Bretton Woods arrangements were constructed to avoid precisely these problems. John Maynard Keynes, whose influence transcended all others at Bretton Woods, sought to take the price of money out of the play of the market. He was not a planner nor one who believed in the government setting prices – except with the price of money. There is an external and an internal price for money. The internal price of money is the interest rate. Its external price is the foreign exchange rate – what one nation's price of money is in terms of another's.

Keynes's *General Theory,* published in the mid-1930s, and after which the Keynesian Revolution is named, focuses on the internal or domestic economy, ignoring for the most part external economic relations in the international economy. Central to his work is the interest rate – the internal price of money, its function and how it should be determined. Keynes presents a persuasive case that the interest rate should be established by the central bank in order to achieve the objectives of high levels of employment. He insists that the interest rate be taken out of the play of market forces and that it be one of the few instruments of policy retained by the government. In the Keynesian *General Theory* this one price, and just this one price, is set by government.

He extended this rationale at Bretton Woods. If the external price of money – the foreign exchange rate – remained within the play of market forces, then the interest rate would be affected. It would be dragged into the play of market forces, and undermine the centrepiece of the *General Theory*. The creation of fixed exchange rates, established among governments in international accord, was designed to remove the external price of money from market forces in order to promote international trade and in order to permit governments to follow their own domestic monetary policies with interest rates they established. The Bretton Woods designers saw the two prices of money as linked: if one were set free on the market, inevitably so would the other. This would not be a terrible fate if one believed the market was more astute at setting the internal and external prices of money. But that is not what Keynes believed, nor was it the consensus of those who accepted fixed exchange rates at Bretton Woods.

This all collapsed between 1971 and 1973 when the fixed exchange rate regime fell under its own weight and the absence of imagination on the part of the industrial economies which for more than a decade put off treating the fractures in the Bretton Woods fixed-exchange rate system. When a market-determined exchange rate system replaced the fixed exchange rate, external prices of money began to gyrate more widely with each cycle of exchange-rate fluctuation. By the end of the 1970s domestic interest rates were pulled into this maelstrom and were used to stabilize exchange rates. Just as Keynes predicted, once the external price of money was left to float freely on the market, governments would begin to lose control over their domestic interest rates – the internal price of money. In the 1980s and 1990s the two have become linked more closely as markets and policy managers have absorbed the teachings of the 1970s and now try to calibrate domestic interest rates to exchange rate movements.

The answer to this conundrum is to create a new exchange rate system that combines the best of the fixed and the floating rate systems. This would be one in which the exchange rate bands were wide enough to accommodate the market but not so wide as to destabilize domestic interest rates. Coupled with this should be a coordination of interest rate policy so that individual countries can pursue their own domestic interest rate strategies but not at the expense of the destabilization of other nations' interest rate policies, as happened between Germany and Great Britain in 1993.

The important factor in the movement of short-term financial capital is the *relative* interest rates in any two countries. Their level is inconsequential. It should be possible, therefore, to engage in policy coordination over relative interest rates while slowly moving downward the absolute level of interest rates. Presently no one government can lower interest rates too much without threatening a run on their currency via capital flight. But coordination could permit this.

Such policy coordination is not terribly cumbersome. In fact, the coordination need only occur among the United States, Japan and the European Community (with Germany being pre-eminent in the European Community). This is not a large group. Nor is it one which does not already have formal and informal venues in which consultation goes on continuously. The key actors know each other very well, think along similar lines and share a common financial culture. In fact, this is one of the simplest and easiest of any policy coordination ideas to implement precisely because of the shared values among the decision-makers.

Nations have not pursued this collaborative interest rate policy because they have jealously guarded what they continue to believe is their exclusive franchise over the value of their money. But this has been only partially valid for nearly two decades. The quicker countries abandon this fiction the sooner they will be able to ask the appropriate questions about financial governance in the last decade of the twentieth century.

The problems posed by this new supranational economic order extend beyond the boundaries of economic stability. Political stability is also threatened by a global regime in which the nation state has been weakened in its influence over economic welfare. This is true for the old as well as the new parliamentary democracies. The new parliamentary democracies in the post-Cold War era conflict with a supranational economic order that leaves scant room for economic improvement and imposes a unified ideology of free markets on an historical setting to which it is ill-suited. For the established market economies, a government that cannot control the internal value of its money – the interest rate – when its currency is under stress, or direct its economic destiny, has limited call on the public for support. In both instances, abstract forces emanating from the global economy seem to exercise more influence over personal economic futures than do elected governments.

The fragmentation of modern society, and the accompanying resurgence of nationalism that is seen most acutely in Europe, is in no small measure a result of the weakened economic influence of governments. Economic insecurity, rising levels of unemployment and fear of the future all converge to destabilize political systems when they are seen to be ineffective in dealing with the erosion of economic vitality. Blaming the other, hunkering down and replaying old tapes of ethnic hatred are the result of governments allowing the untamed forces of economic supranationalism to have their way with national economies.

Globalism begets tribalism in a world in which governments no longer exercise dominion over their economies. The paradox of the minutiae of nationalisms coexisting with the most modern of globalisms takes on meaning when tribal rituals fill the void left by public inaction and inattention. The threats to social stability spawned by the global economy cut deeper into society than mere economic welfare. In the post-Cold War era, this threat is nationalism and its tendency towards the balkanization of society. By not attending to economic globalism, governments encourage the incubation of a nationalism that confronts them with a new security threat.

Note

1   *Wall Street Journal*, 12 November 1985, p. 28.

7

Creative Debt Relief: The Swiss Debt Reduction Facility

Alfred Gugler

Citizens groups in a few countries have proved particularly adept at challenging and pressuring their governments to initiate innovative responses to the debt, finance and development crises that the Bretton Woods institutions have helped to foster. A prominent country in this regard is Switzerland which until recently did not belong to the World Bank and IMF. Swiss groups led a spirited but ultimately unsuccessful campaign to defeat a national referendum on Switzerland joining the Bretton Woods institutions. After failing in this effort, a broad coalition of Swiss development NGOs carried out a campaign that led to one of the most comprehensive and innovative programmes to wipe out debts owed by developing countries, and to convert some of the debts into new development funds controlled by NGOs and citizens groups in debtor nations. The Swiss NGOs involved in the implementation of this debt relief programme, together with the Swiss government, are now attempting to share this debt reduction experience with other countries in the hope that others might follow in their footsteps.

A Broad-based NGO Debt Campaign

It all began in 1989, when more than twenty-five Swiss development NGOs and church-related organizations came together in order to form a coalition to carry out a national debt campaign. This had been preceded by more than a year of discussion and reflection on the best way in which Switzerland could contribute to an easing of the debt crisis of the Southern countries.

After long and controversial debates it was decided to choose a pragmatic route, whereby the need for long-term structural changes in the world economic order would be combined with the demand for short-term improvements in financial flows through a substantial debt reduction.

Thus, the petition launched by the NGO coalition called on the Swiss government to establish a 'debt relief fund' of at least 700 million Swiss francs (approximately US$470 million) in order to write off both the official debt owed to the government and private banks in Switzerland by the low income countries. In addition, the petition asked for more equitable economic and financial relations with the South, particularly with respect to prices of primary commodities and capital flight.

The Debt Reduction Facility

Thanks to massive social mobilization, the debt petition campaign was able to gather the impressive figure of 250,000 signatures. Due to this substantial political pressure, the Swiss government drafted a bill based on the petition within a very short period of time. In March 1991, the Parliament passed the bill without any amendments.

Although the Swiss NGOs did not agree with a number of aspects of the bill, they had to acknowledge that the proposed concept and set of measures were quite comprehensive and sensible.

The newly established Debt Facility aims to support eligible countries in their efforts to reduce their commercial, official, bilateral and multilateral debt. The debt reduction operations are designed to restore normal financial relations with creditors and to improve the prospects for economic and social development of these countries. Only recognized debt claims of a non-military nature are taken into account for buy-backs.

The potential beneficiaries of the debt relief programme are highly indebted low-income countries (the so-called 'Enhanced Toronto countries'), programme countries of Swiss ODA which had to restructure their debt in the Paris Club, and all least developed countries that are not included in either of the two previous groups.

To become eligible for debt relief under the Facility, the countries must be engaged in a medium-term economic reform programme. In addition, their governance situation must be acceptable, and they should have an adequate debt management system.

Measures Applied and Operations Concluded

The Debt Facility has an endowment of 500 million Swiss francs (approximately US$350 million) to finance both bilateral and multilateral debt relief operations. It is expected that at least US$1.8 billion of debt will be retired under the Facility. Measures to reduce debt include:

- buy-backs of commercial bank debt and contributions to the IDA Debt Reduction Facility;
- contributions to the clearing of arrears and, where appropriate, the financing of obligations to the international financial institutions; and
- complementary measures, such as provision of fresh money in conjunction with debt relief and fresh money for countries having avoided a large debt overhang and/or a breakdown in their external creditor relations.

In 1992–3, two operations for the buy-back of tail-ends of officially guaranteed export credit debts were conducted. They covered claims on twenty-seven countries, with a large share in sub-Saharan Africa. The total volume of debt that can be retired through this buy-back, including the part under guarantee held by the Swiss Export Guarantee Agency, amounts to approximately US$900 million.

In addition, Switzerland has co-financed four internationally coordinated debt buy-backs prepared and implemented by IDA, with a total amount of US$9 million. At the end of 1993, the Swiss government decided to contribute a further lump sum of US$14 million to the IDA Debt Reduction Facility for upcoming operations of the same type.

When a country fulfills the preconditions for debt relief, the Swiss government enters into negotiations with the debtor government. The debt in foreign currency is forgiven at 100 per cent. As a rule, however, the Swiss government negotiates the establishment of a counterpart fund, wherein part of the debt is converted into local currency. The redemption rate is determined on the basis of a variety of factors: secondary market price, budgetary constraints of the debtor government, fiscal and monetary policies, social policy and absorptive capacities of the private sector. Generally, the conversion factor negotiated in these bilateral debt agreements is relatively low, but it can vary considerably: the lowest rate thus far was for Zambia (8 per cent of face value), the highest for Jordan (30 per cent).

The Concept of Creative Debt Relief

'Development requires debt relief' was the slogan of the NGO debt campaign that was at the origin of the Swiss Debt Reduction Facility.

The underlying idea was that for a great number of developing countries the external debt burden was so heavy that it blocked their economic and social development. Therefore, substantial debt relief was indispensable to provide these countries prospects for development.

Aside from the quantitative aspect of easing the debt burden, the slogan also possessed a qualitative dimension: the idea of creative debt relief. This meant that debt relief could be used as a tool for fostering development in a broad sense. The NGOs had suggested in their petition that the governments of the South should redeem a small part of the external debt in local currency into a so-called counterpart fund to be administered and utilized by domestic NGOs. In this way, the macroeconomic benefits derived from debt reduction were to be passed on to the micro level. However, what was proposed was not just 'more of the same', that is, more individual development projects. The idea was also to allow domestic NGOs to create long-term financial instruments, like capital or trust funds, thus enhancing their financial autonomy as well as their organizational and management capacities. Additionally, the part of the local currency proceeds not directly used for funding projects could serve as the capital base for a financial institution on the micro-level or, for instance, as a loan guarantee fund (see the Zambian case described below). In short, what the NGOs were proposing was what some have called 'the next generation of debt swaps'.

What Does a Programme of Creative Debt Relief Look Like?

A creative debt relief operation as implemented under the Swiss Facility includes four components:

1. *A bilateral debt relief agreement.* The Swiss government negotiates the debt relief including the provision of the local currency (counterpart fund, or CPF) with the debtor government. The agreement eventually signed between the two parties generally provides for, apart from some general provisions and a specification of the debt to be converted, the redemption rate, the payment modalities, the sector(s) in which the resources should be invested, and the structure and composition of the body responsible for the management of the fund.

2. *The body responsible for the management of the CPF.* Ideally, the CPF should be managed by an independent body representing the whole range of NGOs and POs (people's organizations) that are active in the priority sectors specified in the agreement. Generally, the rep-

resentatives on the CPF board or committee will come from the most representative national umbrella organizations or NGO networks. The contracting parties, i.e. the two governments, will usually also have a seat on the CPF committee.

Within a certain period of time after its constitution, the CPF body has to work out rules and regulations for its own functioning and for the allocation of the fund's resources. These include, among others, general investment and funding policy guidelines, funding application guidelines and project selection criteria.

3. *Projects and programmes to be submitted for funding*. Within the priority sectors defined in the agreement, the scope of projects and activities eligible for funding should be defined broadly enough as to allow all the interested NGOs and POs to file applications. An interesting and innovative field of application is the promotion and strengthening of the organizations themselves. Resources from the CPF can contribute to enhancing the management capacities and the financial autonomy of operational NGOs or service support organizations. This may be achieved through the creation of endowments, through infrastructure investments or by funding educational activities.

4. *The development partnership*. A creative debt relief programme should be embedded in the long-term relationship between NGOs in the South and development cooperation agencies in the North. Only a long term relationship provides the necessary insight into the local conditions and a sufficient knowledge of the strengths and weaknesses of specific organizations. Especially in the preparatory phase, that is prior to the signing of the bilateral agreement, when the organizational structure of the CPF is designed, close cooperation and regular exchange of information between the NGO partners in the South and the North are of great importance. This allows both sides to be informed at any time about the intentions of their counterpart's government and thus to avoid unpleasant surprises. After signing the agreement, the role of individual Swiss NGOs is to inform their partners about the contents of the agreement and to support them in preparing and filing funding applications.

How Are Such Programmes Being Implemented?

The key element of a programme of creative debt relief is the agreement between the two governments. The various steps can be divided into three main phases: the preparation of the debt relief agreement; the actual establishment of the fund, including its management structure; and the implementation of its funding activities.

In the preparatory phase a number of issues must be clarified by a fact-finding mission or by other means. For example, it is important to know whether the debtor government is ready to provide local currency for debt relief, if there are any official guidelines for debt conversions or any specific precedents and what redemption rate could be expected. Another set of issues is related to the management of the CPF: Which organization(s) could represent the different NGO communities in the CPF committee or board? Are these groups willing to get involved in such a scheme? And finally, it is important to know which sectors should be prioritized, and what kind of programmes and projects might be funded.

The results of these investigations are then discussed with the relevant Swiss government agencies and form the basis for the debt negotiations. In some cases, it is not possible to submit a detailed proposal for the management structure or the composition of the decision-making body of the CPF before the start of the negotiations. In such cases, the bilateral agreement will specify the principle of local NGO involvement or the number of NGO representatives on the committee, and these will be selected after the agreement has been signed. In some instances, it may be useful to undertake a planning mission after the signing of the agreement in order to discuss with the CPF committee issues like the funding policy to be applied or to clarify what kind of technical support may be needed.

The Role of the Southern NGOs

The Southern partner NGOs or NGO networks play a crucial role in preparing and implementing creative debt relief programmes. They can get involved at different stages and at various levels:

- Designing the CPF concept: NGOs or NGO umbrella organizations can be commissioned to flesh out a concept for the management and the utilization of the fund; in other cases, they may only be associated with the designing of such a scheme or consulted with regard to a concept that has been worked out by the Swiss NGOs or the relevant government agency.

- Assisting with the management of the CPF: NGO networks or, if appropriate, individual NGOs may be members of the Fund's decision-making or executive bodies.

- Utilizing the Fund: NGOs and POs may file applications for funding with the CPF according to the guidelines defined by the Fund.

- Surveying, monitoring and evaluation: local service organizations or individual NGO consultants may be mandated by CPF management to monitor or evaluate specific projects or programmes funded by the CPF.

The Experience with Counterpart Funds

There is a wide range of options for the management and use of the proceeds of debt conversion operations. The ideal scheme as it was envisioned by the Swiss NGO's petition would be a privately owned trust or endowment fund, managed and utilized by domestic NGOs. Given the economic, political, and institutional constraints, this ideal form of a counterpart fund will only be realized in a very limited number of countries. There must be a 'tailor-made' solution for each country, based on its specific circumstances. The variety of options ranges from the NGO-managed capital fund to budgetary support for the central government.

By January 1993, seven bilateral debt agreements providing for counterpart funds had been signed or negotiated under the Swiss debt relief programme (Bolivia, Honduras, Peru, Ecuador, Tanzania, Zambia and Jordan). From these, three different models of CPF have emerged. (A fourth scheme has been proposed for the debt negotiations with the Philippines, which took place in March 1994.)

Bolivia: a 'Light' Management Structure
In the Bolivian case, the debt claims to be negotiated amounted to approximately US$35 million. The Bolivian government agreed to redeem eleven per cent of this amount in local currency, that is about US$4 million. This money, which represents the CPF, was transferred to an interest-bearing account with a local commercial bank.

The agreement stipulates that the CPF shall be used to finance development projects and programmes in the following two sectors: conservation of natural resources and micro-enterprise promotion with a special focus on credit programmes.

For the administration of the fund, a special committee (Comite de Fondo de Contravalor) has been set up. It is composed of a representative each of the Ministry of Planning and Coordination of

Bolivia, the Swiss Development Cooperation office in La Paz, the Bolivian Federation of Small- and Medium-Size Industries, a national NGO network and the National Environment Fund (FONAMA).

The Committee has worked out regulations for its functioning and guidelines for funding applications and for project selection. Based on these guidelines it selects and approves projects and programmes submitted to it. The decisions are taken by consensus. For the monitoring and evaluation of projects financed by the fund the Committee can appoint sub-committees. Within six months of its existence the Committee had approved eleven projects for which it had committed the total of US$4 million in fund resources. Two of these are credit programmes. All the projects or programmes are implemented by NGOs and private institutions.

Peru: a Fund for NGO and Government Projects

Through export credit, debt owed to Switzerland by Peru stood at about US$130 million. By 1993, when the debt reduction agreement was signed, 75 per cent of this debt was written off, and the remaining 25 per cent was converted into pesos. The Peruvian government committed itself to paying the corresponding amount, that is approximately US$33 million, into an account with a Peruvian commercial bank specified in the bilateral agreement. The payment was made up-front in early 1994.

According to the agreement, these fund resources will be used for projects in the areas of social infrastructure, environment and natural resources, and micro-enterprise promotion. The agreement specifies that the CPF money shall be allocated equally to government programmes and programmes implemented by NGOs and other private organizations. This means that government agencies can also file funding applications.

The CPF will be managed by a three-stage structure. The decision-making body is the so-called Bilateral Committee. It is composed of one representative from each of the two contracting parties. It approves (or rejects) funding applications submitted to it by the Technical Committee. It also has to approve the policy guidelines worked out by the Technical Committee, a body that constitutes the second component of the CPF. This forum comprises representatives of the Peruvian Executive Secretariat for International Cooperation, the Swiss Development Cooperation, the National Fund for Social Compensation and Development (FONCODES) as well as two NGOs representing the environment and micro-enterprise sectors which the Peruvian government did not want to have specified in the agreement. The Technical Committee is responsible for the screening of project and programme funding applications and makes recommendations to the Bilateral Committee. The third component of the CPF management structure is the Secretariat which is in charge of the day-to-day business of the fund and is directly answerable to the Bilateral Committee.

Zambia: Promotion of Financial Instruments

The face value of the debt negotiated with Zambia amounted to roughly US$17 million. Given the low payment capacities and the severe budgetary constraints of that country, the redemption rate was set at a relatively low eight per cent of face value so that the counterpart fund volume amounted to a mere US$1.3 million in *kwachas*.

As in the other cases, this money will be transferred to a private bank account. Contrary to the other agreements negotiated to date, the Zambian one specifies the organizations that shall receive part of the funds for projects identified in advance and proposed to the Zambian government during the debt negotiations. One of them is an infrastructure project implemented by the United Church of Zambia. It relates to the cleaning of a canal that represents the only means of transport and communication for 50,000 people living in a secluded region.

The other project has some very interesting and innovative features. The money coming from the CPF will serve as capital base for the Women's Finance Trust of Zambia (WFTZ). WFTZ is a financial institution affiliated with the New York based Women's World Banking (WWB). Its purpose is to support poor women micro-entrepreneurs in Zambia by granting small loans or facilitating access to commercial bank loans through loan guarantee arrangements. WFTZ also provides financial and technical counselling and training. The resources provided by the CPF will be used by WFTZ for a loan guarantee fund and/or a credit programme. The interest earnings will be utilized to cover part of the operating costs of the institution.

Philippines: Long-term Funding for NGOs

In the Philippine case, the debt negotiations have not yet taken place. Philippine and Swiss NGOs have proposed a different scheme which takes into account the particular institutional and political situation of that country. In the other countries with debt relief agreements, the CPF is designed as a short- to medium-term project financing fund; the option proposed for the Philippines, however, is that of a long-term capital fund. This means that only the return on capital, that is the interest, would be used to fund projects and programmes. The idea underlying this proposal is to provide the Philippine NGO community with a tool that permits a sustainable financing of their activities.

One interesting aspect of the proposed scheme is the process that has led to its emergence. In an initial stage, the Debt-for-Development Unit of the Swiss NGOs commissioned a Philippine NGO consultant to design a first rough concept for an NGO-managed endowment fund. The results of this initial project were then discussed with the consultant and checked during a fact-finding mission in the Philippines. The findings of the mission were discussed at a seminar with all interested Philippine NGOs and networks. Following that mission, a working group was set up in the Philippines in order to further discuss and refine the initial proposal. The finalized scheme will constitute the basis for the negotiations between the Swiss and the Philippine governments. It is the result of a process of intensive debate and permanent exchange of information between the Philippine and Swiss NGOs and the Swiss government.

According to the proposed scheme, the CPF will be managed by a Program Committee and a Secretariat. The Program Committee, which is the decision-making body, will be composed of representatives of all major Philippine NGO networks. The Swiss NGOs will also have a seat on the board. The board will decide on the investment and funding policy of the fund and approve specific projects. The endowment shall exclusively be used to finance NGO activities in the productive sector. The Secretariat is responsible for screening funding applications and making recommendations to the Program Committee.

Debt Conversion Negotiations: Problems and Constraints

The negotiations on debt relief and the establishment of counterpart funds that have been conducted until now by the Swiss government with seven countries have revealed a certain number of problems and constraints at different levels.

Redemption rate and disbursement modalities. Although Switzerland practises a rather prudent and conservative conversion policy, taking into account as much as possible monetary and budgetary constraints of the debtor countries and trying to avoid any inflationary effects, the redemption rate and the payment modalities have in most cases caused some controversies, although never unsurmountable difficulties. Understandably, the debtor governments try to limit the costs related to the debt reduction operations as well as the implicit subsidizing of domestic (and in some instances also foreign) NGOs to a minimum. In some cases where the budget constraints proved to be very severe or the negotiators' position very tough, Switzerland had to accept payment in several installments (Honduras: two annual tranches; Ecuador: three tranches). Or, as in the case of Zambia, it had to be accepted that the agreed local currency would be disbursed only in 1994, since, as was argued by the Zambian government, it was not possible to programme it in the 1993 budget.

Private bank account. In most cases, the governments were not very happy with the Swiss negotiators' proposal to transfer the local currency to an account with a commercial bank. They would usually have preferred to open an account with the central bank which was not interest bearing. On this issue, Switzerland is usually not prepared to make any concessions, since the central bank option would give the government control over the counterpart fund and make the participation of NGOs more difficult.

NGO participation. In one or two cases, the involvement of domestic NGOs in general or of specific NGOs or umbrella organizations in the management of the CPF or as beneficiaries of the fund resources was contested by the government of the debtor country. However, Switzerland's position on this issue is clear: domestic NGOs must be able to participate in decision-making and to submit projects and programmes for funding. Certain concessions are possible with regard to the proportion of the funds being allocated to government programmes.

Conclusion

To date, Switzerland has forgiven approximately US$35 million of debt, mostly export credit debt, under its debt reduction programme. Through the corresponding bilateral debt reduction agreements, seven counterpart funds have been established or negotiated with a total volume of the equivalent of US$65 million. This corresponds to an average redemption rate of about nineteen per cent. Additional bilateral agreements will be negotiated in 1994 and 1995, up to a total amount of approximately US$550 million. Therefore, as a whole, the bilateral debt reduction will amount to roughly US$900 million. Although this is almost 100 per cent of the outstanding Paris Club debt owed to Switzerland by the eligible countries, it will not reduce their total debt by more than a half of one per cent.

Because this is no more than a drop in the ocean, the Swiss NGOs have always argued that it is justified to use the Swiss taxpayers' money for debt reduction operations only if an imitation effect on other – and more important – creditor nations can be expected from the Swiss programme. That is why both the Swiss NGOs and government are making efforts to disseminate information on the Swiss Facility and to convince other governments to follow the Swiss example and to go beyond the debt reductions presently granted in the Paris Club.

8

A New Framework of Accountability for the IMF

Richard Gerster

The development debate has centred on issues of governance following the end of the East–West confrontation. The reason for this trend rests on the conviction that the development process is strongly correlated to the quality of governance. Governance has been defined by the World Bank in the context of sub-Saharan Africa as the exercise of political power to manage a nation's affairs. The characteristics of good governance[1] in large measure derive from the Universal Declaration of Human Rights, adopted by the United Nations in 1948, and as such may be regarded as the consensus of the international community.

Governance is a concept, however, that can be applied not only to national bureaucracies but also to multilateral institutions. As one such institution, the International Monetary Fund is also challenged by the tenets of good governance. These encompass in particular the decision-making process, the relationship between the institution and the public, particularly regarding access to information and participation, the implementation of programmes and their evaluation, and the question of financial accountability.

The application of good governance principles to the IMF leads to a new framework of accountability. Underlying this is the perception of the Fund as a crucial public institution subject to the tenets of good governance and accountability. Between the IMF, the member state and the public, there is a triangular set of relations. This set of relations displaces the traditional view of separate relations between the IMF and the member state, and between the member state and the public.

The vision of a democratic, transparent, participative, evaluative and financially responsible IMF emerges if one looks at the recent OECD *Orientations on Participatory Development and Good Governance*: this document clearly states that 'the integration of environmental concerns with economic and social goals – fundamental to sustainable development – depends on access to information and the transparency as well as accountability of public sector activities'.[2]

This vision is meaningful assuming that the Fund has a role to play in the world of today and tomorrow. A critical assessment of the IMF comes to the conclusion: 'If we did not already have the IMF, we would have to invent it. To reject the extreme argument for closing down the Fund does not imply that there is no need for change'.[3] Therefore, the vision mentioned above paves the way for proposals for institutional reform of the IMF.

Decision-Making

With 135 developing countries among the 175 member countries of the IMF in 1993, the developing countries constitute an overwhelming majority. The South, however, has a voting share of only 34 per cent: the majority has become a minority. Although the number of developing country members has increased from 93 in 1970 to 135 in 1993, the voting power of the developing countries has decreased from 37 per cent in 1970 to 34 per cent in 1993. Without the unique circumstances of the oil-exporting countries, the reduction in the voting power of the developing countries would be even more dramatic. The main reason for this trend towards marginalization of the South in the IMF lies in the method of determining voting power.

Through IMF membership, each country acquires basic voting power consisting of 250 votes. In addition, each country receives votes based on its IMF quota of Special Drawing Rights (SDRs) equal to one vote per 100,000 SDRs. Over time, these quota-based votes, which favour the economically powerful countries, have increased as a proportion of total votes. The number of votes allotted through basic voting power – the egalitarian element in the IMF voting structure – has remained unchanged since the IMF was founded. Meanwhile, the weight of quota-based voting power – the plutocratic element – has increased, from 87.5 per cent of the total votes in 1947 to 97 per cent with the Ninth Quota Review of 1992. Thus, despite the increase in the number of IMF members from 44 in 1947 to 175 in 1993, the proportion of basic votes to total votes has declined, from 12.5 per cent in 1947 to 3 per cent in 1992.

Each member of the executive board represents either one country or a grouping of countries. Regardless of whether the member represents a single country or a country group, his or her voting weight, a combination of basic and quota-based voting power, goes on the scales as a single, undifferentiated vote. Within a voting group, the economically powerful countries thereby dominate their weaker partners, who can at best express a divergent opinion orally but cannot bring it to bear in the form of a vote. Within the voting group, however, dynamic processes also come into play that temper one-sided domination in favour of compromise.[4]

The strengthening of democratic elements in the IMF through voting reform cannot be achieved by uncritically following the UN principle of 'one country, one vote'. Gains in voting power that greatly exceed the realities of economic power would be worthless. The UN principle, as it now stands, is highly unsatisfactory in a democratic sense. For example, when the 72,000 inhabitants of the Caribbean island of Dominica have the same voting weight as the 1,149,500,000 citizens of China, this reflects national sovereignty and the equal rights of states, but has as little in common with democracy as quota-based voting power at the IMF. The division of voting power into country-based basic votes and quota-based votes is quite rightly justified. But to eliminate the shortcomings, both the weight of the basic votes as well as the criteria for determining quotas need to be reconsidered. In this sense, voting reform at the IMF must evolve and combine various elements.

Basic voting power should again be given the significance it had in the founding years. Total quotas have increased about twenty-fold, from US$7.5 billion in 1945 to about 145 billion special drawing rights – corresponding to about US$201 billion – following the Ninth Quota Review of 1992. This extension of quota-based voting rights would suggest raising the basic votes from 250 to 5000. The weight of quota-based voting power would decrease from its current 97 per cent to approximately 63 per cent, while that of basic voting power would increase from 3 per cent to 37 per cent.

For the developing countries this would mean an increase of their voting share based solely on their basic votes from their current 2.3 per cent following the Ninth Quota Review to over 28 per cent. Taking quota-based voting power following the existing distribution formula into consideration, the developing countries would have a right to about a further 21 per cent vote share following the voting reform. For the South, basic and quota-based voting power together would then amount to a new total of 49 per cent.

Instead of a fixed increase of basic voting power, one could also envision a fixed minimum proportion of basic votes to total votes of, say, one third. This solution would be advantageous in that the significance of basic voting power would not once again be marginalized by subsequent quota increases.

The adjustment of basic voting power requires a revision of the IMF Articles of Agreement because basic and quota-based voting power are expressly regulated by Art. XII, Para. 5. Amendments to the Articles of Agreement require a qualified majority of 85 per cent. Therefore, without United States and European support nothing will change.

Access to Information

High ranking World Bank officials have stated:

> A critical dimension of accountability is transparency, which implies making readily available for public scrutiny all public accounts and audit reports, ... a practice that most governments strongly resist for obvious reasons. There can be little justification for secrecy, and any exceptions need to be carefully circumscribed. Even secrecy about military expenditure is hard to justify and is almost always a cover for abuse. This is not a question of sovereignty, but simply a matter of Good Governance. Every citizen, as well as every donor, can and should insist on it.[5]

The market economy depends on full access to information, and so do accountable political systems. Market philosophy as well as the principles of good governance would lead us to expect an IMF dedicated to transparency with regard to its own activities. On request, the external relations department of the Fund summed up the present situation as follows:

> With respect to access of information, the policies and practices of the IMF are set by the board of governors, the executive board, and the Fund's managing director, as mandated by the IMF's Articles of Agreement. Formal communications between the Fund and a member government take place through the member country's governor to the IMF, an arrangement that has worked well. More recently, as member country parliamentarians, NGOs, and the general public have expressed a desire to know more about the activities and policies of the IMF, we have intensified efforts to make additional information available. In member countries that have programmes with the IMF, efforts are made –

in consultation with the authorities – to have mission chiefs or resident representatives brief the press, parliamentary groups and NGOs on the elements of the program.

Even acknowledging that information disclosure is a joint responsibility of both the IMF and the member state, in reality the IMF cultivates a culture of confidentiality.[6]

The World Bank formally postulates a presumption in favour of disclosure if there is no compelling reason to withhold the information and decided on 26 August 1993 to facilitate the access to information to a considerable extent (see Chapter Twelve). In the Fund there is not even this formal presumption in favour of disclosure. Documents are generally the property of the IMF and even country reports cannot be disclosed without the consent of the Fund. Even the agenda of the board meetings are considered confidential. Thus the great majority of documents are not available to the public or only become accessible when they are outdated.

The close relationship of the IMF to the central banks and the ministries of finance in the member countries promotes secrecy rather than openness as such financial institutions often favour restricted access at the national level. For example, national governments often do not release the results of Art. IV consultations with the Fund to the public, the exceptions being the governments of Australia, Belgium, Korea, Switzerland and, to a certain extent, Italy, Japan and the Netherlands. In a democracy there is no reason to keep this consultation process confidential. Recently, the IMF's annual report includes sections summarizing the main points of the latest executive board's final discussions of Art. IV consultation reports for selected countries. Only on rare occasions is there a legitimate concern to restrict information, as when, for example, there is a Fund recommendation to devalue a currency. Such situations are very exceptional, however, and can in no way justify the general policy not to disclose information and documents.

This culture of confidentiality contradicts the quest for accountability. There is a striking contrast between the introductory quote on the transparency expected from the South and the behaviour of the Fund. Economic wisdom does not grow in secrecy but develops in the course of public debate. In the interest of an accountable IMF, access to information must be put on the agenda: policy documents, structural adjustment programmes and Art. IV consultations should be accessible to the interested public, as far in advance as possible of board discussions and decision-making. In addition, statements and the votes cast by individual executive directors should be disclosed by the member countries concerned on request.

People's Participation

People's participation presupposes freedom of association on the local as well as on the national level. Effective interventions by non-governmental organizations are closely linked to free access to information from national governments as well as multilateral agencies. Only from the perspective of a top-down development model can an argument be made for disregarding people's participation. Such a model of imposing development on people rather than seeking their involvement in it, however, has suffered so many failures in the past that promising programmes and policies cannot but include people's participation. In particular it has become clear that dialogue with governments cannot be a substitute for participation by the people.

In IMF activities, NGOs have not played a substantial role so far. Of course, it must be conceded that a participatory approach will prove more difficult to realize with regard to macroeconomic issues than with specific projects. As a consequence, good governance in the member countries assumes paramount importance and should be treated accordingly by the Fund. Otherwise the IMF may become a tacit ally of political systems that lack public accountability. In addition, the IMF should examine ways and means to integrate NGO experience into the policy dialogue, the programme design and the Art. IV consultations.

One such example of cooperation occurred in May 1993, when the Fund organized a seminar on macroeconomics and the environment with NGO participation. On rare occasions in earlier years, similar events have taken place at IMF headquarters or in member countries. Although the importance of macroeconomic policy for social and environmental concerns is widely recognized within the Fund, there is no permanent forum for a systematic policy dialogue with NGOs, comparable to the NGO World Bank Committee or the observer status of NGOs in the executive committee of the Montreal Protocol for the Protection of the Ozone Layer.

Research on structural adjustment may often lead to controversial results. One aspect, however, is evident: broad acceptance of reforms by all the relevant political actors in a country is crucial to success. Lack of participation severely undermines the quality of operations and provokes opposition. Acceptance, on the other hand, requires prior access to information and consultation with non-governmental organizations. The participation of private, social, economic and environmental actors in the programme design for the Enhanced Structural Adjustment Facility (ESAF) or for regular standby arrangements is therefore in the general interest. To date, Fund missions have met with leading NGOs to discuss broad economic developments in only a few countries. The systematic participation of new actors may require change but brings the advantage of a more realistic programme and better prospects for implementation.

The adage that the IMF supports government-owned programmes is no excuse for overlooking a potentially bad relationship between the government and the people in general and with the NGO scene in particular. Even for purely financial reasons, the IMF must keep the political framework of the programmes in mind and should officially and repeatedly advise member governments to consult with NGOs before concluding borrowing agreements.

Based on Art. IV of the Articles of Agreement, the Fund is obliged to exercise surveillance over the exchange rate policies of its members. Today, the scope of the consultations goes far beyond exchange rate and monetary issues and includes a medium-term perspective and structural policies. Art. IV consultations, during which Fund staff meet annually with the authorities of member countries to analyse economic policies, are an opportunity for NGO participation[7]. As these consultations are held in principle with all member countries, they are one of the rare opportunities for officially presenting adjustment proposals in the home countries of Northern NGOs. In 1993, the Swiss Coalition of Development Organizations had the opportunity to participate in the Art. IV consultation of the IMF with Switzerland and officially submitted a memorandum on reforms for Switzerland in a global perspective.[8]

Independent Evaluation

Programme evaluation plays a role in the Fund as part of its research activities but not as an end in itself. Though it may be more difficult to assess stand-by agreements, stabilization and adjustment programmes, there is no major difference from the structural adjustment programmes supported by the World Bank, the effects of which are evaluated more systematically. The creation of an evaluation unit of high quality would be of benefit to the Fund as well as to the public.

In this light, the creation of an evaluation unit is a necessity. The cornerstone of such a proposal should lie in the virtues of a division of power and include a comprehensive mandate, including evaluation of the programmes, of technical assistance, of surveillance in the North and the South, and analysis of the social and environmental impacts of the Fund's activities; firmly established independence from the Fund's management, requiring that the evaluation unit report directly to the Board and that the head be nominated for at least a five-year term; and the publication of findings and recommendations, including viewpoints that significantly differ from those of the management and of national authorities.

Some of the procedures of the newly established Independent Inspection Panel of the World Bank and its Operations Evaluation Department could be transferred in an appropriate way to the Fund's evaluation office. Much of its credibility will depend on the nomination of the chief evaluator and his or her team of experts.

The executive board of the Fund discussed a proposal by the managing director for the creation of an evaluation office in January 1993. Although a broad majority basically favoured the establishment of an evaluation office, views on the modalities diverged widely. In particular, the profile of the director of the evaluation office, its mandate, its independence within the organizational structure of the Fund, and access to its findings were controversial issues. Formally, it is now up to the managing director of the Fund to present a revised proposal. However, as long as no consensus proposal is in sight or until strong political pressure brings the topic back on to the board's agenda, no progress will be made towards the creation of an evaluation unit.

Risk Sharing

A basic tenet of the market economy is that decision-making is linked to risk taking. 'This link promotes economic efficiency and makes those taking decisions accountable'.[9] This financial side of accountability has been widely neglected in the discussion of the role of the Bretton Woods institutions. The following remarks are of a preliminary nature as their consequences for the IMF and the poor member countries in particular need further study.

Both the World Bank and the Fund enjoy not only backing by their member states but also preferred creditor status. Due to this privilege, the Bank and the Fund can avoid any formal rescheduling of their claims because the arrears to the Bretton Woods institutions must be settled before a Paris Club or London Club negotiation can take place. This insistence on full repayment negates their co-responsibility for the programmes and transfers the entire risk for any misguidance and failures on to the borrower. 'As the shares of multilateral debts are relatively higher in the poorest countries, protecting international financial institutions (IFI) from losses is done at the expense of particularly poor clients, whose lack of experts has often made them extremely dependent on solutions elaborated by IFI staff'.[10]

Since the beginning of the debt crisis in 1982, the preferred creditor status of the IMF could be formally maintained only thanks to bailouts on different levels. On the one hand, the creation of the Structural Adjustment Facility (SAF) in 1986 and its successor mechanisms, ESAF, provided and still provide longer-term, low-interest money to repay ordinary IMF drawings for many indebted countries. SAF and ESAF have refinanced 40 per cent of low-income countries repayments of non-concessional debt to the IMF.[11] On the other hand, bilateral grants often provide the desperately needed hard currency to repay debts owed to the Fund.

There is an increasing diversion of bilateral grant assistance from poverty alleviation to debt service to multilateral institutions, also endangering public support for development aid in OECD countries.[12] Therefore, the risks taken by IMF staff are shifted on to the taxpayers of the industrialized countries as well as onto the people of the adjusting countries in the South.

The far-reaching involvement of the Fund in policy formulation of member countries in balance of payments difficulties is well known. The interaction between the World Bank and borrowers has been described by an executive director as a 'pattern dominated by description, imposition, condition-setting, and decision-making'.[13] In the case of failure, there is no reason why the IMF should not participate in the loss-sharing between the lenders and the borrower.

Unlike the World Bank, the IMF has never borrowed on the private capital market and therefore cannot lose an AAA rating as creditor. At the IMF, the gold stocks retained earnings, reserves and provisions are substantial, permitting room for manoeuvre in providing debt relief to debt-distressed, low-income countries. A total write-down of the IMF's exposure in Africa would require the sale of no more than around 10 per cent of its $36 billion gold reserves.[14] The Bretton Woods institutions, claiming to be the custodians of market philosophy wisdom, can no longer remain immune to their failures and should be made financially accountable. Putting an end to double standards ought to win the support of those who take market principles seriously.

The pressure to lend as an overriding characteristic of the corporate culture of the World Bank has been well-documented by the Wapenhans Report. 'The costs of tolerating continued poor performance is highest not for the Bank, but for its borrowers'.[15] A major possibility to fundamentally change this corporate culture would be to re-link the decisions and risks. Riskless lending just to satisfy pressure from major members will have to end. Therefore, the quest for financial accountability will in the end result in better quality lending.

In practice, it may hardly be possible to determine the IMF's fair share of responsibility for programme failures. The best short-term solution is, therefore, to treat the Fund equally and to include its claims in rescheduling exercises in the same way as those of other creditors. On the part of the multilaterals, an 'explicit acknowledgment' is needed that 'while they must remain preferred creditors they cannot be exempt creditors'.[16] This is a very moderate way of introducing financial accountability into the Fund.

A far-reaching alternative to the present system might be the creation of an insolvency mechanism (see Raffer 1990) linked to an international court of arbitration. Analysts consider the appointment of qualified independent tribunals particularly 'compelling' in the case of 'IMF-World Bank designed and imposed adjustment programs in the affected severely indebted low-income countries which have subsequently failed, but which have left in their wake a debt burden which is unsustainable'.[17] The political will, however, to embark on such new paths has yet to crystallize.

Working for Change

There is no substantial reason for accountability to be more advanced at the World Bank than at the Fund. This asymmetry is mainly due to NGO negligence of IMF activities. The NGO community has paid much more attention to the World Bank than to the IMF. This may be due to the fact that Fund operations are more abstract and cannot be as easily linked to physical events as Bank projects. Since membership in the Bank requires membership in the Fund, NGO advocacy should re-examine its priorities and deal with IMF matters at least as intensively as with Bank matters, with greater accountability as a common goal.

International cooperation and coordination of NGO advocacy is important but only part of the story. The real strength of the NGO movement working for change lies at home, influencing the positions of their national authorities in multilateral institutions. This homework is of crucial importance as there is an institutionalized bias against public accountability of the executive directors in the Bretton Woods institutions due to their dual allegiance to the IMF, on the one hand, and the country or country groups they represent, on the other.[18] This bias against accountability can only be compensated by a clear political will on the part of the member countries. Shaping that will on the part of authorities and parliament is a major task of national NGOs.

In the United States, the Freedom Support Act of 24 October 1992 obliges the Secretary of the Treasury to 'instruct the US executive director of the Fund to promote regularly and rigorously in program discussions and quota increase negotiations' – among other aims – public access to information and broader participation. The Fund should establish procedures for public access to information while paying due regard to appropriate confidentiality; in particular 'Policy Framework Papers and supporting documents prepared by the Fund's mission to a country' are mentioned as examples of documents that should be made public. The IMF is urged 'to explore ways to increase the involvement and participation of important ministries, national development experts, environmental experts, free-market experts, other legitimate experts and representatives from the loan recipient country in the development of Fund programs'.

In Switzerland a parliamentary motion was tabled in the Senate on 17 December 1993 inviting the Swiss government to 'promote institutional reforms in the International Monetary Fund regarding an open information policy, better possibilities of participation by NGOs and the creation of an efficient, independent evaluation unit'. In the House of Representatives a parliamentary motion of 8 December 1993 asks the Swiss government to examine how Switzerland could work towards voting reform in the Fund to improve the influence of developing countries. Both motions are still pending at the time of writing.

Similar steps should be taken in as many countries as possible. Parallel and coordinated political action will lead to a more accountable IMF. The Tenth General Review of Quotas is an excellent opportunity to promote this aim. And the fiftieth anniversary of the Bretton Woods conference provides an appropriate opportunity to take a leap forward towards a more accountable IMF.

Bibliography

1 Landell-Mills, Pierre and Serageldin, Ismal, 'Governance and the External Factor', in World Bank, *Proceedings of the World Bank Annual Conference on Development Economics 1991*, Washington, DC, 1992, p. 306.

2 OECD, DAC *Orientations on Participatory Development and Good Governance*, Paris, 1993, p. 22.

3 Bird, Graham, 'Does the World Still Need the IMF?', in S. Murshed Mansoob and Kunibert Raffer (eds), *Trade, Transfers and Development: Problems and Prospects for the Twenty-first Century* (Edward Elgar, 1994), p. 178.

4 Gerster, Richard, 'Proposals for Voting Reform Within the International Monetary Fund', in *Journal of World Trade*, June 1993, pp. 121–6.

5 Landell-Mills, p. 314.

6 Gerster, Richard, 'Accountability of Executive Directors in the Bretton Woods Institutions', in *Journal of World Trade*, December 1993, p. 99.

7 Gerster 'Accountability ...' p. 103.

8 Swiss Coalition of Development Organizations, 'Art. IV Consultation of the International Monetary Fund with Switzerland, 20–28 October 1993: Structural Adjustment in Switzerland in a Global Perspective', mimeographed paper, Berne, 1993.

9 Raffer, Kunibert, 'International Financial Institutions and Accountability: The Need for a Drastic Change', in Murshed Mansoob, S. and Raffer, Kunibert (eds), *Trade, Transfers and Development: Problems and Prospects for the Twenty-first Century* (Edward Elgar, 1993), p. 152.

10 Ibid, p. 161.

11 Mistry, Percy, 'The Multilateral Debt Problems of Indebted Developing Countries', mimeographed paper for the EURODAD/NOVIB Seminar in The Hague, 6 December 1993, p. 22.

12 Ibid, p.16.

13 World Bank, *Getting Results: The World Bank's Agenda for Improving Development Effectiveness*, Washington, DC, 1993.

14 Oxfam, 'Multilateral Debt as an Obstacle to Recovery: The Case of Uganda', mimeographed paper for the EURODAD/NOVIB Seminar in The Hague, 4 December 1993.

15 World Bank, *Effective Implementation: Key to Development Impact.* Report of the World Bank's Portfolio Management Task Force, Washington, DC, 1992.

16 Mistry, p. 35.

17 Ibid, p. 19.

18 Gerster 'Accountability ...'.

III

Alternatives to the World Bank

9

Farewell Lecture to the World Bank

Herman E. Daly

After six years at the World Bank and having at 55 finally reached the age of both reason and early retirement, I am now returning to academia – to teaching, researching, writing – and chasing after grants. While I am happy about that, I also feel a sense of loss at leaving, especially because I think the Bank will become, and is already becoming, much more environmentally sensitive and literate. It is also, of all the places that I have worked, the one where I have had the best colleagues. The person who more than anyone else has fought for the environment in the Bank for over 15 years is Robert Goodland. Trying to help him, Salah El Serafy, and others, to 'green the Bank's economists' has been a high privilege and sometimes even fun. It is also unfinished business. The vice presidency for Environmentally Sustainable Development in its first year, under Ismail Serageldin's leadership, has been the most encouraging step forward during my time there. When the critical areas of population and energy are brought under the domain of ESD, it will be even more encouraging.

I should confess that this is a farewell from someone who is not going very far away – only nine miles up the road to the University of Maryland, so I hope to keep contact with many colleagues and with the Bank. But, who can refuse an invitation to give a farewell lecture to (take a parting shot at) such a powerful institution – an institution whose role in the world is, for better or worse, becoming ever more important, and whose imminent fiftieth birthday invites the reassessment characteristic of mid-life? I willingly succumb to the temptation both to pontificate and to prescribe a few remedies for the Bank's middle-aged infirmities.

My prescriptions will be of two kinds, internal and external. First, a few antacids and laxatives to cure the combination of managerial flatulence and organizational constipation giving rise to such a high-pressure internal environment. Second, to improve interactions with the external world, I will prescribe some new glasses and a hearing aid. After age 50 these aids to the body become more necessary and should be accepted, or at least listened to, with as much grace as possible.

Internal Issues: the Workplace and Managerial Environment

Many excellent people work at the World Bank, and usually work very competently and very hard, probably too hard. But top-down management, misguided by an unrealistic vision of development as the generalization of Northern overconsumption to the rapidly multiplying masses of the South, has led to many external failures, both economic and ecological. These external failures, due to faulty vision and hearing, will be considered later, but for now I just note that external failure also undermines internal morale. The unrealistic vision of development should be blamed at least as much on academic economic theorists as on World Bank practitioners.

Management should be more open and participatory – at least managers should sometimes ask the advice of their subordinates, even if they are not likely to take it. The Bank should be much more open – there is really not that much to hide – or if there is I am too dumb to see it. The Bank's failures cannot be hid for long. And it is important not to be able to hide those things that it would be tempting to hide, even when temporarily possible. And why one part of the Bank has to hide things from other parts of the Bank, and especially from the Executive Directors, has always puzzled me. I have even heard it said that Executive Directors should be treated like cultivated mushrooms: 'kept in the dark and fed manure'. Surely that is not being open and participatory!

Forget all this useless and unevenly applied nonsense about clearance for speeches and published articles by professional Bank staff when they are not officially speaking for the Bank. All that should be necessary is a disclaimer stating clearly that the author is not speaking on behalf of the World Bank. Of course if you *are* speaking on behalf of the Bank, or using some kind of proprietary information, clearance is obviously necessary. Yes, the World Bank's Administrative Manual Summary 14.20 does indeed say that disclaimers do not exempt one from submitting all publications for Bank censorship because disclaimers are said to be 'unconvincing'. But then I wonder why the Bank itself nearly always puts a disclaimer on published Bank research? Disclaimers are well understood – I can assure you that no one has ever mistaken a paper of mine for a World Bank policy statement!

If some Bank office absolutely must be engaged in censoring and 'clearing' employee's non-Bank utterances, then the Bank's image is better protected by monitoring the pretentious real estate ads of Bank vice presidents trying to sell their expensive houses by including their high Bank position in the description of the house, as if the prestige of their anti-poverty office should adhere to and be capitalized in the value of their domicile. Other worthy candidates for monitoring would be the internal memos of other vice presidents examining the 'impeccable economic logic' of dropping a given load of toxic waste on the poorest countries. Alternatively, some of that monitoring energy might be spent on controlling construction cost overruns on new Bank buildings in downtown Washington. But don't waste time trying to censor some little staff economist who, in his theoretical writings, deviates from the Bank's party line favouring free trade, NAFTA, or anything else. Fortunately, some managers are wise enough not to waste their time in this way, and my impression is that those whose duty it is to enforce clearance are very uncomfortable doing so. Without deviance there can be no change.

In sum, my internal workplace advice is: open up, loosen up, listen up, speak up and don't work weekends on anything you don't enjoy.

External Issues: Advice for Fostering Environmentally Sustainable Development

I have four prescriptions for better serving the goal of environmentally sustainable development through World Bank policy and action. The four prescriptions are presented in order of increasing generality and radicalism. That is, the first two are fairly specific and should, I think, be relatively non-controversial. The third will be debated by many, and the fourth will be considered outrageous by most Bank economists.

1. *Stop counting the consumption of natural capital as income.* Income is by definition the maximum amount that a society can consume this year and still be able to consume the same amount next year. That is, consumption this year, if it is to be called income, must leave intact the capacity to produce and consume the same amount next year. Thus sustainability is built into the very definition of income. But traditionally, the productive capacity that must be maintained intact has been thought of as man-made capital only, excluding natural capital. We have habitually counted natural capital as a free good. This might have been justified in yesterday's empty world, but

in today's full world it is anti-economic. The error of implicitly counting natural capital consumption as income is customary in three areas:

- the System of National Accounts (SNA);
- evaluation of projects that deplete natural capital; and
- international balance of payments accounting.

The first, SNA, is well recognized and efforts are underway to correct it – indeed, the World Bank played a pioneering role in this important initiative, and I hope will continue to contribute to 'greening the GNP'.

The second, project evaluation, is well recognized by standard economics which has long taught the need to count 'user cost' (depletion charges) as part of the opportunity cost of projects that deplete natural capital. World Bank *best* practice counts user costs, but *average* Bank practice ignores it. Uncounted user costs show up in inflated net benefits and an overstated rate of return for depleting projects. This biases investment allocation toward projects that deplete natural capital, and away from more sustainable projects.

Correcting this bias is the logical first step towards a policy of sustainable development. User cost must be counted not only for depletion of non-renewable resources, but also for projects that divest renewable natural capital by exploiting it beyond sustainable yield. The sink or absorptive services of natural capital, as well as its source or regenerative services, can also be depleted if used beyond sustainable capacity. Therefore a user cost must be charged to projects that deplete sink capacity, such as the atmosphere's ability to absorb CO_2, or the capacity of a river to carry off wastes. It is admittedly difficult to measure user cost, but attempting to avoid the issue simply means that we assign to depleted natural capital the precise default value of zero, which is frequently not the best estimate. Even when zero is the best estimate it should be arrived at not by default, but by reasoned calculation based on explicit assumptions about backstop technologies, discount rates and reserve lifetimes.

Third, in traditional balance of payments accounting the export of depleted natural capital, whether petroleum or timber cut beyond sustainable yield, is entered in the current account, and thus treated entirely as income. This is an accounting error. Some portion of those non-sustainable exports should be treated as the sale of a capital asset, and entered on capital account. If this were properly done, some countries would see their apparent balance of trade surplus converted into a true deficit, one that is being financed by drawdown and transfer abroad of their stock of natural capital. Reclassifying trans-actions in a way that converts a country's balance of trade from a surplus to a deficit would trigger a whole different set of IMF rec-ommendations and actions. This reform of balance of payments accounting should be the initial focus of the IMF's new interest in environmentally sustainable development. The World Bank should warmly encourage its sister institution to get busy on this – it does not come naturally to them.

2. *Tax labour and income less, and tax resource throughput more.* In the past it has been customary for governments to subsidize resource throughput to stimulate growth. Thus energy, water, fertilizer, and even deforestation, are even now frequently subsidized. To its credit the World Bank has generally opposed these subsidies. But it is necessary to go beyond removal of explicit financial subsidies to the removal of implicit environmental subsidies as well. By 'implicit envi-ronmental subsidies' I mean external costs to the community that are not charged to the commodities whose production generates them.

Economists have long advocated internalizing external costs either by calculating and charging Pigouvian taxes (taxes which when added to marginal private costs make them equal to marginal social costs), or by Coasian redefinition of property rights (such that values that used to be public property and not valued in markets, become private property whose values are protected by their new owners). These solutions are elegant in theory, but often quite difficult in practice. A blunter but much more operational instrument would be simply to shift our tax base away from labour and income on to throughput. We have to raise public revenue somehow, and the present system is highly distortionary in that by taxing labour and income in the face of high unemployment in nearly all countries, we are discouraging exactly what we want more of. The present signal to firms is to shed labour, and substitute more capital and resource throughput, to the extent feasible. It would be better to economize on throughput because of the high external costs of its associated depletion and pollution, and at the same time to use more labour because of the high social benefits associated with reducing unemployment.

Shifting the tax base to throughput induces greater throughput efficiency, and internalizes, in a gross, blunt manner the externali-ties from depletion and pollution. True, the exact external costs will not have been precisely calculated and attributed to exactly those activities that caused them, as with a Pigouvian tax that aims to equate marginal social costs and benefits for each activity. But those calculations and attributions are so difficult and uncertain that insisting on them would be equivalent to a full-employment act for econometricians and prolonged unemployment and environmental degradation for everyone else. Politically the shift towards ecological taxes could be sold under the banner of revenue neutrality. However, the income tax structure should be maintained so as to keep progressivity in the overall tax structure by taxing very high incomes and subsidizing very low incomes. But the bulk of public revenue would be raised from taxes on throughput either at the depletion or pollution end.

The shift could be carried out gradually by a pre-announced schedule to minimize disruption. This shift should be a key part of structural adjustment, but should be pioneered in the North. Indeed, sustainable development itself must be achieved in the North first. It is absurd to expect any sacrifice for sustainability in the South if similar measures have not first been taken in the North. The major weakness in the World Bank's ability to foster environmentally sustainable development is that it only has leverage over the South, not the North. Some way must be found to push the North also. The Nordic countries and the Netherlands have already begun to do this.

3. *Maximize the productivity of natural capital in the short run, and invest in increasing its supply in the long run.* Economic logic requires that we behave in these two ways towards the limiting factor of production, that is maximize its productivity and invest in its increase. Those principles are not in dispute. Disagreements do exist about whether natural capital is really the limiting factor. Some argue that man-made and natural capital are such good substitutes that the very idea of a limiting factor, which requires that the factors be complementary, is irrelevant. It is true that without complementarity there is no limiting factor. So the question is, are man-made capital and natural capital basically complements or substitutes? Here again we can provide perpetual full employment for econometricians, and I would welcome more empirical work on this, even though I think it is sufficiently clear to common sense that natural and man-made capital are fundamentally complements and only marginally substitutable.

In the past natural capital has been treated as superabundant and priced at zero, so it did not really matter whether it was a complement or a substitute for man-made capital. Now remaining natural capital appears to be both scarce and complementary, and therefore limiting. For example, the fish catch is limited not by the number of fishing boats, but by the remaining populations of fish in the sea. Cut timber is limited not by the number of sawmills, but by the remaining standing forests. Pumped crude oil is limited not by man-made pumping capacity, but by remaining stocks of petroleum in the ground. The natural capital of the atmosphere's capacity to serve as a sink for CO_2 is likely to be even more limiting to the rate at which petroleum can be burned than is the source limit of remaining oil in the ground.

In the short run raising the price of natural capital by taxing throughput, as advocated above, will give the incentive to maximize natural capital productivity. Investing in natural capital over the long run is also needed. But how do we invest in something which by definition we cannot make? If we could make it, it would be man-made capital! For renewable resources we have the possibility of fallowing investments, or more generally 'waiting' in the Marshallian sense – allowing this year's growth increment to be added to next year's growing stock rather than consuming it. For non-renewables we do not have this option. We can only liquidate them. So the question is how fast do we liquidate, and how much of the proceeds can we count as income if we invest the rest in the best available renewable substitute? And, of course, how much of the correctly counted income do we then consume and how much do we invest?

One renewable substitute for natural capital is the mixture of natural and man-made capital represented by plantations and fish farms, which we may call 'cultivated natural capital'. But even within this important hybrid category we have a complementary combination of natural and man-made capital components. For example, a plantation forest may use man-made capital to plant trees, control pests and choose the proper rotation – but the complementary natural capital services of rainfall, sunlight and soil, are still there, and eventually still become limiting. Also, cultivated natural capital usually requires a reduction in biodiversity relative to natural capital proper.

For both renewable and non-renewable resources, investments in enhancing throughput productivity are needed. Increasing resource productivity is indeed a good substitute for finding more of the resource. But the main point is that investment should be in the limiting factor, and to the extent that natural capital has replaced man-made capital as the limiting factor, the Bank's investment focus should shift correspondingly. I do not believe that it has. In fact, the failure to charge user cost on natural capital depletion, noted earlier, surely biases investment away from replenishing projects.

4. *Move away from the ideology of global economic integration by free trade, free capital mobility and export-led growth – and towards a more nationalist orientation that seeks to develop domestic production for internal markets as the first option, having recourse to international trade only when clearly*

much more efficient. At the present time global interdependence is celebrated as a self-evident good. The royal road to development, peace and harmony is thought to be the unrelenting conquest of each nation's market by all other nations. The word 'globalist' has politically correct connotations, while the word 'nationalist' has come to be pejorative. This is so much the case that it is necessary to remind ourselves that the World Bank exists to serve the interests of its members, which are nation states, national communities – not individuals, not corporations, not even NGOs. It has no charter to serve the one-world-without-borders cosmopolitan vision of global integration, nor to convert many relatively independent national economies, loosely dependent on international trade, into one tightly integrated world economic network upon which the weakened nations depend for even basic survival.

The model of international community upon which the Bretton Woods institutions rests is that of a 'community of communities', an international federation of *national* communities cooperating to solve global problems under the principle of subsidiarity. The model is not the cosmopolitan one of direct global citizenship in a single integrated world community without intermediation by nation states.

To globalize the economy by erasure of national economic boundaries through free trade, free capital mobility, and free or at least uncontrolled migration is to wound fatally the major unit of community capable of carrying out any policies for the common good. That includes not only national policies for purely domestic ends, but also international agreements required to deal with those environmental problems that are irreducibly global (such as CO_2 and ozone depletion). International agreements presuppose the ability of national governments to carry out policies in their support. If nations have no control over their borders they are in a poor position to enforce national laws, including those necessary to secure compliance with international treaties.

Cosmopolitan globalism weakens national boundaries and the power of national and subnational communities, while strengthening the relative power of transnational corporations. Since there is no world government capable of regulating global capital in the global interest, and since the desirability and possibility of a world government are both highly doubtful, it will be necessary to make capital less global and more national. I know that is an unthinkable thought right now, but take it as a prediction – ten years from now the buzz words will be 'renationalization of capital' and the 'community rooting of capital for the development of national and local economies', not the current shibboleths of export-led growth stimulated by whatever adjustments are necessary to increase global competitiveness. 'Global competitiveness' (frequently a thought-substituting slogan) usually reflects not so much a real increase in resource productivity as a standards-lowering competition to reduce wages, externalize environmental and social costs, and export natural capital at low prices while calling it income.

The World Bank should use the occasion of its fiftieth birthday to reflect deeply on the forgotten words of one of its founders, John Maynard Keynes:

I sympathize therefore, with those who would minimize, rather than those who would maximize, economic entanglement between nations. Ideas, knowledge, art, hospitality, travel – these are the things which should of their nature be international. But let goods be homespun whenever it is reasonably and conveniently possible; and, above all, let finance be primarily national.

10

Transforming Aid Through Democratic Participation

Douglas Hellinger and Stephen Hellinger

Participation is the centrepiece of the development process. The relevance, effectiveness and sustainability of development projects, programmes and policies are directly dependent upon the meaningful and broad-based involvement of the citizenry in the decision-making that affects them, their communities and their environments. External assistance that is supportive of this democratic process and the outcomes that it produces can play a significant role in engendering equitable and sustainable economic growth and development, addressing global problems at their roots, and building stable democracies.

Participation means more than sharing in the benefits of development. It means an active, sustained and consequential role – particularly for those who have hitherto been the passive 'targets' and the 'intended beneficiaries' of a development defined by others – in determining how those benefits are to be generated. It means – especially in the case of women, who have been largely responsible for holding together fractured economic and social systems – having a seat at the table where the allocation of development resources is decided. And, just as importantly, it means owning a share of national economic and political power sufficient to ensure that one is not perpetually reliant on outside interventions for access to the decision-making process.

For almost two decades, The Development GAP has advanced the participation agenda in agencies that dispense aid and worked on contracts with the World Bank on urban projects in seven countries in Latin America and Africa. As in our consultancies with the US Agency for International Development (USAID) and other aid agencies during that period and in the early 1990s, we collaborated with organizations representative of local populations in ensuring that the latter participated actively in project design and implementation and in the sharing of project benefits.

While some of our initiatives, particularly one in postwar Nicaragua in 1979–80, met with success, our attempt to institutionalize this participatory assistance approach as policy in the World Bank was less successful. These efforts became increasingly more difficult to realize with the effective imposition during the 1980s of 'economic policy reform' by the Bank, as well as by the International Monetary Fund, the USAID and other multilateral and bilateral agencies. The 'democratic' involvement of citizens in shaping their societies' development was relegated to the marketplace, while the influence of those agencies expanded dramatically as they intervened directly in the economic-policy sphere and prevailed upon financially indebted governments to privatize, deregulate and open their economies.

Policy 'dialogue' has led to the adoption of virtually the same undifferentiated policy of structural adjustment in over seventy countries. Led by environmental organizations, the NGO community began in the mid-1980s to pressure the US Congress and other policy-makers to require the Bank to incorporate local populations and their knowledge of local conditions in the economic development of their countries, starting with large-scale environmentally sensitive projects. The Development GAP, working with its Southern partners, then applied this development methodology to economic-policy formulation. We did this in our advocacy work *vis-à-vis* the Bank and in our involvement of the US Congress in a broad-based consultative process in the Caribbean that yielded an alternative to the Reagan Administration's Caribbean Basin Initiative.

Six years ago, we published a set of proposals for the transformation of the Bank, USAID and the overall US aid programme into agents of more participatory, equitable and effective development.[1] This work, which included a strategy for popular involvement in regional development planning that we had devised for USAID, led The Development GAP into a collaboration with the House Foreign Affairs Committee and then with the Clinton Administration on a fundamental reform of the US aid programme.

The proposed transformation of USAID is the subject of this chapter. It was originally prepared at the request of the USAID Administrator and has been adopted as Agency policy, but has yet to be implemented. Much of its language was also incorporated in the aid-reform bill sent by the Administration to Congress in early 1994. While it was written specifically for USAID, it is pertinent to the operations of most aid agencies and is, in fact, presently under review by agencies of the United Nations and the Organization of

American States looking to promote development made sustainable by popular involvement.

The transformation that we prescribe in these pages can be achieved to a large degree through internal organizational changes. Ultimately, however, external structural changes also have to be made. The Bank, for example, as a highly undemocratic structure responsive largely to the finance ministries and commercial sectors of the North, must be made more accountable to the people of both the South and North if its managers and staff are to be reoriented in their purpose and have the support they need to sustain new emphases and methodologies. Similarly, USAID's best efforts to underwrite sustainable development based on peoples' understanding of their own environments can be continually compromised by the political and commercial agenda of other US government agencies if it does not have a measure of structural autonomy.

Even if USAID were to undergo the necessary external and internal restructuring, it no longer has the resources and thus the leverage, except in a relative handful of countries, to compete with the Bank and Fund (and the US Treasury) for policy influence. Yet, for far less money, the Agency can have a much more profound and lasting impact overseas by underwriting those organizations and activities that form the backbone of a democratic economy. This low-budget support would include: investments in democratically organized grassroots institutions; the defence of their rights when they organize and press for social change; the provision of information (and feedback mechanisms) on international policies and programmes under consideration; and the promotion of and support for national dialogues that yield broad-based perspectives and, at times, consensus on national and sectoral economic policy.

This piece was written to help stimulate this process and to explain how broad-based, equitable and sustainable development can be engendered through a low-cost participatory approach to foreign aid. It is an approach that can make development assistance more effective, in terms of cost and on-the-ground results, by helping to ensure that local populations, particularly women, have the opportunity to commit their extensive resources to the shaping of their own societies. Through the cultivation of this involvement, it helps ensure that development is relevant to local realities and priorities and that environmental and other global problems are addressed at their roots. This approach is of particular importance in societies in transition in which national reconciliation, reconstruction and stability are dependent upon the building of democratic institutions and a national consensus on the goals and nature of the country's economy.

This chapter is intended to form the conceptual basis for the development of an implementation strategy for USAID, but it is our hope that it will contribute to efforts to transform other international financial and donor institutions, as well.

The Process of Inclusion
Local populations in the developing world (as well as in Eastern Europe, Russia and the CIS) must be able to associate voluntarily in a range of organizations through which they can address the issues that affect them and their communities. The involvement in public decision-making on the part of organizations and social movements that directly represents the broadest possible range of interests in the civil society helps ensure that decisions are relevant and have broad-based support. Such organizational involvement, along with the freedom and exercise of individual expression, forms the backbone of a democratic society.

This process of inclusion is also critically important because it strengthens a nation's institutional, and, hence, development capacity, while engendering a commitment of resources that can ultimately sustain economic progress without outside assistance. It is the growth and maturation of participatory organizational structures and effective support institutions, rather than specific projects or programmes, that is the key to a sustainable development process.

If these non-governmental institutions can operate freely, they and their constituencies are in a better position to engage effectively in development decision-making, competing on a more equal basis with organizations representing the interests of economically or socially more powerful groups. The fair competition among interest groups not only adds vibrancy to a society, it can also yield national consensus on many issues and, with it, greater social stability. The more that groups, even those with sharply conflicting interests, are able to listen to and interact with one another, and the more that they feel that they are part of an open and meaningful national dialogue, the more likely they are to support a broader social interest.

Participation and Foreign Assistance
USAID and other donors similarly committed to promoting participatory, equitable and sustainable development can help ensure that all these sectors, and particularly the most broadly representative entities in each, are adequately and continually consulted and incor-

porated in the process of determining the allocation of development resources.

A development process will fail if it is driven by outsiders, whether
it be governments formulating programmes without the full involvement of affected communities or donors conditioning loans on the
application of a particular economic-policy framework. Planners,
technicians, economists and other specialists – both national and
foreign – can play a critically important role in the development
process but only if they serve a broad spectrum of society. No matter
how enlightened and well-intentioned the experts, their policies
will inevitably fail to serve the interests of the poor and marginalized unless they are informed by the values and priorities of ordinary
people and are in some way made accountable to local populations.

In this regard, USAID has important contributions to make. It has
been engaged in promoting various forms of participation in development through the years, more extensively during some periods than
in others. Times have changed, however, since the last concerted
attempt to incorporate participation systematically in USAID programming. The strong emphasis on policy dialogue over the past
decade has resulted in an increased concentration by donors and governments on economic policy-reform issues relative to project
investments.

With this shift has come the need to open up that dialogue to broad-
based participation as part of the democratization of the development
process. It is the development process as a whole and not just specific
projects that must be defined and designed in a participatory fashion.

USAID must take a new, bold and more comprehensive approach
to participation, with the emphasis first and foremost at the strategic
level. In addition to ensuring that there has been full involvement
of the civil society in the formulation of the economic policies that
it supports, USAID must elicit the participation of local populations
in the development of its own priorities, policy objectives and
country assistance strategies. Only in this way can the priorities of
the people and those of the Agency begin to mesh.

In short, a full and sustained commitment to participation as an
operational methodology will mean a transformation of the Agency
into an effective facilitator and supporter of bottom-up, equitable
development. It will require significant changes in the way USAID
is structured and operates, as well as a dedication to overcome the
many constraints and challenges that will be faced as the new
methodology is applied in the field.

Operational Meaning of Participation for USAID

USAID's promotion of participatory development means, in operational terms, the provision of support for those activities and decision-making processes in which affected populations are engaged, directly or through their representative organizations, for the purpose of shaping their economic and social environments. Such participatory processes are essential to the creation of democratic structures and the design of the projects, programmes and policies that serve the broad-based national interest.

In practice, USAID would promote participation in the identification, design, implementation, monitoring and evaluation of development undertakings at all levels, including: programmes of support for community and other local-level endeavours; larger-scale projects, development programmes, infrastructure investments and government policy formulation at the local and regional levels; and national-level development programmes and policies and their formulation. Just as importantly, the Agency should support institutional development, as it is only through their own organizations that people can gain greater control over the development process. Clearly, effective project activity and the building and strengthening of local institutions are mutually reinforcing. A project to train village health workers, for example, must not aim just to improve technical skills, but to encourage the newly trained workers and other villagers concerned about local health to meet and identify common interests and ways to work together to address sanitation and health problems.

USAID must act simultaneously at both the macro and micro levels and do so in a consultative, participatory, inclusive and responsive fashion. Support for participatory local initiatives, representative organizations and social movements can help empower local populations and provide the foundation for more open and relevant development decision-making, broad-based development and democracy. And, in those places where active participation in national and regional planning is possible, these processes help ensure an appropriate environment for the emergence and implementation of participatory endeavours and innovative initiatives at the local level.

To be effective in supporting participatory development, the Agency must also remain flexible in formulating and adapting its own country assistance strategies and programmes over time. In so doing, it must be responsive to ongoing input from local populations and systematize its own learning process. USAID must reach out more broadly to a wide range of organizations representing civil society and not limit its contacts to those with whom it agrees or has a funding relationship. It should also establish mechanisms through which it can be held accountable to those with whom it has consulted, as well as to the intended beneficiaries of the projects and programmes it supports.

Through the consultative process, USAID would be able to effect its own field-based analysis of the development situation in the countries in which it works and would bring a more informed point of view to its discussions with government. This would allow staff to assess better the relevance of government plans to local populations, determine the degree to which public planning has been participatory, and credibly promote participatory planning where it has not taken place. It would also increase USAID's awareness of alternative institutions and programme options.

Participation at the Local Level

Popular participation at the local, or micro, level is an active process through which beneficiaries and other affected populations initiate, control or significantly influence the design, execution and general direction of development activities. While USAID would not necessarily or primarily fund directly at the community level or directly finance small projects, it could enhance the process of participatory development by supporting the expansion of local participatory initiatives, the establishment of programmes in support of these initiatives, and larger-scale, often multi-institutional efforts that have built upon local successes.

With a sufficiently decentralized staff, it would place itself in a position to be continually informed of, and directly exposed to, participatory endeavours and organizations. Smaller assistance and development organizations that are active at the local or regional levels, including NGOs, the US regional development foundations and the Peace Corps, as well as local public-sector agencies, could provide a link to these initiatives.

In supporting development programmes that have grown out of participatory activities defined and started by the people themselves, USAID would be helping to create critical building blocks in the construction of national development and democratic nations. Programmes that build and draw upon the experiences of small producers in both the agricultural and informal sectors, for example, empower the farmers, enterprises and their organizations to take further action, particularly when those programmes effectively respond to their needs for credit, technical advice, appropriate policy support and other assistance. It is this self-generation of activity that is central to a participatory, self-sustaining development process.

The principal vehicle for participation at local levels are peoples' organizations and those institutions that represent or support the poor and their interests. These range from women's community fish-retailing groups to area-wide federations of farmers' associations. They include rural and workers' unions, small-enterprise associations, local rights groups, cooperative structures and organizations of the unemployed, as well as support organizations that provide services and project assistance while involving local populations in decision-making. At the same time, in most countries the formal private sector has well-established mechanisms through which larger financial, commercial and productive enterprises relate to their governments and to the international assistance community.

To play its role effectively in this process, USAID must consult these representative and support institutions to determine locally defined needs, the voids that must be filled in the development process, and the institutions and programmes in the non-governmental, public and private sectors deserving of support. In determining which undertakings merit assistance, USAID should consider a number of factors that relate to the degree and nature of local participation. They include: the genesis of the activity; the level of involvement of women, indigenous populations and others lacking access to development resources; the degree of decentralization of control and responsibility; and its sustainability in terms of the extent to which local institutions have been strengthened and the likelihood of continued and expanded local involvement and commitment of local resources.

USAID can further stimulate participatory development by encouraging cooperation between local organizations and governments and, where appropriate, the private sector. Such endeavours have the advantages of broadening the impact of community-based initiatives and ensuring public involvement in and support for local government programming. They also can link organizations with complementary functions and capabilities to maximize the impact of public investments.

This involvement can, in turn, expand the analytical capacity of local citizens' organizations and facilitate their involvement in public decision-making processes. The latter might include municipal, district, provincial and other local and regional planning exercises designed to yield plans for projects and programmes, the execution of which USAID could support through appropriate participatory organizations. USAID's experience in working at the municipal level may facilitate its introduction of participatory planning processes at local levels.

Participation at the Regional and National Levels

The strengthening of local participatory initiatives and institutional capacity also facilitates the involvement of the poor and the infusion of their experiences, perspectives and priorities in macro-level decision-making. To the extent that USAID is involved in supporting local participation, it is in a position to ensure that such input informs regional and national planning processes.

It is critically important that USAID and other donors encourage, facilitate and underwrite such participatory planning exercises. This is particularly true in light of the social and environmental consequences of economic-policy programs promoted through the years by the donor community. Exclusion from national decision-making disempowers local populations, undermines local participatory efforts and breeds alienation from, and destructive conflict in, the formal development process. Large-scale projects, planned and designed in isolation and without public scrutiny, can disrupt local activities, dislocate local populations, and wreak havoc on the natural environment. Inappropriate programmes can reroute critical resources away from the poor and disenfranchised and towards the more privileged and powerful. Economic policies can create an environment in which it is difficult for small producers, workers and their families to survive, placing ever-greater burdens on women as the sustainers of national economies. Over the past decade, members of the formal enterprise sector, and particularly those producing for the domestic market, have also been frustrated by their exclusion from the making of economic decisions that have often had the effect of destroying indigenous productive capacity.

On the other hand, there exists a rich experience in the utilization of participatory techniques in sectoral, national and, particularly, regional planning exercises. Approaches to effecting participation in these planning processes include, but by no means are limited to, town meetings, consultations with representative functional, sectoral and regional institutions, and fora with the leadership of a broad range of local and national organizations. The identification of appropriate development projects, programmes and policies requires the participation of representatives of a wide range of organizations, population groups and constituencies in dialogue with government. At its best, this dialogue is an ongoing process in which development contexts, problems, needs, priorities, resources, institutions, capabilities and solutions are discussed and a consensus is formed.

USAID should also ensure in its support for what comes out of these processes that the projects that are implemented are themselves designed, implemented and monitored in a participatory manner. Large-scale infrastructure projects, for example, must be subjected to up-front social and environmental assessments that directly involve the public, and to public reviews utilizing adequate appeals mechanisms. Once project goals are agreed upon, joint planning and management councils representing all interested parties can provide effective means for resolving conflicts and forming consensus, while small management groups or local councils can provide people with a way to promote their rights and interests. Along the way, meaningful choice in the form of a wide range of options must be available to people, who must be consulted early and continually to build account-ability into the system. Openness, transparency and ongoing access to information must also characterize the project cycle, as must the formulation of macroeconomic and sector-reform policies in order to make meaningful participation feasible. A proper enabling envi-ronment is the key because, without the appropriate services, infrastructure and policy framework, peoples' initiatives at the local level cannot be successful.

If these processes are in fact participatory, they present USAID with real opportunities to underwrite democratic change and development. It can support new and evolving policy frameworks, confident that they are well grounded in local reality and do not reflect either narrow private- or public-sector interests or the biases of donor agencies. It can, in accordance with its own resource availability, invest in those areas of national development that emerge as national and regional priorities. And it can work with those institutions that are representative of broad-based local interests or that practice partic-ipatory decision-making in carrying out component parts of the national plan in accordance with established criteria.

Participatory External Assistance

As an important development actor in many country contexts, USAID, along with other donors, has the potential to be either a con-structive or destructive force in the area of participatory change. To be constructive, USAID itself must act in a participatory fashion. This means three things operationally.

First, in order to promote participation, USAID must be open to supporting participatory endeavours and those which emerge from participatory decision-making processes at the national, regional and local levels rather than promoting and financing programmes that do not reflect the perspectives and priorities of local populations. Clearly, there are limitations to USAID's involvement which should be commensurate with: the capacity of executing institutions to absorb and effectively manage and utilize funds; the projected or proven viability, effectiveness and sustainability of the endeavours undertaken; the nature and availability of the Agency's resources; and the extent to which these endeavours will empower the poor through increasing equity in the system and protecting the natural resource base for future generations. Particular attention should be paid to participatory endeavours involving marginalized groups.

Second, in those many cases in which governments do not engage in participatory decision-making, USAID must encourage and facilitate such exercises or reach out itself to consult broadly with local populations and their organizations. Again, special attention must be paid to those historically excluded, particularly women and indigenous populations. Through systematic and sustained consultation, USAID can obtain a broad view of a nation's needs and assets and move towards a country assistance strategy less influenced by elite interests and its own priorities.

Third, what USAID learns through supporting participatory activities and processes in various national contexts must also inform and modify, on an ongoing basis, the institution's policy objectives, areas of concentration, programmatic thrusts, approach to global issues and operational style and structure to more effectively serve its clients. It will also place USAID in a unique position in its relationship with other donor agencies, including the multilateral development banks. It will be able to introduce field-based information and analysis into the country and overall assistance programming of other donors, thereby improving the quality and relevance of donor coordination.

Obstacles and Challenges

As USAID moves toward the implementation of an assistance strategy in support of participatory development, it will confront various difficulties, constraints, challenges and costs. These will be found within the societies in which USAID works, as well as within the Agency itself, both in the field and in Washington. A cursory review of some societal constraints and some of the challenges facing USAID field staff might be helpful in putting the concepts presented above in perspective. These problems and challenges can be divided into seven categories.

1. *The lack of preparedness of local populations, communities and groups to participate.* The poor know their immediate environments, but they often lack information and understanding about circumstances, options and technologies outside their communities. They are also often distrustful of outsiders, who have frequently intervened in their lives without making positive contributions. For participation to be successfully elicited – particularly in programmatic and policy decision-making and especially among women, indigenous populations and other marginalized citizens who have seldom had their voices heard – sufficient trust must be established, information provided, options presented and transparency and accountability proven. Effective organizational vehicles are also essential.

2. *The role of local elites.* Elites tend to control information, decision-making and resources at local levels. They also have the power of intimidation, and the poor usually have little bargaining power when their interests conflict. Elites need to be engaged, co-opted, circumvented or educated, depending on the situation.

3. *Differences within local populations and among interest groups.* As in our own society, social, economic, ethnic and other groups often have sharply conflicting interests. In the processes of consultation and participation, some voices are heard more clearly and often than others, and it may be difficult to reconcile divergent views. Furthermore, these views, taken separately, may not add up to positions that serve the broader social or national interest. By levelling the playing field, thoroughly analysing the legitimacy and viability of the proposals set forth, and synthesizing the feedback received, governments and donors can improve the quality of public decision-making. Moreover, participatory planning processes in which the poor and other segments of the population are represented around the table by their respective organizations can often move public decision-making towards consensus and outcomes that serve the greater good.

4. *Conflicts between the needs, priorities, perspectives and expertise of local populations and those of planners, economists and other technicians, both in government and donor agencies.* In most cases, public agencies have their own preconceived ideas of their countries' development problems and solutions. At best, they may view public participation as a means of transmitting local information and views to project and programme implementors after the design phase of the endeavours has been completed. Bureaucratic systems, always difficult to change, exacerbate

this problem. Donors often further complicate matters by introducing their own varied priorities through the assistance process. By developing their priorities in conjunction with local populations, however, governments and donors can close the gap between local needs and demands, on the one hand, and bureaucratic imperatives, on the other. If participation is to be effectively promoted, it will also be necessary to identify potential conflicts between the local populace and planners as well as to establish clear rules of the game for the process of give and take among the various parties. An equal challenge will be to find ways to encourage and support discussions and negotiations within a framework established by local populations.

5. *Government resistance to engaging in and supporting participatory processes*. While some governments might welcome the opportunity to engage in processes that yield broad-based support for development programming rather than adhere to economic programmes promoted by foreign donors and international financial institutions, it is equally clear that many would resist efforts to truly democratize the development process. In the latter circumstance, donors promoting participation are forced to rely more heavily on their own consultations in the field in determining what to support and to act as advocates for local populations, bringing public views to bear on their negotiations with government. In playing such a role, they will often need to reconcile conflicting local views on project, programme and policy issues. There are clearly limits, however, on the extent to which this role can be played by a donor. In the end, USAID must keep open the option of working with other institutions if government agencies cannot be convinced to be sufficiently inclusionary in their decision-making.

6. *Identifying appropriate participatory techniques*. Cultural and political circumstances, as well as the nature of the activity for which USAID is considering support, will determine the type of participatory technique employed. The quality of almost all public decisions, however, will be enhanced by public input, review and accountability, whether they relate to the development of a foreign-investment code, the construction of a power plant or the design of a new road system.

7. *Time-consuming nature of participation*. Participation involves consultations, planning processes, the building of local capacity and the application of political acumen in a variety of ways, all of which take time to be effective. On the flip side, however, it increases the quality, relevance and sustainability of development activities and can greatly diminish the amount of work required later in dealing with the

negative fall-out from ill-conceived projects, programmes and policies. These trade-offs exist at all levels of activity, including the development of donor policies and country assistance strategies.

With sufficient commitment, skills and flexibility, USAID can overcome many of these problems. This will require a significant transformation of the Agency, however, as many of the problems faced by field staff derive from the USAID bureaucracy itself. Extensive discussions are needed in-house to adequately flesh out current institutional constraints to effectively promoting participation and other required changes.

Note

1   Stephen Hellinger, Douglas Hellinger and Fred M. O'Regan, *Aid For Just Development* (Boulder: Lynne Reinner Publishers, 1988).

11

A Creative Approach to Structural Adjustment: Towards a People-centred Development

Marcos Arruda

'Structural adjustment' is the name of a set of policies designed by the World Bank and the International Monetary Fund. These international financial institutions and the General Agreement on Trade and Tariffs (GATT) are known as the Bretton Woods institutions. In collaboration with national governments of debtor countries, the Bank and the Fund insist upon adjustment of national economies to certain priorities and 'realities' of today's world. The stated goals of structural adjustment are: to combat inflation; to re-establish the equilibrium of the balance of payments of debtor countries; and to prepare the ground for relaunching economic growth. 'Sustained' growth is seen as the primary, long-term objective of adjustment programmes. The Bank and the Fund identify development with sustained economic growth which is to be promoted by the market with no interference from the state, its engine being the private sector. This concept can be summed up by the term 'market-centred, profit-oriented' development.

A growing number of people in both the South and the North are weary of the suffering resulting from the reforms promoted by their governments, inspired and supported by the Bretton Woods institutions. Citizens' organizations have had some influence in changing the attitude of the World Bank and the IMF, from one of arrogance and unaccountability to increasing concern with the opinion of society outside and beyond governments. The fact that the policies of these institutions have met with failure in many cases and have had such painful social and environmental consequences is forcing the institutions to enter discussions outside their traditional constituency. They are beginning to recognize that civil society has the right to express its views, concerns and expectations by means other than just national elections.

This chapter examines the World Bank and IMF approach to structural adjustment, and presents a brief critique of this approach by exposing both the inadequacy of their stated goals and the inconsistency between the goals and the means chosen to achieve them, concluding with a summary of an alternative approach to economic transformation and sociopolitical change in both North and South.

The World Bank and IMF Approach to Structural Adjustment

Detecting problems and obstacles to development has not been the only puzzle for those hoping to improve the economies of the South. Most controversial has been the analysis of those problems and the policies to adopt in order to overcome them. It is here that the various economic and social agents part company. On one side are those who can be called 'power agents'. They include governments of the North and South, large private corporations and multilateral organizations like the IMF and the World Bank. On the other side are citizens' organizations of all sorts and socially-oriented church and ecumenical groups which identify with the poor.

The first group, with a specific interpretation of the origins and characteristics of the crisis, adopted a set of programmes whose stated aims were 'stabilization' and structural adjustment programmes (SAPs). Though they may vary from country to country, these programmes share a common ideology: free markets and private-sector growth will further develop a country. Export production is increased; the economy is opened up to foreign firms and products; imports are cut; public spending is reduced; credit is restrained; tariffs and taxes are increased; currency is devalued; all industry is privatized; markets are deregulated; and protective regulations and barriers to investment and trade are eliminated.

Some of these policies may be adequate in specific situations, if they are introduced at the right pace and sequence, on the basis of a serious evaluation of costs and benefits and with a consistent plan to share their fruits equitably among the various social sectors. But taken together, these policies form a macroeconomic package which aims at pushing the 'adjusting' economy in a certain direction. There is abundant literature on the impact of individual policies on the economy, society and the environment. But the question of whether those policies are or are not adequate for the Southern countries, and what can be done to overcome the major problems afflicting their economies must be examined primarily in terms of the origin of the crisis and the assumptions, goals and motivations of those enforcing adjustment policies.

Alternatively, an exploration of the concerns and expectations of the 'non-power agents' – who comprise a majority of the world's population but who do not have access to productive property, management and political-economic decision-making – gives us a foundation upon which to build a vision of another kind of development, other economic priorities and the general elements of an alternative development strategy.

The World Bank and the IMF have a peculiar view of the origins of the crisis which has afflicted the majority of developing countries since the early 1980s. According to a World Bank document,

> The widespread economic crisis of the 1980s halted the advance in poverty reduction in many developing countries. In the early years of adjustment lending there was optimism that adjustment programs would be temporary, and that with the resumption of growth, poverty would continue to diminish and the adverse social effects of adjustment would be remedied.

Elsewhere, the Bank states that the balance of payments problems affecting developing countries are 'the result of the sharp deterioration in the terms of trade for oil-importing countries and from the legacy of weaknesses in domestic policies and institutions'.

The assumptions contained in both quotations are, first, that in the decades before the 1980s, poverty reduction was the primary concern of developing countries; second, that market-led economic growth automatically generates a reduction in poverty and 'remedies' the adverse social effects of adjustment; and, third, that the debt crisis was not a crucial factor and, therefore, was not worth mentioning. In other documents the World Bank recognizes that debt is a problem, but it also argues that rules are rules and therefore debts must be repaid.

Social movements and citizens' organizations in both North and South tend to reject these assumptions. They argue that no special attention was given to the poor in the 'development' or the 'adjustment decades', not even in regions, such as Latin America, which were achieving accelerated growth. They say that there is ample evidence to prove that market-oriented economic growth does not by itself generate poverty reduction, but rather leads to income concentration and rapid destruction of the environment. They question the adequacy of adjustment policies and point out that foreign-induced indebtedness was a crucial factor contributing to the socioeconomic crisis of the 1980s. A solution to the crisis would have had to include effective policies to overcome the debt crisis. However, these have generally been either absent or marginal in structural adjustment policies.

Citizens' groups point out that there was actually no special concern for the poor in the programmes for which money was borrowed that resulted in massive foreign indebtedness. The belief that capital accumulation and economic growth should first entail income concentration until the economy reaches a point where the benefits of that accumulation and growth would 'naturally' trickle down to the working majorities was widely publicized. The real priority was to create an attractive environment for foreign investment, which was seen by the elites of both the North and South as one of the main engines of economic development. However, the unpopular nature of these policies and the resulting inequality generated widespread social unrest. In order to control this social unrest, Northern governments, particularly that of the United States, showed no hesitation in promoting military regimes. These were precisely the governments which, lured by the claims of international bankers and the grandiose rhetoric of multilateral agencies, decided to take foreign loans to promote huge infrastructure and industrial enclave projects. Such borrowing, side by side with capital flight, corruption and luxury imports, have been largely responsible for the impoverishment and decapitalization that has afflicted the debtor countries since the early 1980s.

Citizens' groups also argue that the poor were not on the agenda of the 1980s. Stabilization and adjustment policies and loan conditionalities date from the early part of the decade. Originally the policies were promoted by the IMF and had a predominantly monetaristic character: they were more concerned with the equilibrium of monetary and financial indicators than with production and distribution of goods or the structural obstacles to self-reliant development. The plight of the majority was left out of the adjustment agenda. Later, the World Bank moved in, offering longer-term adjustment loans tied to rigid conditionalities. The debtor nations had to reorganize their economies around the priority of foreign debt servicing. Exports were accelerated to provide capital to service the debt, yet the export drive was unable to generate enough foreign exchange to cover interest payments and countries were then forced to borrow not for productive investment but to pay interest on the debt. As a result, a vicious cycle of indebtedness has been established, whereby the more the debtor countries pay, the more they owe. Governments and international financial institutions became the main creditors of the majority of least developed countries. Private creditors have also relied on those financial institutions as proxies and debt collectors on their behalf. As a result, citizens' groups argue, the debt crisis has been used by the Northern elites to get a tighter grip over the economic and financial destinies of the Southern countries. Citizens' organizations legitimately ask why the poor are even poorer after decades of 'development', 'aid' and foreign investment.

Critique of Structural Adjustment Based on the Market-centred Development Paradigm

Social movements and citizens' organizations acknowledge that the World Bank moved forward when it established poverty reduction as one of its 'overarching goals' in the early 1990s. However, they argue that the way SAPs are designed indicates that the primary goal of foreign aid has proved to be the subordinate integration of the Southern economies within the world market economy, not the economic basis for a more self-reliant, equitable and sustainable human development. In effect, SAPs serve to adjust the indebted economies to the priorities of the North. Issues such as income distribution and the concentration of wealth, exclusion of poor majorities from the right to own property and control productive resources, private sector inefficiency and oligopolistic control over markets, and political authoritarianism to guarantee the implementation of SAPs, remained outside the scope of the Bank's diagnosis. The insistence upon all-embracing deregulation and loan conditionality dismantled the state and transferred much of the power of designing national macroeconomic policy to the multilateral agencies.

Some of the consequences of adjustment have been recession in the domestic sector, growing unemployment, massive impoverishment of urban and rural workers, growing bankruptcies of businesses related to domestic markets, weakening of workers' organizations, cuts in health, education, housing, transportation and social services and social unrest. The loss of real resources of developing countries in terms of negative net transfers, higher interest rates, unequal competition in international services and restricted access to Northern markets in 1990 amounted to US$500 billion or the equivalent of seven Marshall plans.[1] The fact that the South has become a net exporter of capital to the North led to massive decapitalization of Southern economies and the growing impoverishment of their societies.

A Market-centred SAP Is Incompatible with People-centred Development

What this social breakdown shows us is that development cannot be market-centred and people-centred at the same time. The market was originally defined as an impersonal set of economic forces, 'the invisible hand', which ideally would be capable of allocating scarce resources according to real needs. But by monetizing social relations and subordinating everything and everyone to the market, capital converts the worker, the consumer, the human being into commodities. In the advanced world capitalist system, a small number of large corporations and strong governments have gained monopoly power over national and international markets, creating a visible hand to guide the 'invisible hand'.

Market-centred SAPs have not been able to reduce or eliminate poverty, precisely because they do not tackle the roots of poverty and inequality.[2] Insofar as macroeconomic structures and policies continue to create and reproduce the matrix of poverty and marginalization, compensatory social projects and social investment funds may offer temporary relief, but no long-term solution.

The lack of a strategy for adjusting the world economy, including Northern economies, to the goals of equitable and sustainable development and poverty eradication has also been responsible for the widespread failure of SAPs. As Northern economies go through another stage of technological and managerial modernization based largely on the capital they have been able to draw from the South, they are themselves confronted with new and more acute social disparities and tensions. At the same time, they practice dumping, impose tariff barriers against industrial imports and enforce other restrictive practices against the Southern economies. As a consequence, the gap between the rich North and poor South is increasing but, in the new world order of globalization, two new entities are emerging, one constituted by the elites of both hemispheres, and the other encompassing the Southern majority and a growing number of impoverished or chronically unemployed workers in the North. The assumption at the heart of the old development paradigm is that the private sector is the only effective economic agent and, freed from constraints and regulations, it can ultimately resolve all problems of economies and people. NGOs challenge this assumption, asking how the World Bank's intention of ensuring 'the participation of the poor in operations directly affecting them' can be put into practice if the private sector, with profit and market control, rather than working people and their creative capacity, is to be 'the engine of growth'?

The Bank has recognized, in its most recent review of SAPs in sub-Saharan Africa, that adjustment has 'left much to be desired in terms of restoring growth and social welfare', and admits that investment levels have dropped significantly in countries implementing its programmes. Nevertheless, the Bank tends to offer the same prescriptions for overcoming ills that it has only recently been willing to acknowledge.

Could economic planners have foreseen these outcomes? Why have the promoters of Bank policies so grossly miscalculated? Why have they repeated the same mistakes for years, using the same inadequate recipes that have consistently proven ineffective? Citizens' organizations and academic institutions have produced abundant literature clearly demonstrating the high risks of those policies and the inadequacy of their goals. Around the world, people are testing new ways of organizing themselves and their economies. They need space, incentives and financial support which multilateral institutions are in a position to provide.

Alternative Vision, Alternative Policies

For two-thirds of the world population, who suffer the effects of poverty, marginalization and dispossession, there must be an alternative development model. The challenge is threefold: there must be a profound understanding of the complexities and contradictions of the current economic system; a new vision for a new development paradigm, to succeed, must be established in a participatory fashion; and it must be implemented in a way in which it will be incorporated and organically built into human lives, relationships and economies. The presence of the material conditions for change is not enough for change to happen; the time must be ripe and the will for change must be present together with adequate forms of organization to effect true and lasting change. In a world of blatant inequalities in the distribution of power, knowledge, information and resources, it is essential to design macro-socioeconomic policies that give special attention to the elimination of poverty, exploitation and marginalization – particularly among women, youth, children and the ethnically oppressed – and to reverse the process of environmental destruction.

Alternative Goals
From the perspective of the world's impoverished majorities, desirable goals of an adjustment that truly tackles the roots of the socioeco-

nomic crisis are: poverty eradication; self-reliance; food security; socially, culturally, politically and environmentally sustainable development; continuous improvement of the quality of personal, communal and social wellbeing of every citizen; the sharing of ownership, access and control of productive resources; and the sharing of the responsibility to design and implement development goals.

Citizens' organizations tend to make their fundamental assumptions explicit and essentially non-doctrinaire. They believe there is enough evidence to prove that the dynamics of the liberal market by itself leads to monopoly control and to a lack of democracy. Therefore, only the right combination of market mechanisms, government regulation and the active participation of civil society can bring about an equitable and sustainable development. Furthermore, they argue, there is no single blueprint for this combination. It has to emerge from the dynamic interaction of the various sectors of each society, including the organizations of the poor, in a truly democratic and participatory manner.

A different kind of adjustment – a 'people- and community-centred adjustment' – based on the vision of an equitable, participatory and sustainable human development, would be one step towards equitable structural transformation. Such a policy would include the elements below, which offer new priorities and new local, national and international policies.

New Priorities

1. *Beyond economic growth.* A people-centred adjustment would subordinate the equilibrium of macroeconomic indicators to macro-social as well as ethical development goals. It would see the individual and the social human being as the ultimate purpose and the subject of economic activity. The adjustment process would be envisaged as a response first to local and national human development needs, with macroeconomic policies as instruments to achieve these goals. This requires an exchange of ideas between grassroots groups, NGOs, governments and multilateral agencies. To shift the pole of development from the global economy to popular communities and units of production is crucial, so as to generate a participatory process of development planning and implementation from that level upward.[3]

2. *Getting to the roots of poverty.* A people-centred adjustment would promote social policies, human resource development, participatory democracy and human rights as integral components of macroeconomic policy from the outset, wherein the role of the state

in socioeconomic policy is clearly recognized. The fight against hunger and poverty and their determining factors would be at the core of the new macroeconomic policies and not simply a marginal concern. Social and environmental problems would be addressed as part of each policy and development strategy, and not only as a separate compensatory programme. In the short run, it would be desirable to combine compensatory programmes with structural, employment- and income-generating strategies to bring marginalized workers back into the economy. Indicators of human development, democratization and quality of life should be adopted as barometers of the success of development policies and projects. Development agencies should be asking how to respond to the needs of low-human development (which includes life expectancy, health, food and nutrition, education, income distribution and basic indicators about the situation of children and women), instead of 'low-income' communities, countries and regions.

3. *Human empowerment.* A people-centred adjustment would seek to restructure the domestic economy towards sustainable human development by adopting investment and credit policies aimed at strengthening the balanced development of domestic industry, agriculture and services, economic and social infrastructure and the domestic mass-consumption market. It would seek to promote the democratization of control over productive, financial and commercial resources and activities, so that market mechanisms can gradually be combined with mechanisms of cooperation between economic agents, regions and economic sectors.

4. *Education for self-reliance.* The overarching goal of a people-centred adjustment and development is to promote each and every citizen's and community's capacity to manage their own lives and destinies in a perspective of self-reliance and cooperation with other persons, communities and peoples. This can only become a reality if integral education is taken as an essential dimension of human development. Integral education includes basic education, understood as the satisfaction of basic learning needs related to the material foundations for a better quality of life. But it postulates permanent education, not strictly functional, including the development of all the learning capacities of the person. It is not over-specialized, because its programmes embrace all the relevant areas of life and work of the persons, and their inter-relationships. It also includes the production of autonomous local and national research and development capacity, as the means to enhance self-reliance and cooperation among communities, nations and peoples.

New Local and National Priorities

1. *Policy by and for the people.* A people-centred adjustment would make corrective and development policies the result of a broadly democratic dialogue, wherein transparency prevails, and all social sectors concerned, particularly popular organizations and NGOs, are included. This requires that both the Bretton Woods institutions and governments recognize and make space for the views of popular organizations and NGOs.

2. *Community-based design.* A people-centred adjustment would take local communities as the basic unit for the design and implementation of adjustment and development policies. Participatory research on the overall needs, resources and human capabilities of each community would serve as the basis for a comprehensive plan that, among other things, would deal with the most crucial emergencies and the mechanisms needed to guarantee ownership by the local communities, and durable success, of the development strategy. At the national level, services would belong to the realm of a democratic government and, above all, of organized society. This is crucial for the achievement of sustainable, community-based human development.

3. *Increase ownership of development through fiscal reform.* A people-centred adjustment would promote effective measures, including adequate fiscal, employment- and income-generating policies, to achieve a quick redistribution of income – thus 'democratizing' effective demand. An important measure would be to make costs, prices and profits more transparent, thus enhancing the freedom of choice of consumers and workers. Such policies should envisage the participation of all concerned in the ownership and management of productive resources, thus rekindling domestic-oriented supply and increasing 'ownership' of adjustment and development. A comprehensive, democratic agrarian reform – formerly an important element in the development agenda of the World Bank and later dropped – should be given priority.

4. *Regulate competition.* A people-centred adjustment would adopt legal measures to regulate competition, democratize productivity gains, prevent oligopolistic practices and overhaul cartels and restrictive business practices. A democratized state should be empowered to induce corporations – in particular foreign firms, by means of regulations, fiscal and other measures – to abide by these new priorities.

5. *Adjust SAPS.* A people-centred adjustment would redesign and regulate a number of policies included in current SAPS in ways that could effectively benefit the poor. It would confront the cost-push factors of inflation, and not just the demand-pull factors, thus seeking

to reduce inflation without suppressing wages. It would adopt targeted subsidies, based on a careful survey of needs, which provide adequate coverage and supply the basic goods needed by poor families. It would introduce comprehensive human development indicators and the concern with 'full-cost' measures to gauge the adjustment effort. It would seek currency stability, rather than continuous currency depreciation.

6. *Adopt selective privatization.* A people-centred adjustment would adopt a selective privatization policy, seeking to democratize control over industry and rid the state of enterprises that do not benefit the public sector and the population, while keeping highly profitable and strategic industries under public control. It would base privatization and its rhythm on a prospective impact assessment as to the economic, social and environmental costs and benefits in each industry, with special emphasis on the poor. It would make privatization a regulated and transparent process aimed at market democratization, so as to promote the broad distribution of privatized industries in order to avoid further concentration of wealth.

New International Priorities

1. *Break the cycle of debt.* Debt repayment should not be a priority goal. Consistent measures should urgently be adopted in order to invert the current net outflow of real resources from the South. A people-centred adjustment would aim at rescheduling debt payments according to people-centred development priorities. The recuperation of the local and national economy would be seen as the only effective means to generate sustainable capacity to pay the foreign debt. Development loans should be granted at better-than-market terms and should be aimed at the local and national economic reconstruction, not at repaying financial obligations. Creditors should accept a share of the costs of disindebtedness and should not press debtor countries to the extent that they have to resort to new loans to service the debt. All military debt should be made transparent; the World Bank and the IMF should support social movements' pressure on government and creditors for its outright cancellation.

2. *Make trade sustainable.* A people-centred adjustment would subordinate the external sector to the priorities of the domestic sector and the communities that make up the national economy. It would orient targeted incentives, subsidies and credits to the domestic sector first, particularly to the development of a popular economy, whose economic agents can have the highest social and democratic multiplier effect. It would also plan a socially and ecologically sustainable development of the export sector, seeking equitably to

combine the interests of the nation with those of foreign exporters and the labour and consumer markets abroad. Trade liberalization, its pace and sequence, would benefit the poor and the consumers by providing lower-priced consumer goods and adequate prices for small and medium producers. International trade policy-makers should envisage suppressing the prevailing double standards – protection of 'intellectual property' among others – which have proven severely harmful to developing countries. Each measure adopted in the Southern country should be related to a consistent measure of liberalization of Northern markets. The state should also have the power to define strategic priorities and sectors which should be regulated or remain protected. Its action should be guided by the priorities of food self-sufficiency and complementary cooperation with producers of the same region.

3. *Move from 'development aid' to 'participatory development'*. A people-centred adjustment would adopt a strategy of gradual replacement of 'development aid' with participatory investment. Structural transformations in the international economy, and particularly in the North, including mechanisms to ensure an international redistribution of income, knowledge and access to resources, are necessary preconditions. Such investment would be oriented to projects that have been defined and designed by local communities and would aim at supporting initiatives coming from the people whom the projects are supposed to serve. Such investments would only foster projects that are economically, socially and environmentally sustainable.

4. *Increase access to information and participation*. A people-centred adjustment would promote open access to information on policy and project loans, including the publication of social and environmental impact assessments. It would also establish mechanisms of periodic participatory evaluation of the adjustment process, focusing on the costs and benefits for the different sectors of the economy and the population and the different regions of the country, as well as for society as a whole. This would be the basis for a participatory planning process concerning both the following phase of adjustment and the global development strategy.

Conclusions

In a time when production and communication are becoming globalized processes, international financial institutions are important spaces for dialogue and negotiation on issues of common interest.

The Bretton Woods institutions are not immune to pressure by the social movement and citizens' organizations of North and South. Changes in their approach to structural adjustment and the indebtedness problem, faced by countries whose population is predominantly poor, require a new development paradigm. Intellectual arguments are important, but concrete experiences of people's education, promotion and empowerment are the crucial factor. They have the power to prove that ordinary workers, ethnically oppressed people and others, when given access to the means, are creative and capable of becoming 'owners' of their own development and wellbeing.

Notes

1   UNDP, *Human Development Report*, 1992, p. 67.
2   According to UNDP, control over the global income by the 20 per cent richest increased from 70.2 per cent to 76.3 per cent (6.1 percentage points) between 1960 and 1980, and to 82.7 (6.4 points) in 1989. The per capital income ratio (richest to poorest) in 1988 was 140 to 1.
3   José Luis Coraggio, 1993, 'Desarrollo Humano, Economia Popular y Educacion: El Papel de las ONGs Latinoamericanas en la Iniciativa de Educacion para Todos', CEAAL, Santiago, especially Part IV, 'Economia Popular y Necesidades de Aprendizaje'.

12

The World Bank's Revised Information Policy and New Inspection Panel: Public Accountability or Public Relations?

Lori Udall

At the heart of the campaign to reform the World Bank and other multilateral development banks (MDBs) is an attempt by citizens' groups, NGOs and local communities to force the MDBs to become more publicly accountable and transparent in their operations. For years, World Bank projects and programmes during critical stages of planning and design have remained shrouded in secrecy with virtually no public input or scrutiny. In the Bank's borrowing countries, local communities that are directly affected by Bank-financed projects have often been denied access to the most basic information about these projects. At the same time, taxpayers in the World Bank's major shareholder donor countries, whose money supports and underwrites the Bank, also have little knowledge of or control over how their money is being used.

The lack of information, public participation and public scrutiny of World Bank operations, among other things, has contributed to a growing number of unsustainable and unsound projects. The most notable of these is the Sardar Sarovar (Narmada) dam in western India. The grassroots opposition to Narmada and ensuing nine-year battle is rooted in a belief that indigenous and rural poor people have a right to democratic control over their own future and development. The Narmada project has come to symbolize a destructive and outdated development model which still is promoted by the development banks. The Bank's involvement in Narmada actively prevented community participation and debate while contributing to the most extensive human rights violations associated with any internationally financed development project.

Over the last ten years, NGOs in the Bank's donor and borrower countries who share a common vision of community-based development have forged partnerships to force major changes on the World Bank.

NGOs believe that if project planning and design were open and transparent, fewer disastrous projects would ever be approved. In 1993, after facing severe criticism from international NGOs, donor governments and legislators for deteriorating project quality and lack of public accountability, the World Bank was forced to revise its information policy and to create a mechanism whereby people directly affected by Bank projects could send complaints regarding violations of the Bank's policies, procedures and loan agreements.[1] A battle in the US Congress over the authorization of the US$3.7 billion contribution to IDA 10 catalyzed the quick establishment of the new policies, after environmental NGOs testified before Congress that the United States should not continue to pour billions of dollars into the World Bank without major institutional reform.[2] However, six months after the new policies were created, public accountability at the Bank seems as far away as ever, causing many to question whether these 'reforms' were merely another public relations exercise.

Alternatives to the World Bank's Current Information Policy

The battle over access to information is rooted in a belief in the fundamental value of public participation, in which people have a voice in their own development and control over their own lives and futures. While the World Bank has paid lip service to public participation in its projects and policies, community participation in development decisions and planning is meaningless without access to basic information.

Since 1989, the World Bank has had an information policy in favour of disclosure of information in the absence of a compelling reason not to disclose.[3] Despite this policy, in practice the Bank has consistently restricted almost every type of document regarding Bank projects, policy-based lending, economic programmes as well as much environmental and social information. Attempts to access information, particularly by people directly affected by Bank projects and programmes, have been met with arbitrary refusals and red tape. While there may be reasonable grounds to restrict a small body of documents which contains confidential or sensitive information about the Bank's borrowers, most information is not legitimately withheld.

The failure to disclose information has often resulted in a total lack of local consultation and public participation at the project level, ill-conceived and poorly planned projects, deteriorating project quality and, in some cases, massive local opposition to projects. Aside from Narmada, projects such as the Kedung Ombo dam in central Java, Indonesia and the Pak Mun dam in Thailand are stark reminders of these deficiencies.

Intense and growing public pressure from local and international NGOs, donor governments and legislators resulted in the World Bank reassessing its information policy. In October 1992, the Bank convened an internal working group to study and make recommendations regarding proposed revisions to the information policy. In March 1993, the working group issued weak recommendations which would have little practical effect at the project level in increasing transparency or openness.[4] However, inside the working group, a dissenting group of Bank staff issued an 'alternative view' which recommended far-reaching changes in the Bank's policy – changes which would release almost all project documents and all environmental and social information.[5] Despite this effort, the mainstream working group recommendations formed the basis for the policy revisions and were sent to the World Bank's Board of Executive Directors[6] during a period of US Congressional scrutiny. They were approved in August 1993.[7]

Two public documents that describe the new information policy are 'Bank Procedures on Disclosure of Operational Information' (BP 17.50) and a booklet by World Bank external relations entitled 'Policy on Disclosure of Information'.

Project Documents Continue To Be Withheld

Instead of releasing pre-appraisal project documents which are needed by local people and communities to offer input or generate debate on a proposed project, the Bank's new policy creates a new document called a project information document (PID). PIDs are created specifically for public consumption: they will probably be sanitized, stripped of any candid description of the reality on the ground. While the Bank claims that the PIDs will contain the same information as pre-appraisal project documents and would be lengthened as more information becomes available, recent examples of the PID reveal their claims to be false. Most have half the detail of pre-appraisals. The PID also creates extra and unnecessary work for Bank staff who already have to write many project documents and appraisals. If the

Bank is in good faith in its attempts to improve project quality, then it should be open, from start to finish.

The new Bank Information Procedures state that when an interested party requests more information on a project under preparation, Bank staff may release factual, technical information or portions of such documents, after they have asked the borrower government. This approach allows for a case-by-case handling of information requests which will undoubtedly result in unequal treatment of those requesting information and an unequal application of the presumption in favour of disclosure of information. By bringing in a third party, it also leaves open the possibility of greater delays and arbitrary decision-making regarding release of information.

The creation of the PID is insufficient to alter meaningfully the way the Bank does business or to involve substantially local communities in project planning and design. The policy should be revised to allow for the release of virtually all project documents particularly those in the early stages of project planning.[8] All of these documents should be made available to affected communities and the public in the country where the project is located. The documents should also be available in the public information center upon request. Sensitive or confidential information in early project documents could be put into other documents such as the memorandum of the president which is used by the board of executive directors in considering a project.

Country Generated Documents – Environmental and Social Information

During the preparation of many projects, various environmental and social documents are prepared by the local project authorities or consultants which have important value to local communities and people directly affected by development projects. Most of these documents (such as environmental impact assessments) are considered the property of the borrower country. Currently many of these documents are withheld from the public – action which can hardly be reasonable or justified since public input can sharpen or significantly alter a project's design or result in mitigation which may have been overlooked.

According to Bank policy, environmental impact assessments and environmental analyses are now available both in country and in the Bank's new public information center.[9] Many reports from developing country NGOs, however, reveal that there is still difficulty in getting copies of even these basic documents. Moreover, there is a broad range of other environmental and social documents which should be made available to the affected communities. Additional environmental documents which should be made available but aren't include: draft environmental impact assessments, feasibility studies, studies of project alternatives, baseline data, flora and fauna surveys, national environmental action plans, tropical forestry action plans, national forestry policies, forestry studies and cost/benefit analyses.

Social documents which should be made available include draft and final resettlement plans, indigenous people's development plans, timetables for resettlement, maps of resettlement sites, compensation rates and schedules, government resettlement policies, rehabilitation plans and poverty alleviation plans and programmes.

Retroactivity and the 'Case-by-case Basis'

The new information policy is not retroactive – which means it does not apply to projects which were already approved before the policy came into effect on 1 October 1993. This time constraint is a serious problem since most of the controversial projects were already approved before that time. Requests for information on these projects will also be dealt with on a case-by-case basis. This has already allowed for arbitrary refusals by task managers, operations staff and member governments. This has and will result in an unequal treatment of those requesting information. Legal limitations to disclosure cited by the Bank's legal counsel can be easily and legally overcome if the Bank informs member countries that it intends to release staff appraisal reports and project documents and seek blanket approval for release.[10]

The World Bank's Inspection Panel

The idea of an independent appeals commission to monitor controversial World Bank projects and investigate citizens' complaints was originally proposed by NGOs in 1990.[11] However, the concept did not really gain momentum until after the Morse Commission issued its independent review of the World Bank-financed Sardar Sarovar dam in western India.[12] Mounting local and international opposition to Sardar Sarovar, as well as the disparity in information between what NGOs and the India operations staff sent to executive directors, left the executive directors with little choice but to hire an independent body, the Morse Commission.

The Morse Commission was unprecedented, as the Bank had never previously hired a completely independent group to investigate an ongoing project. The Bank opted not to use the Operations Evaluation Department (OED), an internal Bank office which conducts ex-post facto evaluations of projects. It was not in the mandate of this department to conduct an evaluation of an ongoing project and some Board members also said that the only way to conduct an investigation credibly was to hire people completely independent of the Bank.

The Morse Commission established a precedent for a body operating independently from Bank management and Executive Directors, and working on an independent budget. Their review, which was seen as credible and independent by the outside world, became a source of embarrassment for the Bank because of its severe criticism of Sardar Sarovar, the Bank's appraisal process and a wide range of other Bank projects involving forcible resettlement. The manner in which Bank management dealt with the findings and recommendations of the Morse Commission made matters worse: in their response to the review issued to executive directors, operations staff misrepresented what was said in the Morse Commission review, confirming the need for a permanent independent mechanism.

The Morse Commission's independence was no accident. The Commission was not based inside the Bank and, after the terms of reference were agreed upon and a contract was signed, the Commission did not take any instructions from the Bank management or executive directors. A key element in its independence was its budget of US$1.2 million, which allowed the team an extensive travel budget and capability to hire consultants and researchers and support staff. Another key element was the fact that the report was published independently of the Bank and simultaneously made available to the public, the executive directors and Bank management.[13] The Morse Commission holds the copyright for the report. The Commission also had access to all Bank information on the project and the cooperation of all parties concerned including Bank staff, local NGOs, the Indian government and international NGOs.

Inspection Panel Is Not Independent

By Spring 1993, discussions regarding the creation of an independent mechanism took place inside the Bank and among members of the board for the first time. By September 1993, a resolution establishing an 'inspection panel' was approved by the board of executive directors.[14] However, the shortcomings in the resolution are so extensive that few expect it to be a truly credible panel.

With the exception of having access to all Bank information, the panel as currently codified in the resolution has none of the features of the Morse Commission. Instead, executive directors have approved a resolution with very little capability to improve public accountability, project quality or to gain public confidence. In the current resolution, the panel's actions and procedures are heavily restricted by Bank management and the executive directors, threatening the panel's credibility and independence. The role and rights of the public are marginalised by the resolution, and even the rights of the person filing the complaint are minimal.

A major flaw in the current resolution is the ability of the executive directors to block outside citizen complaints.[15] Currently, complaints can be filed by an NGO or group of people that can demonstrate that its rights or interests have been or are likely to be directly affected by a World Bank-financed project. Complaints can also be filed by an executive director. As the resolution is currently worded, when the panel decides to take up a complaint from an outside party, it will send a recommendation to the executive directors. At this point if only one executive director objects, there will be a vote to determine whether the complaint should be taken up. This clearly undermines the independence of the panel. Since the panel will draw up its own criteria, standing, and further define the procedures for filing a case, it logically follows that the panel should be able to decide which cases to investigate. (In contrast, the Operations Evaluation Department reports to the board but makes its own decision about which projects it will evaluate.) The fact that the board can block a complaint means that rather than being guided by policy and carefully drawn up guidelines, the issue of whether to take up a complaint will become embroiled in the North/South politics of the board and will remain at the mercy of individual board member's prejudices or biases.

Another major flaw is that the budget for the panel is now only US$1.6 million. The Morse Commission used US$1.2 million investigating only one project for a ten-month period. Even Bank staff admit that many projects in India are much worse than Narmada; as many as twenty complaints could be filed with the panel in the first year. A well-endowed panel is also important to ensure independence and to ensure that reports of the panel will be published and publicly released. Hiring of consultants and researchers is an essential part of investigating a problem project and must be paid for out of the budget of the panel. The panel should also have the budget to publish reports and findings independently and to travel extensively to project sites and to conduct field visits to the surrounding areas. The panel should not have to go back to the Bank repeatedly for reimbursements; this would leave the panel open to manipulation by the Bank, particularly if the Bank did not approve of expenditures and used it as a device to constrain the panel's activities.

One of the most serious flaws of the panel is the lack of public disclosure at the time of the report's release to executive directors and Bank management.[16] The way the resolution currently reads, the panel's findings will not be released to the public until two weeks after the board votes on it. Even more disturbing is that the complainant will not receive the report until after the board votes on it. This will result in no opportunity for public input from the time the report is released to the board until after the board has already made a decision. For NGOs and activists who have been involved in influencing board decisions, this is unacceptable and will undermine the independence of the panel. The fact that the decision and the vote remain shrouded in secrecy until it is too late for public input invites manipulation, unauthorized editing and misrepresentation of the findings. Based on Bank management's attempts to misrepresent the findings of the Morse Commission, this sets a dangerous precedent.[17] Compared to proceedings and judgements of other international tribunals, this falls far short of customary notions of due process and accountability.

There is currently a process within the Bank to turn much of the existing detailed Bank procedures and policies, called 'operational directives', into staff guidelines which are not mandatory. Although this is not a direct shortcoming of the panel, NGOs fear that the streamlining of operational directives may undermine the panel's effectiveness because the Bank's mandatory policies and procedures, which are the standard the panel is empowered to investigate, will be gutted.

Since the resolution was passed, the Bank has given NGOs plenty of reason to feel excluded. The nomination process has been conducted in virtual secrecy for a two-month period. Names of candidates were put forward to the president's office by executive directors and Bank management and lists of around fifty names were considered by the managing directors in Lewis Preston's office. This list was reportedly narrowed to fifteen and then five without any public consultation.[18]

Parts of the resolution are still quite vague and these areas could feasibly be expanded upon and improved by the chairperson. The more detailed procedures and criteria for filing a complaint, the more investigations and the whole complaints process will also need to be further defined in accordance with the above recommendations.

The resolution needs to be revised and further elaborated upon in order for the panel to have any public accountability. However, until the resolution is substantially revised to allow for more public input and transparency similar to the Morse Commission and timely public disclosure of reports, the panel will be one more World Bank public relations exercise.

Notes

1 See Resolution No. 93–10, Resolution No. IDA 93–6, The World Bank Inspection Panel, 22 September 1993. See also 'Expanding Access To Bank Information', 31 August 1993 and Bank Procedures, Disclosure of Operational Information, BP 17.50, September 1993.
2 The tenth replenishment of the World Bank's 'soft loan window', the International Development Association. See Testimony of Lori Udall on Behalf of Environmental Defense Fund; Barbara Bramble, on Behalf of National Wildlife Federation before the Subcommittee on International Development, Finance, Trade and Monetary Policy.
3 See The World Bank and International Finance Corporation, *Directive on Disclosure of Information*, July 1989.
4 World Bank, *Report of Working Group on the Review of the Directive on Disclosure of Information*, 29 March 1993.
5 World Bank, op. cit., annex c.
6 The World Bank's board of 24 executive directors represent the shareholder countries of the World Bank. The executive directors are responsible for the conduct of the general operations of the Bank and they approve all World Bank projects and policies.
7 World Bank, 'Expanding Access to Information: Proposed Revisions To the Directive On Disclosure of Information', 10 June 1993. See also World Bank, 'Expanding Access To Bank Information', 31 August 1993 and Bank Procedures, Disclosure of Operational Information, BP 17.50, September 1993.
8 Bank project documents which should be made publicly available include, but are not limited to, initial executive project summaries, executive project summaries, draft appraisal reports, staff appraisal reports, mid-term reviews, briefing documents prepared for Executive Directors, project completion reports and project performance audit reports.
9 Bank Procedures: Disclosure of Operational Information, BP 17.50.

10 Other documents which should be publicly available include loan and credit agreements, draft sector policy papers, IDA replenishment agreements and background papers, legal opinions, project briefing documents prepared for executive directors.

11 Eric Christensen, Natural Resources Defense Council, 'Green Appeal: A Proposal for an Independent Environmental Commission of Inquiry at the World Bank', September 1990.

12 Bradford Morse and Thomas Berger, Sardar Sarovar, *The Report of the Independent Review* (Resource Futures International, 1992).

13 Bank management did have an opportunity to comment on an earlier version, although there was no editorial control, and only some comments were accepted, mostly small factual errors.

14 World Bank, The World Bank Inspection Panel, Resolution No. 93-10, Resolution No IDA 93-6, 22 September, 1993.

15 Op. cit., Resolution, page 8.

16 Op. cit., Resolution, pages 9–10.

17 After the Morse Commission issued its report in June 1992, World Bank management issued a response entitled 'Next Steps', which was sent to executive directors which totally misrepresented what the Morse Commission had said. Bradford Morse and Thomas Berger were compelled to write a letter to Preston to preserve the integrity of their report in which they charged Bank management with misrepresenting the main findings of their report.

18 An exception to this was the US Treasury Department which consulted with various US NGOs before putting forward names for the inspection panel.

13

Grounds for Divorce: Why IDA Should Delink from the World Bank

Lori Udall

There are probably very few people who would disapprove of the stated objectives of the International Development Association (IDA) – poverty reduction, economic growth and development, and environmental protection and improvement in the least credit-worthy countries. Set up in 1960, fourteen years after the World Bank Group opened its doors, IDA provides concessional lending to the poorest countries. In contrast, the International Bank for Reconstruction and Development (IBRD), the largest component of the World Bank Group, lends at commercial rates.[1] Despite these fundamental differences, IBRD and IDA are totally intertwined politically, financially and administratively. They share in-house resources, staff, a Board of Executive Directors and similar lending portfolios. They also share underlying institutional constraints and shortcomings.

More than thirty years after its creation, the gap between IDA's stated objectives and its actual performance is vast. While IDA claims to focus its lending on poverty reduction and the poor, research over the last ten years has revealed that its loans and programmes not only do not reach the poor or involve local communities, but many actually harm poor communities. For example, a large percentage of IDA funds are used to finance large-scale infrastructure projects such as dams, thermal power plants and road projects which are forcibly displacing hundreds of thousands of rural poor and indigenous people from their homes. The most infamous of these is the World Bank-funded Sardar Sarovar dam in western India which is forcibly displacing over 100,000 tribal and rural poor people without adequate compensation or resettlement.[2]

IDA's Articles of Agreement specify that its lending should be for specific projects related to poverty reduction and environmental protection except in unspecified 'special circumstances'. Despite these specific guidelines, IDA has followed IBRD's practice of becoming extensively involved in structural adjustment programmes in Africa and elsewhere – programmes which have a devastating impact on poor populations. While structural adjustment programmes are supposed to help countries with their balance of payment deficits, as currently designed, the poor are hit hardest by the conditionalities attached to these programmes such as cuts in domestic expenditures on health, education and human services. Moreover, abundant recent research reveals that structural adjustment programmes have not achieved the objectives of reviving IDA recipient countries' economic prospects. In 1991, thirty per cent of IDA gross disbursements went for structural adjustment programmes.

IDA's inability to reach the poor has also been exacerbated by the same chronic institutional deficiencies as IBRD, such as a lack of public accountability and access to information, a failed appraisal process and pressure inside the Bank to lend money which overwhelms all other considerations. These problems have been extensively documented by NGOs and even by some of the Bank's own internal documents.[3]

The myth of IDA's assistance to the poor and the poorest countries is further underscored by the fact that a large portion of IDA money actually returns to donor country corporations in the form of procurement contracts. Most of these contracts go to the world's ten richest industrialized countries. For example, net disbursements of IDA to borrowing countries in the Bank's Fiscal Year 1992 were US$4.471 billion. Of this US$2.347 billion was paid out again in procurement contracts associated with IDA credits. IDA disbursed more money back to Britain (US$285 million) than to Bangladesh (US$253 million) and more money to Switzerland (US$73 million) than to numerous sub-Saharan African countries such as Senegal (US$43.7 million), Guinea (US$7.3 million) and Sierra Leone (US$64.4 million).[4]

When a multilateral institution fails to live up to its objectives after 30 years, member governments should consider major changes.

Some NGOs have called for the closing of the World Bank. During 1993, many NGOs and legislators in donor countries were calling for both IDA and IBRD funding to be cut. However, considering the political realities of multilateral arrangements and continued requests from Southern governments for funds, an alternative approach would be to consider the delinking of IDA from World Bank management and reorganizing it into a separate and smaller institution. While the costs of delinking IDA from the World Bank might be high, the consequences of *not* making such a change in the long run could be catastrophic.

The Battle Over the IDA 10 Replenishment

Every three years, IDA funds are replenished in a series of negotiations which end in pledges by donor governments. The resulting IDA agreements contain a discussion of issues which donor governments believe should be highlighted during that replenishment period. Since its inception, there have been ten replenishments of IDA. In 1992, the tenth replenishment, donor governments pledged US$18 billion to IDA.

A unique aspect of IDA in contrast to IBRD is that it is funded entirely by member government contributions.[5] The largest shareholders in both IBRD and IDA are the United States, Japan, Germany, France and the United Kingdom. While public and financial accountability may never become a reality at the World Bank, donor country taxpayers who foot the bill for IDA are increasingly demanding to know how their money is being spent. During the battle over the IDA's tenth replenishment, many NGOs felt that at least by opposing IDA funds, they could prompt some change in the institution. Pressure for IDA to become more publicly accountable, open and transparent reached a critical stage for several donor countries during 1992–3, when NGOs worldwide called on donor governments to significantly cut IDA funding until the institution was substantially reformed.

The tenth IDA replenishment was a turning point for many NGOs and activists worldwide who had been working to reform the World Bank. Donor governments had successfully negotiated unprecedented environmental and social conditions in the agreement, yet, because environmental conditions from the ninth replenishment of IDA funds remained unfulfilled, many observers were skeptical of the chances of implementation of these newest conditions. And so, while IDA deputies were conducting their final negotiating sessions, NGOs were gearing up to oppose the replenishment in the US Congress and in several European parliaments. In December 1992, there was so little confidence in IDA that international NGOs opposed an extra US$5 billion for the 'earth increment' – a vague concept to which IDA had agreed to increase its environmental lending.

Additionally, two 1992 internal Bank reports – 'The Independent Review of Sardar Sarovar' (The Morse Commission) and 'The Portfolio Management Task Force' (The Wapenhans Report) – issued devastating critiques of the Bank's operations, the failed appraisal process and promotion of unsound projects.[6] While the Morse Commission was a serious indictment of one project funded partly by IDA, the

Wapenhans Report revealed that these problems were widespread. Wapenhans reported that 37 per cent of World Bank projects (including IDA projects) were unsatisfactory, a dramatic increase from only 15 per cent in 1981. The report revealed that the credibility of the Bank's appraisal process was under pressure. Wapenhans cited the pressure inside the Bank to lend money as overwhelming all other concerns and as one of the causes of the poor appraisal process and resulting problem projects. 'Underlying many of these aspects is the Bank's pervasive preoccupation with new lending', the Wapenhans Report stated.[7]

After the Bank's October 1992 decision to continue funding the Narmada dam project in spite of the recommendations of the Morse Commission to step back from the project, NGOs retaliated by launching a worldwide campaign to cut IDA funds. As IDA deputies were winding up their negotiations in December 1992, an international NGO statement was issued calling for significant cuts in IDA funds. The statement was signed by 140 NGOs from 20 countries, many of whom were from IDA borrower countries.[8] Indian grassroots NGOs, including the group representing the displaced people of Narmada – Narmada Bachao Andolan – issued an 'Appeal to Donor Governments to Reject the IDA 10 Replenishment'.

In 1993, US NGOs testified before Congress calling for reprogramming of IDA money to other funding mechanisms which would be more publicly accountable and democratic, and for Congress to authorize IDA appropriations one year at a time, instead of for the full three years.[9] Ultimately, Congress authorized IDA for two years only, and IDA funds were cut by US$200 million from the US Treasury Department's pledge. In its appropriations subcommittee report, Congress sent a clear message to the Bank that future funds for IDA were conditional on increased access to information and accountability mechanisms.

Even though IDA has always had a difficult time getting its funding approved by the US Congress,[10] it has still managed to get its appropriation every year. However, there is every indication that in the future, appropriations for wasteful, unaccountable and unreformable institutions will not be forthcoming.[11] Based on the floor debates and appropriations and authorization committee reports, the mood in the US Congress is not charitable toward IDA as currently designed. Legislators in other major donor countries including Japan, the United Kingdom, Sweden, Finland and Canada have raised questions about the poor performance of IDA or introduced motions to cut IDA. In Finland, appropriations for IDA were cut by 30 per cent in 1993.

While many European and African NGOs oppose the approach of cutting IDA funds, no NGOs argued that IDA was actually doing a good job in reaching the poor or promoting environmentally or socially sound development or meeting its objectives. In fact, the only sound argument put forward for not cutting IDA funds was that debt-ridden African countries desperately needed quick-disbursing non-project IDA funds to service their debts and pay for precious commodities such as petroleum and medicine.[12] While this may be a strong argument for the short term, it seems a perverse and illogical reason for sustaining IDA in the long term. A delinked IDA could also issue quick disbursing payments without being linked to destructive structural adjustment programmes as currently designed.

Many researchers and writers state that when IDA was created it was grabbed by the Bank in order to continue lending to countries which could no longer borrow at commercial rates.[13] According to Cheryl Payer, at the time of IDA's creation, the loss of credit-worthiness of India and Pakistan, two of the Bank's largest borrowers, was threatening the relevance of the the World Bank in the international financial community.[14] In this light, IDA's stated objectives may have been doomed from the beginning.

By separating IDA from IBRD, there is an opportunity to salvage the institution and reestablish its objectives. IDA could continue as a concessional mechanism, but evolve into a smaller, more accountable and democratic institution. Separating IDA from Bank management would clearly have to occur in conjunction with debt relief if sound development objectives were to be pursued. The barriers to separating IDA would probably be more political than logistical, since its articles of agreement clearly define IDA as a separate and distinct organization. However, the political barriers should not be underestimated; those with an interest in IDA's contribution to the World Bank's credibility and agenda would vigorously oppose such a measure.

The proposal to make IDA a separate institution has in fact been forwarded more than once during its history. During the pre-IDA discussions, several European countries stated that they wanted an IDA that was open to countries that were not Bank members and that could give grants. Earlier suggestions were that the institution deal only in grants and should be created as a special United Nations fund for economic development.[15] Later in 1969, a special commission on international development (known as the Pearson Commission) also recommended that IDA be reorganized and set up separately from the Bank, particularly because of its special relationship to and appropriations from donor countries.[16]

Financial and Administrative Issues Related to Delinking IDA

The financial and administrative problems of separating IDA from the World Bank would be extensive, and this subject is clearly in need of further research and debate. The 50-year anniversary of Bretton Woods would be a prime time for congressional or parliamentary hearings on the matter.

The strongest argument for the continued marriage of IBRD and IDA is one of administrative and financial convenience; however, this 'convenience' is clearly a costly one for developing and developed countries alike. For example, the cost of two IDA credits totalling US$250 million towards the disastrous Sardar Sarovar (Narmada) dam in India could have been used to buy or move to new IDA headquarters. The administrative cost of separating IDA from IBRD may be substantial at first, but it could save billions in the long run by avoiding such unsustainable and unsound projects. Moreover, since IDA is a separate legal entity with its own articles of agreement and bylaws, the separation of IDA from the World Bank is legally possible.

IDA's full administrative costs are difficult to tabulate since staff, facilities, technical and country knowledge are shared with IBRD. For example, in countries which receive both IDA and IBRD money, project and underlying country work is connected to both IDA and IBRD operations.[17] World Bank estimates of IDA administrative costs covering the three-year period FY89–91 are calculated at US$296 million, and a combined total for both IBRD and IDA of US$810 million.[18]

Since IDA credits are concessional and payments on an IDA credit are not started until 10 years after the credit is approved, then spread over 30 to 40 years, net income and repayments are not a significant source of income. IDA's expenses are currently paid in management fees to the World Bank; the fees represent IDA's share of the costs generated by the operations of the World Bank and IDA.[19] IDA's administrative costs are covered by service charges and commitment fees charged to its borrowers. IDA charges its borrowers a commitment fee of 0.5 per cent per year on the undisbursed balance of new credits and a service charge of 0.75 per cent of the disbursed and outstanding balance.[20] Initial administrative costs for separating IDA could be paid for out of the current cumulative operating surplus of IDA which totals hundreds of millions of dollars.

A new and separate IDA could also reduce current expenses incurred by becoming more oriented towards country ownership of projects and programmes, increased hiring of local consultants and local field-based staff, scaling down its total operations and funding smaller-scale projects, and reducing extensive travel of Washington-based staff.

The Delinked IDA and Debt Relief

Any agency which purports to be aimed at poverty reduction and the poor should first and foremost be assisting debt-ridden countries (particularly in sub-Saharan Africa) with debt relief. Sub-Saharan African IDA recipient countries are so seriously and deeply indebted that many researchers believe that the long-term prospect for sustainable development in this region is increasingly dim. External debt for the region is now at US$178 billion. Many researchers and observers believe that comprehensive debt relief for sub-Saharan Africa would provide much more relief and opportunity for long-term sustainable development when compared with the relatively small amount of IDA funds which now flow to that region.

Debt owed to bilateral lenders accounts for 39 per cent of the region's debts; debt owed to multilateral development banks (MDBs) is 23 per cent of Africa's foreign debt and 30 per cent of its debt service payments in 1991.[21] In recent years, while bilateral lenders have increased their debt relief and debt rescheduling efforts through the Paris Club, neither the World Bank nor IDA (nor any of the MDBs) have ever forgiven or rescheduled any debt owed them.[22] Many researchers believe that even if all bilateral debt were forgiven, it would not be sufficient unless MDBs took action to forgive or reschedule their debt. Moreover, MDB debt costs much more to service than bilateral debt because of the strict repayment terms. For IDA, many of the credits owed will not become due for several years, but IBRD debt is a heavy burden currently being paid.

While IBRD has a few programmes such as the 'Fifth Dimension' and the IDA Debt Reduction Facility which help poor countries reschedule their commercial debt, neither IBRD nor IDA has ever attempted to investigate avenues in which it would relieve its own debt.[23] IDA debt relief initiatives in the beginning would have to be in conjunction with IBRD debt relief, even before the delinking begins.[24]

While IDA debt is not as urgent as IBRD debt, because many credits have not reached maturity yet, the new IDA could still be involved in several debt-relief activities. The new IDA should be actively involved in reducing its own debt through cancelling the undisbursed balances and writing off disbursed balances on failed and unsatisfactory projects. The new IDA could also be involved in rescheduling debt currently reaching maturity, and in debt forgiveness.

The writing off of failed projects would have a house-cleaning effect and relieve many African and Asian countries where the level of failed projects is high. Cancelling loans and debts for failed projects financed by IDA could account for several billion dollars in debt. In India alone, cancelling debt owed for failed IDA projects could relieve that country of US$3 billion in debt. Some payments for debt on old projects could come from the the IBRD reserves.

IDA debt reflows are expected to increase in the mid-1990s when a large group of credits will become due. Member countries should prepare to discuss what debt relief measures could be taken in anticipation of this. IDA 11 replenishment negotiations could include specific provisions for increased research on debt reduction and on writing off failed projects.

The New IDA Lending Criteria

The new IDA should be governed by a set of lending criteria based on fundamental principles of public accountability, democracy, community needs, local ownership and public participation. It should also be delinked from structural adjustment lending and large-scale infrastructure projects such as dams, roadbuilding, thermal power plants and projects involving forcible resettlement of large numbers of people. There should be an increase in lending for health, human services, education, institution building, poverty reduction, environmental training and direct lending to community co-ops, NGOs and the poor.

The new IDA would be a scaled-down Bank with emphasis on debt relief, country ownership, efficiency, lending on a much smaller scale and project quality rather than quantity. Delinking IDA from World Bank management would provide a fresh opportunity to amend IDA's articles of agreement to include provisions on human rights and environmental sustainability. The articles of agreement could also be amended to include NGOs and grassroots representatives as members of IDA's board.

Project ownership There should be clear evidence of project ownership by local communities and government agencies. One of the key findings of the Wapenhans Report was that borrower country officials often felt they did not 'own' the project because projects were often conceived by Bank staff and imposed on them. Wapenhans reported that the 'negotiation stage is seen by many borrowers as a coercive exercise designed to impose the Bank's philosophy and to validate the findings of its promotional approach to appraisal'.[25] In the new delinked IDA, projects would only be funded if they were locally driven and promoted with project preparation, appraisal and designs conducted by local government agencies, with input from NGOs, local communities and in-country consultants. Project ownership would both assure the project's ultimate success while helping to avoid costly project failures and bad debt.

Reaching the poor A top priority for the delinked IDA would be its support of poor populations through programmes promoting local food security, self-reliance, access to credit and land, and the poor's own social sector activities.

Public participation and access to information These two elements are at the core of the World Bank reform campaign and are essential for project ownership and project success. The new IDA would not fund projects in which either of these mechanisms were absent.

Career incentives Currently IDA staff are rewarded for project quantity rather than environmental or social quality. A delinked IDA would create incentives in these areas.

Small loans window The delinked IDA could have a small loans window which would lend small amounts of money to poor people or local co-ops. Several model examples of successful small loan windows are the Grameen Bank and Women's World Banking.

Notes

1 The World Bank Group is composed of the International Bank for Reconstruction and Development (the loan window which lends at international commercial rates); the International Development Association (the 'soft loan' window which lends at highly concessional interest free rates which are paid back over a 30 to 50 year period), the International Finance Corporation (IFC) (the arm of the Bank which lends for commercial activities); and the Multilateral Investment Guarantee Agency (MIGA) which offers political-risk insurance coverage to private investors.

2 Due to intense local and international opposition to the project, the World Bank cancelled its last loan to Sardar Sarovar in March 1993. It had already disbursed US$250 million in IDA credits to the project. For a full discussion of environmental and social problems related to Sardar Sarovar, see Bradford Morse and

Thomas Berger, *Sardar Sarovar: The Report of the Independent Review* (Resource Futures International, 1992).

3 See for example Willi Wapenhans, *Report of the Portfolio Management Task Force* (World Bank, 1992).

4 See Testimony of Bruce Rich on Behalf of Environmental Defense Fund before the House subcommittee on foreign operations, export financing and related issues, 1 March 1993.

5 Donor countries pledge money to the IBRD most of which is never actually paid in. Based on the donor government pledges, IBRD raises money on the international money market.

6 Bradford Morse and Thomas Berger, *Sardar Sarovar: The Report of The Independent Review* (Resource Futures International, 1992). See also W. A. Wapenhans, *Report of the Portfolio Management Task Force*, 1992.

7 Wapenhans, op. cit., page iii.

8 *International NGO Statement Regarding the Tenth Replenishment of IDA*, December 1992.

9 In earlier Congressional hearings before the House subcommittee on foreign operations, export financing, and related issues, Environmental Defense Fund (EDF), National Wildlife Federation (NWF), Friends of the Earth and Sierra Club testified that no money should be given to IDA. Based on several factors, including a negative response from African NGOs, later in the year, EDF and NWF took a compromise position before the subcommittee on international development, finance, trade and monetary policy which called for a one-year authorization and reprogramming of IDA appropriations beginning in 1994, if the Bank failed to meet a series of tough new benchmarks. For details see statement of Barbara Bramble on behalf of NWF, 5 May 1993 and statement of Lori Udall on behalf of EDF, 5 May 1993.

10 The authorizing legislation for IDA 1 was voted down by the US House of Representatives, and the administration had to mount a lobbying effort to reinstate it. Congressional approval of IDA appropriations was also delayed in 1968.

11 In FY 1993, the US did not appropriate any money to the European Bank For Reconstruction and Development (EBRD) because of reported waste and unnecessary expenditures on its headquarters in London.

12 See for example Church World Service and Lutheran World Relief, 'The International Development Association: Flawed but Essential', statement before the house banking subcommittee on international development, finance, trade and monetary policy, 5 May 1993.

13　Stephen Hellinger, Douglas Hellinger and Fred M. O'Regan, *Aid For Just Development* (Lynne Rienner Publishers, 1988), pp. 145–6.
14　Cheryl Payer, *The World Bank: A Critical Analysis*, New York and London: Monthly Review Press, p. 32.
15　The World Bank, *IDA In Retrospect* (Oxford University Press, 1982), p. 2–3.
16　Commission on International Development, *Partners in Development*, report of the commission, Lester B. Pearson (Praeger Publishers, 1969).
17　International Development Association, *IDA's Administrative Costs, IDA 10 Technical Note No. 7*, April 1992.
18　International Development Association, *IDA's Administrative Costs, IDA 10 Technical Note No. 7*, April 1992, p. 2.
19　Op. cit., *IDA in Retrospect*, p. 21.
20　Op. cit., *IDA's Administrative Costs*, p. 1. Since 1989, IDA has not charged commitment fees.
21　Jonathan E. Sanford, *African Debt: Recent Initiatives and Policy Options for Multilateral Bank Debt* (Congressional Research Service), 9 July 1993, p. 1.
22　The World Bank's articles of agreement allows the Bank to reschedule or refinance repayment terms of existing loans.
23　The World Bank instituted the 'fifth dimension' programme in which debt-ridden IDA countries could borrow money to help repay the interest cost of their old IBRD loans. The money borrowed would be part of a structural adjustment loan and the borrowing country would have to be undergoing a structural adjustment programme. The IBRD also established an IDA debt reduction facility which gives grants to IDA countries to repurchase debt owed to commercial lenders usually at a discount.
24　For an in-depth discussion on MDB debt relief see Percey Mistry, *The Multilateral Debt Problems of Indebted Developing Countries*, October 1993.
25　Wapenhans, op. cit., Appendix B.

14

Human Capital: The World Bank's Approach to Education in Latin America

José Luis Coraggio

Many of the critiques of the World Bank's structural adjustment policies have highlighted their negative impact on social programmes such as education. As the Bank presses governments to cut spending on social programmes, the critics have pointed out, public education can suffer. It is less well known that the World Bank has become a major player in reforming education and other social policies in developing countries. Indeed, in June 1993, the Bank's vice president for Latin America and the Caribbean declared: 'For us, there is no greater priority in Latin America than education,' and he offered figures on staggering increases in Bank education lending to back up the statement.

Yet, the Bank's education lending and the implementation of its policies by Latin American governments has been flawed for at least two reasons. First, when a powerful institution like the Bank enters social fields, it tends to crowd out the smaller United Nations specialized agencies, many of which have greater expertise. Secondly, the Bank's view of education derives from its approach to economics – a view which is distorting the educational programmes of a number of countries in Latin America and the Caribbean.

In March 1990, the World Bank sponsored a meeting held in Jomtien, Thailand, along with UNICEF, UNDP and UNESCO. In this gathering, these agencies presented the goal of education for all (EFA). The meeting focused on the need to deliver basic education to children, youth and adults in order to build flexible 'human capital' while alleviating poverty. Using public funds, EFA would assure that everyone had access to a basic package of skills and knowledge to improve his or her opportunities for productive work in the global economy.

The new 'human development' paradigm of the UNDP influenced the EFA agenda and the Bank's approach. The paradigm offers the concept of human capital development, arguing that one must invest heavily in education in order to invest in people. World Bank officials say that they buy into this approach, but they have proceeded to distort it to serve their structural adjustment paradigm. The Bank's basic economic premise is that an unfettered global market best decides which jobs are located in which countries. The main goal of their education efforts is to prepare people for the jobs that the global economy offers. However, in much of Latin America, these jobs are low-skill, poorly paid jobs that produce goods and services for North Americans, Europeans and Japanese. The education that prepares workers for these jobs is, therefore, inherently limited and narrow. This chapter offers a brief critique of the Bank approach to education and suggests a reorientation of the approach to EFA that is based on a different notion of the role of education in fulfilling human needs.

Multilateral agencies at the Jomtien meeting hoped to achieve EFA by the year 2000 – a goal they recognized would require cooperation among themselves and with various governments, both to deliver services according to the new policy guidelines and to proceed to a quick and efficient resource allocation among other agents (NGOs, self-managed community services and related private enterprises). However, as actual implementation of EFA unfolds, there seems to be an agreement among all participants that it can be achieved better if all resources are pooled, with the World Bank leading the way. This seems to be justified by the Bank's operational capability, its leverage on governments (reinforced by the conditions imposed on government by it and the International Monetary Fund), and by the amount of resources it commands.

Despite the Bank's enormous size, the total pool of funds channelled for EFA by both development banks and aid agencies combined would never add up to more than five per cent of the total budget any one nation spends on education. Yet because the World Bank – to whom most developing countries are indebted – is leading the way, EFA promises to have a dangerously strong impact on strategies for education and, with it, various other social policies in regions around the world.

The World Bank is composed primarily of economists, not educators. Their goal is economic efficiency, freer markets and the greater globalization of capital. Their results are, therefore, inherently skewed towards purely quantitative measurements of 'success'. To offer but one example: after a decade of systematically gathering educational quantitative research and policy analysis, the World Bank has concluded that public primary education should become the centrepiece of EFA. This conclusion is arrived at using strictly economic indicators, such as personal income returns. Based on this data, an additional year of education at lower levels of schooling has been found to bring about a larger increase in income than investments at higher levels of education. From this it is concluded that an investment of funds at lower levels of schooling is likely to yield a larger increase in national income. But such an increase in income assumes that the main resource of a developing country will be its cheap and flexible labour pool, producing goods and services for export. The true increase in income will therefore be realized not in the developing country but by consumers that import its goods.

If one is to examine the elements that comprise a sustained learning and development process that truly benefits the targeted country, the conclusion would be totally different: more public support of higher education would be required. Without this support, there will not be enough highly qualified technicians, engineers, communicators, social workers, designers and scientific researchers – all of whom contribute to the ongoing education and development of a nation.

The World Bank's vision of education is one-dimensional, with no consideration for the social, economic and cultural factors which determine the motivations and attitudes of both students and teachers. There is no consideration given to the value of the personal relationship between teacher and student, and, as such, education by text or computer is seen as more valuable than education imparted by an experienced, talented teacher. Before designing new education programmes, we must decide what kind of citizen we want to educate, as well as what kind of worker or entrepreneur. All this is overlooked by the Bank's shortsighted, microeconomic approach to education.

Although we should welcome an economic conception that puts human beings at its centre, the World Bank operational conception of 'human capital' must be changed if it truly is to reflect long-term development goals. As it now stands, it mainly refers to a stock of 'human resources' – inputs for private capital which aims to reduce its demands for labour. Such an approach is in contradiction with the discourse on human development, subscribed to by the World Bank at Jomtien, which claims that people are entities to be developed in and of themselves, and not 'inputs' to be 'processed' by others. Rather, the formation of human capital should be a process whereby people, organized in productive communities, are empowered and increasingly responsible for their own greater development.

The strong concern expressed at Jomtien with the need to address increased poverty via greater education is welcome. However, insofar as education and other social policies do not provide a structural solution to the root causes of poverty, they will tend to maintain and strengthen the dependency of the poor on state expenditures and, in the long run, recreate the fiscal crisis of the state.

If one is to accept the priorities of human education for all declared at Jomtien together with the general priority of poverty alleviation declared by the World Bank, and the assumption that education must be central to any development policy, there are viable alternatives to those proposed by the Bank. Not long ago, the World Bank recognized that investments in infrastructure had a larger productivity ratio if accompanied by investments in education. In the same line of reasoning, educational policies must be integral to social and economic policies if they are to be instrumental to the betterment of everyday life. This goal – a new 'human development paradigm' that moves beyond the outdated economic paradigm, to which the Bank's structural adjustment approach is pivotal – is, of course, hard to reach, given the Bretton Woods institutions' 50-year legacy. Still, these multilateral agencies could be of great help if they overcame their entrenched approach to development.

In its 1990 report on urban policy and economic development, the World Bank concludes that 'urban poverty will be the most significant and politically explosive problem of the next century'. New approaches are needed to deal with new urban realities. In Latin America, the developing world's most urbanized region, these new approaches will be critical to the region's development. Therefore, when adopting the human development paradigm, policies must be geared to systemic urban development – not simply a narrow focus on the poorest, isolated rural communities, which comprise less than one-fifth of the population.

Structural adjustment policies imposed by the World Bank have resulted in the dislocation of many people who used to belong to the urban middle class to below the poverty line. Yet, because these people, who comprise 50 per cent of the population (and a good part of the new poor and the remaining middle sectors in precarious situations) have had access to an education, maintain a high life expectancy and still hold on to some of their durable goods – all indicators the World Bank uses to determine eligibility – they would not be 'poor enough' to be targeted by the EFA programmes. Yet, for many of these people, their education is obsolete or incomplete. If developing human capital is a goal, existing human capital must be recycled and upgraded, not wasted and destroyed.

From a macrosocial perspective, and beyond some sectoral measures of reforms, such as decentralization of education, adapting the curriculum to local needs, improving textbooks, etc., the EFA policy should be designed in order to guarantee its own sustainability in three ways:

a) increasingly generating its own resource base;

b) enhancing individual and collective motivation to learn and produce new knowledge; and

c) nurturing the political will necessary to prioritize education as an investment capable of multiplying development opportunities.

The following recommendations are made in this regard:

1. *Education must be linked with economic development from the outset.* Only in this way can the new knowledge, attitudes and skills be applied to satisfy basic learning needs, such as the skills and abilities to work, to take care of health and to democratically participate in society as a whole. Educational policy cannot be seen as responding to narrow, preconceived needs with predetermined outcomes; they themselves generate needs and demands, stimulating (or paralyzing) the desire to learn and the hope for personal and social development.

2. *An urban popular economy must be promoted, given the insufficiency of the capitalist sector and the public sector to provide opportunities for all.* The growth of the urban economy will not only provide fresh resources to maintain the educational system, but will maintain and strengthen the perceived value of acquiring an education. It is doubtful that private enterprise, national or foreign, will find it profitable to invest in a permanent education of their labour force. Therefore, state intervention in this field is critical until a new productive culture is well-established.

3. *'Human capital' must not be treated as an 'input' whose cost should be minimized for the sake of greater efficiency.* Humans – including teachers – must be valued for their own sake. Teachers are instruments of the historical memory of the popular sector, administrators of social programmes, grassroots organizers and researchers. In brief, in Latin America they are key agents of community development. Yet the World Bank would eliminate many of these skilled professionals in order to achieve 'education for all'.

4. *Greater consideration must be given to higher education and its inter-relationship with basic education.* To obtain a basic education programme for all that is externally efficient, we need not only literate people, but also private entrepreneurs to hire them, engineers to build the society, social workers to heal the wounds of poverty, plus researchers, administrators and intellectuals. All of them must be qualified and inclined to work with and for a strong popular economy.

5. *Programme design must be oriented towards the community as a basic unit.* If one returns to the initial aim of a basic education for all (instead of a primary education for the poor), one will achieve a bottom-up, development-from-the-community approach. This requires a democratic nation state to enable, foster and support the work at the local level. This means working with and for the local communities rather than focusing on isolated segments of them (i.e. the poorest, school-age girls). In this context, attempts merely to alleviate extreme poverty by providing goods and services to the most disadvantaged individuals and/or families can only be sustained by a continuous injection of external resources that are now in short supply. This, in turn, reinforces economic political dependence of the beneficiary groups. Instead, by designing education and other social programmes at a community level, one develops a creative mix of various levels of knowledge and abilities of the population.

6. *Given the shortage of resources, EFA must focus on those urban or urban–rural communities that can efficiently induce similar developments in other communities through technical and economic relationships as well as through cultural affinities.* Target communities should commit themselves to make a contribution to a social fund of financial and human resources to develop other areas.

In sum, the implementation of EFA in Latin America and the Caribbean requires a synergistic approach to education. This means setting in motion all the modalities of education and learning at the same time, incorporating the different elements of the community as active elements of the teaching–learning process, thus creating a community learning context.

Although it would be useful to consider these hypotheses as alternative educational policies, the fundamental goal is not to further enlighten the intelligentsia, but to foster open participatory practises, capitalizing on the best experience of NGOs as well as of the other international agencies. The bureaucratic rules of the World Bank make it a rigid structure that prefers to work with other equally bureaucratized institutions. Yet rigidity and bureaucracy are counterproductive when dealing with qualitative issues such as education. A more participatory process is required when educational policy for so much of the world is at stake. This process must include more transparency at the national and local level, where public policy alternatives to those put forward by the Bank can be openly presented, discussed and assessed by all parties involved.

IV

Promoting Economic Justice:
Other Institutional Changes

15

A Global New Deal

Richard J. Barnet and John Cavanagh

Lee Kuan Yew, the shrewd, tough former Prime Minister of Singapore recently made a chilling prophecy about the impact of globalization on the United States: 'America's top ten per cent will still enjoy the highest standard of living in the world. But the wages of the less educated citizens will drop to those of workers in developing countries with equal or higher education.' If he is even half right, the wages workers in poor countries receive becomes a matter of intense interest for people in the United States.

Over the past three years, poor countries have increased their share of world exports a full three percentage points, and they now control a fifth of the global export market. Hundreds of millions of men and women in the developing world have entered the labour market to compete directly with workers in the advanced industrial countries, making the same goods and rendering identical services at rising levels of productivity, but for a fraction of a US wage.

Global production chains organized by transnational corporations provided the impetus for export-led development in what we used to call the Third World, and this strategy has for many years been encouraged by the industrial nations through bilateral aid policies, the International Monetary Fund and the World Bank. But the United States has been slow in reacting to the negative impacts this rapid redistribution of power in the global marketplace is having on our own society. Countries with still low per capita income but with skilled and efficient work forces capable of producing high quality goods and delivering sophisticated services at low cost have served as magnets for all sorts of work once performed in the United States. As large firms shift more and more jobs to poorer countries where wages are kept low and productivity is high, large numbers of jobs in the United States continue to disappear. The threat to move abroad is also used to bargain down wages and benefits of the many more Americans who still hold a job. In these two ways the increasing mobility of corporations is having a profound effect on both employment prospects and working conditions in the United States.

The problems presented by globalization are compounded by a second development: technological progress that makes 'downsizing' of the labour force both feasible and necessary. Computers, robotics and other innovations in planning, production, administration and marketing across a wide range of manufacturing and service industries now enable firms to increase output and cut costs by shaving payrolls. The pressures to do this are increasing along with the opportunities. Companies that once assured a secure place in the global marketplace for themselves by developing new technologies in consumer products and industrial equipment must now accept the reality that marketable innovations will be copied in an astonishingly short time. One result is that global competition is focusing more and more on cost-cutting.

Strategies to raise wages and working conditions and to stimulate jobs in the United States can succeed only if they address these two aspects of the problem: global competition and labour-dispensing changes in the workplace. Wages in many poor countries are kept artificially depressed – that is, they lag far behind gains in productivity – because basic worker rights, such as the right to organize unions and to bargain collectively, are denied. Unless the wage-productivity gap is narrowed in the poorer industrializing nations, the impact will continue to be felt in the advanced industrial countries as unemployment and deteriorating working conditions.

In the 1930s, as the United States was building a national market that integrated prospering and less developed regions of the United States, the Roosevelt administration established a new set of social standards to soften the destructive side effects of becoming a more integrated nation. For the first time the federal government, prodded by a powerful labour movement, prescribed a minimum wage, maximum hours of work and later a comprehensive set of health, safety and environmental regulations; all were enforceable across the entire continental expanse of the United States. One purpose in establishing uniform labour standards was to prevent the likely alternative, a spiralling down of wages and working conditions across the nation.

For similar reasons global economic integration requires a 'new deal' on a global scale. Wages in poor countries need to rise significantly to keep pace with productivity gains. If this does not happen, we can expect Lee Kuan Yew's prediction to come true: the majority of Americans will see a further drop in wages and working conditions. International agreements to remove the political impediments to a fairer distribution of productivity gains in poor countries ought to be high on the American agenda not only on human rights grounds, but also to protect workers and living standards in the United States. However, as we will discuss, there are difficulties in reaching and enforcing such agreements, and progress will take time.

Moreover, a major diplomatic effort to secure global recognition of basic internationally recognized worker rights deals only with disparities in wages and working conditions and does not address other causes of increasing unemployment, job insecurity and the erosion of wages and benefits in the United States. A domestic strategy to stimulate the creation of jobs more rooted in local communities supported by social policies that can relieve some of the pressures on the US job market is also needed.

The Effects of Global Competition

It has often been said that low wages in poor countries do not interfere with the smooth functioning of the global trade system because the more efficient, higher-paid workers of the 'north' will retain their competitive edge over the more easy-going, less skilled and poorly paid workers of the 'south' by virtue of their greater productivity. But as has happened often in recent years, new developments are challenging elegant economic theory.

Recent advances in technology together with sophisticated worker training now enable firms to shift high-tech operations to countries where productivity levels are rising fast, but wages are kept low as a matter of government policy. Because of their access to a large pool of cheap but increasingly productive labour, Malaysian, Korean and Chinese firms are exerting increasing pressures on US, European and Japanese firms to move operations out of the advanced industrial world. The Ford Motor Company can now replicate its most technologically advanced factories in Mexico and other developing countries and can train its local workers to be almost as productive as US workers for a fraction of a US wage. So can global firms in many other industries.

Twenty years ago, competition from poor countries was limited to certain light-manufacturing industries, such as textiles and consumer electronics. Today, thanks to technological innovations, business enterprises have many more options to pick and choose workers from all over the world to fill a whole range of agricultural and manufacturing jobs – and, increasingly, service jobs, too. Because of the explosion of sophisticated communications hardware, people can be employed anywhere to punch and store data, and the search for productive, low-paid workers is becoming as intense in the service industries as it is in manufacturing. For example, it is now cheaper for Manhattan law offices to fax draft letters to an anonymous woman employed by a data firm in Barbados than to hand it to the secretary in the next office.

Advances in telecommunications make it simple to farm out even sophisticated data-processing. Equidata Philippines, Inc., founded by an American in 1985, employs well over 100 college-educated data-punchers who must punch a minimum of 10,000 characters an hour, for which they are paid US$150 a month plus free medical care – and a few grams of rice if they do not miss a day of work. The compensation package comes to about a sixth of what an entry-level processor in Europe could earn. Employees at Saztec, one of the oldest 'custom software' firms to set up shop in the Philippines, the researcher John Maxwell Hamilton reports, punch everything from American patient records for hospitals in Pomona, California, to the Helsinki, Finland, national library book catalogue. With the collapse of the Soviet Union, global companies are farming out advanced engineering work to highly skilled Russian and Ukrainian scientists and engineers who are now global bargains.

According to an International Trade Commission study, in 1986 Brazilian workers were 59 per cent as productive as US workers, but they earned 17 per cent of a US wage. Shirtmakers in Bangladesh are about 60 per cent as productive as American shirtmakers, according to another study, but they are paid between 3 and 5 per cent of what their US counterparts earn. In Mexico during the boom years from 1987 to 1992, productivity rose by at least 24 per cent while wages climbed only 13.5 per cent.

The reason that wages do not begin to keep pace with productivity gains is that governments and corporations in the countries we are discussing keep labour costs artificially depressed by denying workers the basic rights prescribed in International Labor Organization conventions, the United Nations covenants on Human Rights and local statutes. Thus the government of Mexico routinely ignores systematic violations of its own labour laws. It has carefully cultivated a non-confrontational Confederation of Mexican Workers (CTM) as a pillar of the ruling party, and has assisted firms in breaking up attempts at independent organizing. At the same time, governments in Chile, Papua New Guinea and a few other poor countries do afford most basic worker rights, and trade union movements there have been able to improve wages and working conditions. Because the global economy is becoming fiercely competitive, richer nations that observe basic worker rights are losing out to regimented societies where workers do not have the right to organize or to bargain collectively, much less to strike.

The United States is feeling the increasing effects of low-wage competition in many different ways. Since 1973, average real wages in the United States have fallen 9 per cent. Union representatives in a number of industries recount how at the bargaining table US firms have used the threat of relocation to force down wages and to secure agreement on other corporate strategies to cut labour costs. NAFTA's passage enhances these opportunities for corporations. In a 1992 *Wall Street Journal* survey of 455 business executives, 40 per cent said that if NAFTA were passed, they were 'likely' to build their next production facility in Mexico; a quarter said that they were 'likely' to use NAFTA to bargain down wages in their US facilities.

The sweatshop is back in virtually every major US city. According to a 1989 Government Accounting Office report, over half of the 7,000 apparel factories in New York, which employ an estimated 50,000 workers, are sweatshops; in Chinatown garment workers receive barely half the union wage. There has also been a significant increase in child labour and job-related injuries of children in recent years. The wage-depressing impact of global competition has been most keenly felt by low-skill workers who constitute the bulk of the US work force.

Thanks to the mutually reinforcing impact of corporate mobility in a world of great wage disparities and the exploding opportunities to make use of robotics and other advanced technologies to cut labour costs, the Fortune 500 companies cut more than 4,400,000 jobs from their global payrolls in the 1980s. To be sure, robotics create some new jobs – picking up tasks that are too inconvenient, costly or difficult to assign to robots – but these jobs are often temporary because robots are becoming more versatile and sophisticated.

The twentieth-century technological advances that have facilitated the global shifts of production and changed what factories look like have yet to trigger what the economist Robert Heilbroner calls a 'transformational boom'. Unlike such past breakthrough technologies as the automobile, the airplane, the transistor and the computer, all of which created a wide range of new needs and new ways to satisfy them, advanced information technologies appear to eliminate more jobs than they create.

The 'information revolution' has created many jobs in computer software, entertainment and related industries, but it has enabled the elimination of even more jobs in banking, insurance, corporate and government administration, and retailing. Biotechnology, on which great hopes are pinned, is anything but labour-intensive; Amgen, the largest biotechnology company, employs a mere 2,639 people. The labour-displacing impact of the genetic engineering industry is potentially huge. Synthetic substitutes for vanilla, cocoa and other natural products are forcing millions of farmers in hot, poor countries off the land, adding to the employment crisis in congested cities in Asia and Latin America. Bioengineered strains of major crops and the development of cows with greatly expanded milk-producing capabilities threaten to aggravate the problems small farmers already face across the world, thereby swelling the number of global job seekers. The impacts are felt all over, including the United States.

The Impact on the United States

None the less, millions of Americans are successfully connected to the new world economy, and these winners in the struggles to deepen the involvement of the United States in global commerce experience the winds of change as a caressing breeze. A substantial number of information-related jobs command high salaries, even though most do not. Professionals with the skills and connections to make use of the global marketplace and investors able to take advantage of opportunities in exotic places on the other side of the world have made fortunes. High-skilled workers in many export industries have done well, and for these and others expanding trade will bring increased prosperity.

Indeed, America's increasing dependence on the global economy is creating centres of new growth, some of them near depressed farming communities or right next to faded industrial centres. Consider the small and medium-sized cities in the Southwest corridor of the United States that have lured 23,000 new manufacturing jobs in the last two years, many of them supplied by non-US companies. Yet in the same period the Northeast and West Coast have lost 450,000 factory jobs due in large measure to cost-cutting to meet foreign competition. The gaps between the enclaves of prosperity that benefit from global connections and nearby neighbourhoods left with little but memories of happier times are widening. The major issue posed by globalization is whether the ranks of the winners will grow fast enough to keep pace with the rapidly growing multitude of losers.

There has been much theorizing about how global economic integration will eventually benefit increasing numbers of Americans. It was strongly argued in the NAFTA debate that while the new export platforms in poorer countries may pose a short-term threat to US workers, eventually export-led growth will turn these countries into major markets for US goods. In the words of *Business Week*,

> The 'supply shock' of cheap goods from the new capitalist countries will generate a 'demand boom' for sophisticated goods and services, creating new jobs and economic wealth in the industrial countries. These countries have huge infrastructure needs, from power generators to air traffic control systems. They also will have billions of consumers with improving incomes.

The greatest hopes for a global consumer spending boom are pinned on the expanding middle class of Asia. The wealthiest ten per cent of India constitutes a nation as large as Germany with considerable buying power. More than 200,000,000 Chinese now have the wherewithal to buy a wide range of consumer products produced abroad and the Chinese government is letting down the barriers to foreign goods. Treasury and central bank officials in Washington, Ottawa, London, Bonn and Paris, strongly supported by top managers of global corporations, are banking on optimistic prognoses for these new markets. Accordingly, they are making a major effort to accelerate the deregulation of trade and investment flows and create greater equality everywhere in the treatment of foreign capital and goods of foreign origin. NAFTA and the Uruguay Round of the General Agreement on Tariffs and Trade provide reliable legal protection for cross-border investment and remove many barriers to trade. But no comparable effort has been made to reduce the gross inequalities in wages, working conditions and environmental standards that have a critical impact on global competition.

There are a number of reasons to be sceptical about a strategy for 'putting America back to work', to use the well-worn political promise, by relying heavily on a 'demand boom' in countries where most people are still dirt poor. First, it is not prudent to assume that China and India, once their firms have acquired enough technology and experience, will be willing to let corporations chartered in the rich countries take large enough shares of their lucrative new markets to bring vast numbers of jobs to America and Europe. Their own massive labour force, the accelerating migration from the countryside and high unemployment rates are among the reasons why they will not be so accommodating. Second, Japanese, Korean and other Asian tigers and would-be tigers are especially well situated to flood the large Asian markets with a wide variety of high quality goods at competitive prices. In Shanghai, the Yaohan Department Store Company of Japan is building a department store with about twenty per cent more selling space than Macy's flagship store at Herald Square. Yaohan's president, Kazuo Wada, plans to build 1,000 supermarkets in China before the end of the century.

Third, even if US corporations take over a significant share of these markets, and – as is more likely – a more substantial share of the Latin American market, production to meet this new demand is no more likely to take place on US soil than it is now unless the incentives to produce outside the United States are reduced. Philip Morris' Japanese subsidiaries, for example, import Philadelphia cream cheese from Australia, soft white cheese from Denmark and Italy, and chocolate from Germany and Switzerland. Johnson and Johnson, Kellogg and other US firms are selling their products to the new consumers of China right now, but the goods are made in their Chinese factories.

A Global New Deal

To achieve economic growth, social stability and a sustainable environment in the twenty-first century requires fundamental rethinking with respect to both global economic arrangements and domestic policies. An international effort to reduce global inequalities by bringing up wages through respect for worker rights in the newly industrializing countries can become the centrepiece of a global new deal. But at the same time new job strategies are urgently needed to provide opportunities for the millions of workers who have (and will) become the victims of corporate relocation and 'downsizing'.

Reducing global inequalities by bringing the bottom up in the developing world (rather than by speeding the decline of living standards for the majority in mature capitalist economies) depends upon accelerating the removal of political and social barriers to freer labour markets. Wages have tended to keep pace with productivity in Europe (and, until the last couple of decades, in the United States) because strong trade union movements have demanded this linkage and secured it through collective bargaining.

Since NAFTA does not impose an obligation on Mexico to guarantee the rights of workers to form independent unions and to bargain collectively, the agreement itself will not help to close the wage-productivity gap, and therefore it is not a desirable model for other agreements. Whether Mexican workers will share more equitably in Mexico's rising productivity now depends on the unilateral decision of the party that has ruled that country for more than sixty years. As written, NAFTA does not discourage other countries from trying to attract foreign capital with underpaid labour. ('Underpaid' in many situations has a precise meaning. In the early 1990s the minimum wage in Indonesia for a seven-hour day was US$1.06, but according to the Ministry of Labour US$1.22 was required to meet workers' 'minimum physical needs'.)

Advancing the rights of workers to form unions and to bargain collectively can and should be a major US objective in global trade talks and in regional talks in Asia and the rest of Latin America. These needed reforms would not of course result in worldwide wage equalization. Nor is that their purpose. But were workers to have legal recourse to bargain up wages to keep pace with productivity gains, US-based companies would have less incentive to move abroad, and they would lose much of their power to bargain down wages and working conditions in the United States.

A basic question is how to develop a sufficient consensus on global standards to get them adopted. An equally difficult question is how to enforce such standards.

There is a body of internationally recognized worker rights and standards in the labour-related provisions of the UN Declaration on Human Rights and in International Labor Organization conventions. These include guarantees of free association, collective bargaining, the right to strike, workplace health and safety, and protections against child labour, slave labour and all forms of discrimination. Not only do many governments that have subscribed to these provisions ignore them, but they lure foreign investment by advertising their poorly paid work force and their strike-free environment.

Since 1984 US trade law has conditioned the granting of 'trade preferences' (duty-free status for goods from developing countries) on their respect for internationally recognized worker rights. Paraguay and Chile were denied these preferences because of their treatment of workers. In a number of cases threats by the US government to withdraw trade preferences have led to important reforms in working conditions in a number of developing countries. Because the United States threatened El Salvador with loss of trade benefits on account of widespread abuse of workers, that country is now working with the International Labor Organization to create a more comprehensive labour code. The government of Sri Lanka, reacting to similar pressure, agreed to open up its garment industry to collective bargaining. Indonesia announced a twenty-nine per cent increase in its minimum wage after the United States threatened to remove trade preferences.

Not surprisingly, a number of Third World governments have denounced such pressures as interference in domestic affairs. At the recent United Nations Conference on Human Rights in Vienna, a heated debate between the rich and poor countries arose over human rights in the workplace. Some governments in the developing world argued that 'cultural differences' made it impossible to establish global standards, and they charged that the industrial countries often claim that worker rights are violated as a pretext for keeping their goods out of the US market.

Several governments, led by the Scandinavian countries, have argued for years that violations of basic worker rights be considered an unfair trade practice in GATT. More and more citizens' groups now also advocate this linkage, so long as fundamental reforms make the enforcement mechanisms of this global agreement more open and democratic. In the NAFTA debate, US Representative Richard Gephardt and a number of his colleagues joined with a broad range of citizens' groups representing labour unions, environmental activists, consumer, farm and religious organizations from the United States, Canada and Mexico to advocate the linkage of trade concessions and worker rights, provided the enforcement mechanism was fair, democratic and open. (Mexican groups argued that sanctions should take the form of fines levied on the offending corporations rather than withdrawal of trade preferences which hurt the population as a whole, including the oppressed workers.)

The multilateral lending institutions, the International Monetary Fund and the World Bank, also offer a suitable venue for taking up the issue of worker rights. Since alleviation of poverty, healthy industrial development and political stability are stated goals of these organizations, introducing greater freedom into labour markets is an appropriate objective.

There are also other ways to stop the downward pull on wages exerted by repressive labour policies in poor countries. The World Bank and the IMF could alter the role they have played over the last few years in supporting low-wage strategies in a number of countries. Since the debt crisis of the 1980s, private banks have conditioned their new lending on the debtor nation's willingness to accept structural adjustment programmes mandated by the World Bank and IMF. Typically, these programmes prescribed wage freezes, cuts in government social and job programmes, and devaluations of currencies which increased the prices of imports from the United States and other countries. The IMF now requires similar austerity measures in the former Soviet Union and Eastern Europe.

These policies not only reinforce the incentives of US firms to move their activities to low-wage countries, but they also serve to limit the growth of mass consumption markets that the United States hopes to penetrate. The United States remains the major supplier of capital to these institutions, and these deflationary policies, which widen the gaps between rich and poor within developing countries, causing widespread hardship for the majority of people in many of them, are not in the interest of most American workers and taxpayers, nor are they helpful to many businesses.

On its fiftieth anniversary, the World Bank should seriously consider a development strategy that promotes economic growth by broader distribution of purchasing power through more equitable sharing of productivity gains. Such a strategy might well include redistributive land reforms, easier access to financing for small farms and businesses, and incentives for farmers and manufacturers to produce for domestic markets. A shift in World Bank policy would not only be a significant advance in human rights across the planet, but it would promote more equitable competition in world trade.

The IMF could also play an important role through a programme of substantial debt reduction to slow the outflow of resources from poor to rich nations. (If debtor countries were not so strapped for capital, they would have more bargaining power *vis-à-vis* foreign firms and would have less incentive to keep wages artificially low.) Debt reduction schemes have already been implemented in Costa Rica, the Philippines and several other countries, but they have been tied to IMF austerity measures. By altering these conditions and insisting on respect for worker rights, debt relief could help raise living standards for the majority.

For four decades the prosperous nations of western Europe have realized that their own self-interest is served by making substantial development funds available to the poorer countries on the periphery (Ireland, Greece, Portugal and Spain). Countries that differ too greatly in wages, workers' rights and standard of living, Europeans have reasoned, cannot be successfully integrated; the economic and social problems stemming from such inequalities, including mass migration from poor to rich countries, become serious problems. The same reasoning applies to the integration into the world economy now under way of large areas of Latin America and Asia and parts of Africa.

The differences cannot be wiped out in the discernible future, but demonstrable progress in that direction is a critical component of healthy economic integration since rising living standards in the weaker members are necessary, as we have shown, if the global pool of people with money in their pockets is to grow fast enough to be able to absorb the increasing flood of global goods.

In the past more direct efforts have been made to deal with the negative impacts of the increasing mobility of global corporations. In the mid-1970s, in an effort to increase the public accountability of transnational corporations, the United Nations undertook negotiations for a code of conduct applicable both to business enterprises with cross-border operations and host governments. Under the UN draft code corporations were required to respect worker rights, stop bribing public officials, disclose potential dangers of products and production processes and carry out a number of other obligations in exchange for government promises to offer equitable treatment to foreign firms. This effort was effectively derailed by the Reagan Administration.

In the meantime more progress is likely to be made by encouraging corporations to adopt their own codes of conduct. Consumer groups and labour unions are in a position to monitor compliance provided corporations are pressed to make the necessary information available to the public. Under pressure from US trade unions, for example, Sears and Levi Strauss agreed not to contract production to firms that used prison labour or committed other specified violations of worker rights. Persistent violations in China have prompted Levi Strauss to announce that they will phase out all production contracts in that country. But while voluntary codes are commendable, they are only one step towards providing needed protection to communities, workers and consumers. Given the enormous power large corporations wield in virtually every aspect of modern life, a democratic system requires ground rules that reinforce principles of accountability under which performance can be monitored and enforced in a number of ways. Although there are many technical and political problems involved in negotiating, drafting and enforcing codes of conduct, the effort to develop a consensus for new ground rules for business enterprises operating in the new world economy should not be dropped.

Conclusions

The redistribution of power in the global marketplace that enables poor countries to offer a better standard of living for their people is both inevitable and desirable. Development, defined as industrialization and export-led economic growth, has been a declared goal of the United States ever since the end of World War Two. It was entirely predictable that the United States would lose the pre-eminent position in the world economy it held fifty years ago because both the consumption of resources and the distribution of wealth in the international system was so skewed. The flow of resources and power to a number of newly industrializing countries – even though within these countries the distribution is far from equitable and in some cases becoming more skewed – is welcome not only for moral considerations but for reasons of long-term economic and political stability.

But if the rapid integration of the global economy is not to cause new hardships for the vast numbers of people in the world who need decently compensated work in order to live, new rules of the game to promote fairness and innovative strategies to deal with the negative consequences of globalization are needed in advanced industrialized nations and in newly industrializing nations alike.

16

Lilliputian Power: A World Economy as if Communities Mattered

Michael Shuman

The last thing on the minds of the architects of the Bretton Woods institutions was the impact of their handiwork on communities. Yet it is at the community level where the international economic order ultimately must be judged. In villages, towns and cities, real people work, play and raise children, and it is here where they encounter the real effects – both good and bad – of the globalized economy. In recent years the rapid globalization of once local corporations has placed communities in a terrible dilemma: either cut wages, gut environmental standards and offer tax breaks to induce corporations to build new factories or offices, or prepare to become an economic ghost town. Even 'progressive' mayors and city officials find themselves hobnobbing with the captains of industry to pony up the best bribes for corporations to stay in or relocate to their locales. Yet this is a competition with no winners, as communities everywhere bid down the quality of life.

What alternatives do communities have? How can they increase their leverage over mobile corporations and regain control over their economies? Is there a way communities can ensure for themselves full employment, ecological sustainability, economic justice and broad democratic participation?

The community perspective on restructuring the global economy is important for three reasons. First, there's the matter of goals: any truly progressive agenda must begin at the community level. Local government is the most basic instrument for collective political expression, where citizens have the most access to legal power and are most likely to become democratically engaged. Communities are also where people have the greatest ability to structure and improve their personal and professional relationships, where they can make the most difference in improving their daily lives. Today national leaders chant poetic praises about the value of communities, but in practice they sacrifice them on the altar of free trade. A fundamental goal for a new economic order, therefore, is to ensure that communities have sufficient power to secure their own wellbeing. A new global economy must serve communities, not vice versa.

Second, communities can no longer wait for national governments to save them. The most efficient way to discipline corporations, of course, is to enact a worldwide system of standards for corporate behaviour, either as an enforceable code of conduct or as a social charter in trade agreements. But even with an unprecedented transnational organizing effort on every continent, it will be at least five to ten years before these legal instruments are in force, and another decade before the inevitable kinks in enforcement are worked out. There is no reason to expect that the learning curve for multilateral efforts to control corporate misbehaviour will be any shorter than the five-decade learning curve for the most global of trade agreements – the General Agreement on Tariffs and Trade. Yet the problems communities face call for urgent attention. They cannot afford to wait fifty years to halt the destruction of their economies.

Finally, there's a tactical reason to consider community alternatives: local action is a critically important means to create a more equitable global order. By working alongside labour, environmental and consumer groups, and by becoming a more powerful player in future negotiations of GATT and other global economic instruments, the representatives of communities (elected officials, civil servants, non-governmental organizations and unorganized citizens) can accelerate the pace of reform.

What exactly, then, can communities do to exert control over globalized capital?

Strategies for Change

There are at least five ways communities can reclaim their economic destiny: they can lobby national and international institutions for better rules of the road for the world economy; they can place regulations on products and corporations that come into their jurisdiction; they can choose to invest municipal monies in and enter contracts with firms that adhere to high standards; they can connect corporations to the community by buying them out; and they can delink selectively from the global economy.

Lobbying One obvious – but commonly overlooked – approach for communities to discipline global corporations is through persuasion and politicking. All of the changes in global trade, finance and monetary transactions discussed in this book ultimately require action by national and international institutions. Local governments, working with citizens' groups, can learn from their corporate colleagues how to press these bodies to act with greater sensitivity to local interests. They can orchestrate citizen pressure through education, debates, films, newspapers and letter-writing campaigns. They can set up lobbying offices in the national capital and in key cities abroad like Brussels, Geneva and Tokyo. They can try to unseat politicians who are unsympathetic with the community agenda and organize support for pro-community candidates.

It is ironic that 'non-political' institutions like private corporations have no qualms about trying to influence national and international decision-making, while 'political' institutions like local governments are inclined to steer clear of politics. Seeing themselves as subservient to national policies and as lacking the 'competence' to address international concerns, many local officials are reluctant to express opinions over the shape of the global economy.

A recent survey in the United States revealed that the country's 36,000 municipalities have deployed a total of 116 registered lobbyists in Washington, DC.[1] Most US cities see no need to hire lobbyists because they expect their advocacy to be performed by the National League of Cities (NLC) and the US Conference of Mayors, which receive millions of dollars of municipal dues in part to support their lobbying operations. But the NLC has nine lobbyists, and the US Conference of Mayors has eight. With the attention of these advocates split on hundreds of issues, it's easy to see how they can get overwhelmed. Thus, for example, even though most US cities recognize the value of cutting Pentagon spending and rechannelling the savings back to municipal needs, they have only deployed a handful of staff to press the issue. The top twenty-five defence contractors, in contrast, have 265 registered lobbyists on Capitol Hill working around the clock to protect and expand the military's coffers.

Outside the United States the problem is much worse. The US Constitution at least protects the rights of local governments to lobby through the First Amendment. Other countries with stronger central governments are free to gag dissenting local voices altogether. In the 1980s, for example, when the Greater London Council and other Labour-run local councils sought to counter the Thatcher revolution, the Tories simply abolished them.

If communities are to regain their economic independence, they must formulate and amplify their views on a new Bretton Woods order. They might hold annual hearings on how the global economy is effecting their local economies, and how they could constructively change the global economy. The hearings might lead to the publication of a 'State of the City in the World' booklet, laying out a policy agenda for the coming year, which would be distributed to every member of the community. Communities might push this agenda by sending paid lobbyists to their national ministries and legislatures, as well as to the decision-making bodies of GATT, the World Bank and the IMF. Whatever communities do, it will be better than continuing their collective silence and effectively allowing corporate voices to monopolize the global debate over the rules for the world economy.

Regulation[2] A second way communities can discipline corporations is to regulate products passing through their jurisdictions or businesses deciding to locate there. Product regulation is straightforward and common. Many communities enact tough standards for products entering their jurisdiction to protect public health, safety, welfare and morals. Sometimes communities also ban products produced under unacceptable circumstances, such as through child or prison labour. Most countries, however, frown upon these 'extraterritorial' ordinances, fretting that they might trigger retaliatory actions or trade wars.

Communities have relatively broad powers to regulate corporations with plants, offices and stores located within their jurisdictions. To varying degrees in different countries, municipalities can enact higher minimum wages, better working conditions and stronger environmental standards than their national governments do. They can require regular reports on, say, energy and resource use, levels of pollution and waste, numbers of labour violations, and worker health and safety records. Of course, these regulations do not circumvent the original problem: the more regulations communities impose, the less likely corporations will locate there.

Communities, therefore, have sought to provide carrots in the form of subsidies, tax breaks and regulatory relief to induce corporations to come or stay. According to the Chicago-based Midwest Center for Labor Research,

> During the 1980s, 90 percent of major new plants constructed [in the United States] and 50 percent of major plant expansions benefited from one or more forms of public investment: Industrial Revenue Bonds, Urban Development Action Grants, Community Development Block Grants, infrastructure improvements, property tax reductions or abatements, Jobs Training Partnership Act funds, or various state funds for financing and training.[3]

States and cities also have used a 'stick' approach to punish a corporation that leaves. The city of Chicago sought to enjoin the parent company of Playskool in 1983 from shutting down on the grounds that it had promised not to sell off its assets for twenty years. The case was ultimately settled out of court, when Playskool promised to keep the plant open one more year, to set up a job-placement centre for unemployed workers and to contribute US$50,000 to support displaced workers.

After General Motors announced its plans to relocate a plant from Ypsilanti, Michigan, the city sued to stop it. A lower court held that the city had an implied, common-law obligation to compensate the community. A higher court reversed the ruling and the case is now on appeal. This court decision would have been less vulnerable to challenge had the city passed an ordinance to regulate corporate closures. A community might demand that all companies with more than, say, fifty employees provide at least three months' notice and two months' severance pay before closure.[4] Violations would be punishable by a fine, large enough to enable the city to pay severance to displaced employees. In fact, between 1979 and 1982, ten state legislatures considered bills that would have required corporations to give one to two *years* notice to the community before closure.

Another stick is to require any corporation shutting down to offer its factory to the workers or to other investors in the community. Pittsburgh, Pennsylvania, passed an ordinance mandating that firms about to close a factory issue an economic impact statement exploring alternatives, including the possibility of an employee buy-out. (A Pennsylvania court, however, invalidated the law on the grounds that the city exceeded its power.) Washington state considered a 'social compact' bill in 1992 that would have given workers the 'right of first refusal' – that is, the right to be the first purchaser (at market value) of a plant about to be sold. Some states have created special funds to assist with worker buy-outs: Illinois and Michigan have revolving loan funds for such purposes, and California, Illinois, and Michigan authorize the use of industrial development revenue bonds for buy-outs.

Some states allow state or local governments to use their powers of 'eminent domain' to take over plants about to be closed. The US and state constitutions require that such takeovers serve a public purpose and the owners receive 'just compensation', but compensation can be below (often far below) market value. The states of Illinois, Ohio and Pennsylvania permit government takeovers whenever plant closure or relocation will adversely effect the local economy.

All together, these laws can provide a powerful arsenal for local governments to raise the costs of corporate exit and deter sudden departures. The limitation of the strategy, however, is obvious: the more onerous the restrictions, the less likely corporations will set up shop in the community in the future.

Selective investment and contracting One way communities can escape corporate retribution for regulation is to place financial rewards and punishments on firms not located in the jurisdiction. This can be done through public investment and contracting decisions. Most communities invest surplus revenues and the pension funds of public employees, and most buy goods and services and enter contracts with private corporations. These proprietary decisions are usually made on strictly economic criteria: which investments will provide the greatest long-term rate of return? Which goods and services are cheapest? Which contractors are most reliable? But some communities have begun to add political criteria to these decisions as well, rewarding well-behaved corporations and punishing misbehaving ones.

Perhaps the most successful use of selective investment and contracting was the sanctions movement against South Africa. Over the last twenty years hundreds of municipalities worldwide decided to stop investing or entering contracts with firms doing business in South Africa. In the United States a total of 27 states, 25 counties and 101 cities enacted sanctions. These US jurisdictions decided to reinvest more than US$20 billion in 'clean' firms with no ties to apartheid. Some US communities also refused to do their banking with or buy goods from companies involved in South Africa. The Port of Wilmington, Delaware, refused to unload any cargo from South Africa. Once these sanctions were put into effect, two-thirds of all American companies with ties to South Africa sold off their equity shares and the US Congress passed a Comprehensive Anti-Apartheid Act in 1986, mustering the supermajority needed in both legislative houses to overcome President Ronald Reagan's veto.

An important lesson of the anti-apartheid movement is that a relatively small number of cities can have a dramatic effect on corporate behaviour. Corporations fear the loss of even one major municipal client; the prospect of losing hundreds of clients worldwide is terrifying to them.

For many communities the anti-apartheid campaign was the first time they realized the kinds of power their investment and contracting decisions could give them over corporations. Since then, they have begun to add other 'screens'. A dozen cities and counties in the

United States refuse to buy goods from firms involved in the manufacture of nuclear weapons. Cottage industries have sprung up to promote 'socially responsible investment' and 'green purchasing'.

These initiatives could be the beginning of a social charter drafted and enacted at the grassroots level. A problem with a decentralized approach is that ten cities might adopt ten different investment/ purchasing screens and send ten different (and possibly contradictory) signals to corporations. But one can imagine progressive cities worldwide coming together, formulating a standardized code of conduct, setting up a central clearing house of information on corporate behaviour and agreeing to invest or to purchase products from responsible corporations. A consortium of communities and nongovernmental organizations might attempt to grade corporate behaviour annually, just as investment houses regularly grade corporate economic performance. Any firm with a poor rating would be ineligible for municipal business.

One consequence of this strategy might be the emergence of two global blocs of communities, each endorsing different economic paradigms and each doing business with different corporations. The 'neoliberal bloc' might enjoy cheaper goods and higher rates of return off their investments, but also would have to endure deteriorating working conditions and environmental quality. The 'socially responsible bloc' would give up some economic efficiency for a higher quality of life. Even though the communities and corporations in the latter bloc would start out in the minority, over time, as more workers in the neoliberal bloc lost jobs and pay, as their problems from pollution and unsafe products multiplied, as more ecology, labour and social change organizations emerged to respond to these problems, more and more communities and corporations would probably begin to choose quality over efficiency. The mere existence of an alternative bloc would give progressive politicians and activists a concrete goal for organizing.

Community ownership A more direct way to ensure that corporations do not desert a community is to root ownership there. If a community owns and operates an enterprise, it will only allow relocation when it's clearly in the interest of a community. An owner deeply connected to a home base would examine not only rates of return of relocation in the abstract but also the impacts on local employment and community life.

There are two reasons why a rational community would favour industrial retention more than a private owner. First, a private owner is looking for the highest rate of return, while a community owner need only look for a rate of return above zero. In 1975 Sperry Rand

Corporation decided to shut down a subsidiary called the Library Bureau in Herkimer, New York, because it was not achieving a rate of return of 22 per cent, the ambitious target the parent company had set for all its subsidiaries.[5] Closure of this plant, which employed 250 people, would have decimated the community. So the workers and local residents decided to buy the firm from Sperry Rand. A third of the money was raised by selling US$1-2 shares of stock, and the rest came from loans from local banks and the US Department of Commerce. In its first year of operation under new management the firm earned a 17 per cent rate of return – a return inadequate for Sperry Rand but more than enough for this small community in New York State.

There's a second economic reason a community owner will retain an industry more diligently than a private owner: to avoid devastating transition costs. When a company abandons a community, it rarely has to pay unemployment compensation and welfare benefits. Nor does it have to figure out how ancillary businesses will be kept alive now that fewer people have jobs or disposable income. It almost never has to cope with plummeting property values and a depleted tax base that can no longer support basic services like schools, hospitals, street repairs, electric utilities and police. What economists reify and dismiss as regrettable 'externalities' are in fact significant enough to motivate a community to prop up a business with even a negative rate of return. The lay-off of thousands of steel workers in Youngstown, Ohio, in 1977 cost the federal government US$70 million in unemployment compensation, welfare payments, lost taxes and other costs.[6]

Even in the United States, where hostility to 'socialism' runs high, there is significant precedent for community involvement in the local economy. US state and local governments have created more than 6,300 public–private partnerships to build highways and bridges, to run electric and water utilities, to dispose of hazardous wastes, to operate ports and to perform other services.[7] Because these enterprises are typically engaged in public works, it is hard to imagine their being tempted to move overseas. The New York Transit Authority is hardly interested in running light-rail transit in Manila. But public authorities also can prevent mobility if they acquire or sell industrial plants. Pittsburgh responded to the departure of its steel factories by creating the Steel Valley Authority, a consortium of workers, the community and private investors that converted an old metal-works plant into the City Pride Bakery.

US state and local governments also have set up special funds to promote regional economic development.[8] Twenty-five US states have at least one venture capital fund to finance enterprises that mainstream banks deem too risky and that promise only long-term returns. Michigan has eight separate financing programmes. Many US state and local pension funds are practising economically targeted investments within their regions. The Colorado Public Employees' Retirement Association, for example, plans to place twenty per cent of its investments in Colorado investments. Because these public funds generally are given to private firms that benefit the region, there is still the possibility that the beneficiaries will take the benefits and run. A better policy for preventing capital flight, rarely practiced, would target public investments in *public* enterprises.

Of course, public enterprises need not be necessarily run and operated by governments per se. As the examples above suggest, there are many models for public–private partnership. One alternative is to create a privately held corporation whose shareholders must be community residents. Integrating some community ownership of private firms should be sufficient to convince most of them not to consider moving away to lower-wage, less responsible communities.

Delinking A fifth community strategy to cope with mobile corporations is to unplug, selectively, from the global economy. Not all progressives would support this approach. Many critics of GATT and the North American Free Trade Agreement argue that stronger social charters alone can remedy their defects. The problem is, however, that even so-called 'fair trade' is at odds with self-reliance – and self-reliance is a critically important objective for community wellbeing. Most communities, if they could do so, would like to provide their citizens with adequate jobs, food, education, health care and housing without either relying on outside support or creating new problems for those outside of the community. As Johan Galtung, a leading peace studies theorist, states:

> [T]he basic rule of self-reliance is this: produce what you need using your own resources, internalising the challenges this involves, growing with the challenges, neither giving the most challenging tasks (positive externalities) to somebody else on whom you become dependent, nor exporting negative externalities to somebody else to whom you do damage and who may become dependent on you ... The justification for so doing is clear: we will enjoy the positive externalities, rather than giving them away, and at the same time will be responsible ourselves for the negative externalities.[9]

It's theoretically possible for a community to achieve a desired level of production and consumption based entirely on its own resources and then to use surplus production for export. But the fact is that trade almost invariably brings with it specialization and draws resources away from the production of goods and services that some citizens might regard as essential for local self-reliance. Moreover, the financial flows necessary to sustain imports and exports, which are typically overseen by outside traders, banks and arbitragers, create leakages in the local economy. These problems are exacerbated when trade is unfair – when low-wage, environmentally irresponsible jurisdictions can produce cheap goods that undercut local production. For all these reasons, a community may well decide that the best way to create a robust economic future is to maximize local self-reliance and to minimize trade. There are four overlapping strategies that communities might employ to accomplish this.

The first and most crude is to impose legal barriers against trade. At one extreme a community might forbid the entry of any foreign goods into its jurisdiction. Absolute protectionism, however, is hard to enforce; coercive, goods-confiscating checkpoints are needed at every community entrance. It's also largely irrelevant, since smart producers will gladly set up shops selling foreign goods close to the borders of protectionist communities, and smart consumers within those communities will gladly purchase goods at the border stores.[10] Placing tariffs on foreign goods entering a community is less onerous, but still carries problems concerning coercion, enforcement and cheating. Perhaps the best a community can do is to label foreign goods as such and convince residents of the virtues of voluntarily buying local. The essential argument is this: spending a little more on locally made bread is worth the benefits of keeping local bakers employed, who in turn will spend their income locally.

A second strategy is to create and support diverse local industries. Through the community-support or community-ownership measures discussed in previous sections, local governments can assist industries or create these industries themselves. A community-owned and operated banking system, for example, might be desirable to ensure that deposits were reinvested locally rather than in distant countries.

A third strategy is to establish a local monetary system. A community currency, whether in the form of real coins and paper or government-tallied credits and debits, provides a means of encouraging transactions involving local goods and services. A local government might serve as a central bank, overseeing distribution of the currency and setting rules for how it can be used. It also might disallow exchanges of local for national currency except at specially designated banks that used legally pegged exchange rates. A mark of good local citizenship would be to perform work only for local currency or to use local currency as much as possible for needed purchases.

A final strategy to increase self-reliance is to use local natural resources more efficiently. Investment in solar and wind energy production can prevent the costs of depending on foreign uranium, coal, oil or gas, or importing electricity derived from these fuels. Investment in local agriculture (including greenhouses) can reduce food imports. Investment in technologies for water conservation can reduce the need for diverting far away rivers or depleting nearby water tables. Recycling wastes can eliminate the need for imports of steel, copper, plastic, glass and rubber.

Sceptics argue that the absence of communities that have achieved total self-reliance means that the goal is unattainable and unrealistic. But the goal should be to achieve as high a degree of self-reliance as possible. As communities acquire more wealth and technology, as they grow politically bolder in their willingness to redistribute resources, as they increasingly adopt appropriate technologies, they will certainly be able to become much more self reliant than they are today. All that is necessary is political will – and legal power.

Future Roadblocks and Opportunities

The five strategies outlined above suggest the kinds of basic powers communities need to cope with globalization. Specifically, local governments worldwide must insist on having broad powers to lobby, to regulate product sales and factory mobility, to provide subsidies or tax breaks to corporations, to invest and contract selectively, to create community owned and operated businesses and banks, to label local goods, to create local currencies and to rely on local natural resources.

Unfortunately, most local governments have only a few of these powers, and even those with extensive powers (such as US communities) are reluctant to exercise them. Moreover, the possibility of communities discovering and expanding many of these powers may have just been scuttled by the Uruguay Round of GATT. Consider the likely impacts of this agreement:[11]

- In theory GATT leaves communities free to lobby national and international bodies, but in practice it eliminates much of the leverage communities once had over trade policy. Lobbying at the national level is much less useful than it once was, since national decision-makers now must either accept or reject the

GATT regime as a whole, including all rulings from the new World Trade Organization. And at the international level, communities have little ability to influence global economic decisions, because GATT's decision-making procedures are characterized by secrecy, limited due process and corporate dominance.

• GATT allows pension funds to invest selectively, but limits the ability of local governments to purchase or enter contracts selectively.

• GATT essentially pre-empts local laws concerning product safety with looser, more 'scientific' international standards.

• GATT's prohibition on local government subsidies, which include government loans, loan guarantees, tax abatements, guaranteed purchases, in kind contributions and price supports, might spell the end of community ownership of factories, banks, stores or services.

• Carrots that induce corporations not to move could be deemed trade-damaging subsidies. Sticks that punish corporations that leave might be viewed as protectionist if they effected, as many do, foreign-owned corporations more than domestically owned ones.

• Community labelling practices that induce consumers to purchase local products could be found to contravene GATT's requirement that 'products imported from the territory of any Member shall be accorded treatment no less favourable than that accorded to like products of national origin and to like products originating in any country'.[12]

• GATT might wipe out the possibility for communities to create their own currencies, since the purpose of such schemes is to induce community members to buy local and therefore discriminate against trade.

• Any local laws requiring the use of local resources could be viewed as an infringement on their import and export.

No one can say for sure whether GATT will be enforced in these onerous ways. Like any statute, its provisions must be interpreted by many courts and dispute-resolution mechanisms at the international, national and local level. But if past decisions are a guide to the future, there are serious grounds for worry. The problem is less the pronouncements of the WTO, which will appear slowly, and more those of national and local courts. In the 1971 case of Bethlehem Steel v. Board of Commissioners, for example, the Court of Appeals in California invalidated the state's 'Buy American' Act (which mandated that state and local government agencies purchase goods and enter contracts, if possible, with US firms), partially on the ground that it violated GATT.[13] It is not unreasonable to foresee a certain percentage of courts throughout the world favouring free trade over community empowerment.

Communities need to wake up and reclaim the powers necessary to cope with globalization, to create sustainable and self-reliant economies, and to restore meaningful governance. They must work quickly and effectively – by themselves and in coalitions – to undo the Uruguay Round and to expand their basic powers. If communities lobby, invest, contract and regulate wisely, they can begin to force global corporations to rise to a higher standard, and increase the chances of the world adopting a strong corporate code of conduct. If they insist on creating their own economic activity, anchored to the community through local ownership, they can prevent capital from fleeing to the world's 'maquiladoras', strengthen the security of local workers and reduce the vulnerability of the community to the ever less predictable currents of the global economy. None of these strategies will be easy. But the current strategy, really a non-strategy, in which communities continue to bargain down their quality of life to lure corporations without challenging them, is a guaranteed dead end.

Notes

1 'Main Street USA – Lobby or Lose It', *Global Communities* (Autumn 1991).

2 Much of the information in this section is drawn from: Roger Kerson and Greg LeRoy, 'State and Local Initiatives on Development Subsidies and Plant Closings' (Chicago: Federation for Industrial Retention and Renewal, 1989); and Hany Khalil, 'Top 10 Policy Hits of the 1980s and 1990s: Pushing the Envelope' (Washington, D.C.: Grassroots Policy Project, 1993).

3 Kerson and LeRoy, ibid., p. 49.

4 The Federal Worker Adjustment, Retraining, and Notification Act requires companies with more than 100 or more employees to give at least two months notice of a plant shutdown or major layoff.

5 Gar Alperovitz and Jeff Faux, *Rebuilding America: A Blueprint for the New Economy* (New York: Pantheon, 1984), p. 149.

6 Ibid., pp. 142–3.

7 Khalil, op. cit., p. 3.

8 Ibid., pp. 6–7.

9 Johan Galtung, 'Towards a New Economics: On the Theory and Practice of Self-Reliance', excerpted in Paul Ekins, *The Living Economy: A New Economics in the Making* (London: Routledge, 1986) p. 101.

10 Protectionism also carries a moral hazard. In Arkansas there's a rural county where the anti-liquor laws have remained in effect because of assiduous lobbying by the main church located there. A closer look, however, reveals that county is hardly dry, since liquor stores on the borders of the county do a thriving business. The rumour is that the liquor stores contribute generously to the church's lobbying efforts.

11 A detailed legal analysis of the impact of GATT on communities is forthcoming in Michael H. Shuman, 'GATTzilla v. Community Power', *Cornell Environmental Law Review*.

12 Agreement on Technical Barriers to Trade, Section 2.1.

13 276 C.A. 2d 221, 80 Cal. Rptr. 800.

17

A Just and Sustainable Trade and Development Initiative for North America

The Alliance for Responsible Trade, Citizens Trade Campaign, the Mexican Action Network on Free Trade and the Action Canada Network

On 25–27 March 1993, representatives of citizens' organizations from Mexico, the United States and Canada met in Washington, DC, to discuss proposals for a new social and economic agenda for the continent. The meeting included representatives from environmental, labour, religious, consumer and farm groups.

North America contains almost 14 per cent of the world's land, 7 per cent of its people and 30 per cent of its measured economic activity. From its indigenous peoples to the diverse array of Mexican, Canadian and US communities, the continent is rich in cultures and natural resources. For centuries, rivers and waterways, trading routes, travel and war have brought our people in contact with one another. For centuries some of this contact has enriched us all while other relations have enriched some at the expense of others.

The economic integration of our continent has greatly accelerated over the past quarter century, especially since the mid-1980s with the advent of the US–Canada Free Trade Agreement and the economic liberalization in Mexico that has accompanied that nation's entry into the General Agreement on Tariffs and Trade. Canada and the United States now trade more goods and services with one another than any other two nations, and Mexico has been the fastest growing trading partner of the United States. (For Mexico, the United States accounts for 70 per cent of its trade.)

Clashing Visions

Today, we are faced with a fundamental choice over the future integration of our continent. Two visions that are fundamentally at odds with one another have been placed in the public debate. The first vision is expressed in the proposed North American Free Trade Agreement signed on 17 December 1992, by George Bush, Brian Mulroney and Carlos Salinas – an agreement that would remove most trade and investment barriers between our nations. The 'free trade' or 'neoliberal' vision offered by the NAFTA's promoters claims to be one of accelerated economic integration in the name of enhancing US competitiveness against Asia and the European Community.

The alternative vision offers a democratic programme for North American integration based on principles of justice and sustainability. This vision is emerging from citizens' dialogue across the continent. These two visions clash on three levels:

- **Process** The NAFTA was negotiated in total secrecy by government officials, aided by advisory panels dominated by large transnational corporations. By contrast, the new vision is emerging from a democratic process of dialogue that includes all segments of society.
- **Policies** The clash of policies is laid out within this document. One vital difference is that NAFTA policies focus exclusively on the movement of goods, services and capital. The alternative vision focuses on policies that address social and environmental realities as well as the movement of people, or immigration, that accompany the flows of goods, services and capital. NAFTA policies try to restrict the role of government in society; the alternative vision acknowledges the positive role that government should play in social welfare and in providing incentives to steer market forces towards social gains.
- **Politics** The three national governments and the corporate backers of the NAFTA have attempted to pass the NAFTA by buying support – and buying off the opposition. The political vision of the just and sustainable option is one of building consensus among a rich diversity of communities and social sectors.

As an alternative to the NAFTA, the signatory organizations from Mexico, the United States and Canada commit ourselves to the long-term process of constructing more just and sustainable development initiatives in all nations of North America. This task will be much easier if NAFTA is not approved. New initiatives will address the inequalities among and within our countries, create public accountability for corporate integration and strive to make economic development beneficial to the greatest number of people. These initiatives address the problems not only of the US–Mexico border, but of other areas where large corporations have failed to meet environmental health and social needs. We also open the discussion to the creation of new regional political institutions to address the social consequences of economic integration; we should study the European Community and the European Parliament for lessons on this process.

While these proposals emerge from an ongoing dialogue among three North American nations, we believe that they have relevance to the entire world. The initiatives described here pertain to all nations that subscribe to the criteria of just and sustainable development. We invite other organizations and our governments to work with us in this effort.

The initiatives outlined below are offered as a starting point of a more democratic dialogue, and are based on sound principles. Respect for basic human rights, the promotion of democracy, citizen participation in decision-making, environmental sustainability and the reduction of economic inequalities among and within our countries should be the foundations on which North American development is built.

The Question of Fairness: Addressing Inequalities

Central to the problems of integration are the enormous economic disparities among the nations of North America. Mexico's citizens' groups have accordingly placed the issue of 'compensatory financing' at the core of their alternative development proposals. The experience of the European Community reinforces this emphasis. By providing tens of billions of dollars in structural and regional development funds, the EC has stimulated economic activity in relatively less developed sectors and countries. With these funds, some countries have been able to reduce social and economic inequalities and to strengthen cohesion and infrastructure within their borders and throughout the region. Certain EC projects have had adverse ecological consequences, however, offering both positive and negative lessons for future initiatives.

In North America, several proposals have been put forward to create a North American Development Bank. Some of the proposals offer nothing more than a reinforcement of the same top-down, unsustainable model of development that has characterized industrialization on the US–Mexico border. Some of the proposals also falsely claim that such a bank could be largely self-financing, when in reality much of the environmental clean-up and worker training that is needed will not pay for itself. We do support the development of new regional financing mechanisms, including a new regional bank, as long as such mechanisms address the needs of poor areas and poor people in all three countries. In addition, new institutions should be managed transparently and democratically with broad social, governmental and private participation.

Currently, less funds are available in North America than in Europe for this kind of compensatory financing effort. In addition to new funding mechanisms, however, there are three steps that would help reduce inequalities. Billions of dollars provided to Mexico through multilateral institutions could be better used; billions of dollars that flow from Mexico to the United States in debt service could be reduced; and some existing, small-scale funding mechanisms could be enhanced to address the needs of the poorer majority in Mexico.

Reform Multilateral Institutions
Over the past three years, the World Bank and the Inter-American Development Bank have committed about US$8 billion in loans to Mexico, more than has been provided to any other nation in Latin America. The conditions of the loans promote the export-oriented, privatization model common to these two institutions, conditions that have often deepened the inequalities and exploitation in that country; the loans have not succeeded in narrowing the gap between Mexico and its neighbours to the north.

Our nations should take the lead in thoroughly reviewing the operations of the existing lending institutions, with the long-term goal of reforming them to address inequalities and poverty in countries such as Mexico. We should then jointly call for the United Nations to convene a meeting that would focus on democratizing the institutions that govern the world economy and would explore the need for new institutions to promote equitable, sustainable and participatory development.

Reduce Debt
Mexico remains the second largest debtor nation in the developing world. Payments to service this debt are a major drain on the country's resources. No development strategy can achieve significant progress without substantial debt reduction. Realistic debt reduction plans that are not tied to International Monetary Fund and World Bank conditionalities would free resources to fund development initiatives. Debt reduction schemes should steer the payment of debt service in local currency into a development fund that is administered in a

democratic manner. The Mexican Action Network on Free Trade has designed proposals for such funds that, in addition to debt swaps, could be financed through domestic and foreign contributions and would be administered with substantial participation of non-governmental organizations.

The NAFTA does not address the need for debt reduction. Large foreign debts in both the United States and Canada are also an issue, but since debt restructuring schemes in these countries do not involve World Bank and IMF conditionalities, the debt debate differs significantly from that of Mexico.

Support Small-scale Development Foundations

In recent years, small-scale community foundations have emerged to improve living conditions for poor Mexicans by supporting high-impact social service projects. These foundations have successfully involved poor Mexicans in designing, planning and executing innovative projects. We need to share the lessons of the more successful of such ventures in Mexico and in other countries, and encourage governments and the private sector to assist these foundations. The Mexican Action Network on Free Trade has also proposed the creation of a publicly managed environmental fund to rehabilitate forests, rivers, lakes and other areas adversely affected by past commercial activities.

Trade Adjustment Assistance

None of our three countries has a plan for assisting the millions of small farmers and *campesinos* displaced by farm concentration and economic integration. In Mexico, this land concentration process has been speeded by the reform of Article 27 of the Mexican constitution, which now permits the sale of *ejido* lands. Nor has any of the three countries adequate programmes to assist workers displaced as a result of increased integration. A new guaranteed funding source should be established in each country to supplement the inadequate trade adjustment assistance funds for job retraining and agricultural and infrastructural development in communities, industries and companies affected by growing integration.

Such assistance must be accompanied by a broader package of programmes designed to discourage concentration of businesses and land in the hands of a few large corporations and to encourage support for small and family-owned farms and businesses. Experience worldwide has shown that such efforts are at the heart of sustainable development and lead to the creation of stable jobs at reasonable wages.

International Rules

While the power and mobility of large, private firms to shift jobs, capital, factories and goods across borders have increased – and would increase further under the NAFTA – the ability of our governments to protect the basic economic and social rights of our people has decreased. As governments find it harder to meet citizens' needs for employment and other necessities, corporations have not filled the gap. We must address this shift in power, pressing our governments to create the necessary checks and incentives to ensure that corporate activity contributes to the common good. There are several areas, detailed below, in which action is needed.

Enforceable International Workers' Rights and Labour Standards

A new trinational agreement should incorporate comprehensive, multilateral protection of workers' rights and workplace health and safety standards. Such protection will enable all people to benefit from the economic activity generated by North American development. It will also make the growth of workers' income, including average industrial wages, commensurate with growth in productivity and advance workplace standards and workers' rights throughout the region. We acknowledge that the form this protection takes must address the uneven levels of development among our nations and the disparity in power among our three governments. As a first step, the labour-related provisions of the UN Universal Declaration on Human Rights and ILO conventions are the appropriate standards to be enforced by each country as an essential element of regional economic integration.

Once these standards are recognized, a central feature of any new agreement is making international workers' rights enforceable through a fair, and reasonably swift trinational process. The three countries would negotiate the precise composition of 'internationally recognized' workers' rights, including, at a minimum, the ILO conventions of the right to free association and to organize, the right to collective bargaining, and the right to strike, as well as protections against child labour, prison or forced labour, and all forms of discrimination.

Any government or private party with pertinent information could bring complaints about violations of these rights to the relevant enforcement bodies. We must strive to create a dispute resolution process that restricts fines to the guilty parties.

We should also develop mechanisms that will, over time, raise wages worldwide towards the highest prevailing rates. In the context of a new North America agreement, the minimum wage in the traded goods sectors of the two lower wage countries should move as quickly as possible towards that of the highest wage country. Minimum wages in each country should allow for a decent quality of life.

Environmental Rights and Standards

There is no international equivalent to the International Labor Organization in the field of the environment. As a result, no code exists for international environmental standards. As a first step in this direction, we advocate the trinational negotiation of a set of basic continental environmental rights, such as the right to know (about public environmental threats) and the right to a toxic-free workplace and living environment. We also support launching a process to define minimum regional (or international) environmental standards. As with workers' rights and standards, these safeguards would be set as 'floors' rather than ceilings and enforced with fines or other appropriate trade measures. Our governments should also clarify their commitment to existing international environmental treaties and the inability of trade agreements to override them.

Further, any new North American agreement should be preceded by impact assessments for labour and the environment in the United States, and equivalent assessments in Canada and Mexico.

Codes of Conduct

Historically, most trade agreements have enhanced the ability of corporations to shift investment and goods across borders without imposing responsibilities on firms to address the harmful social or environmental effects of these activities. As companies become more global, we need new codes to increase the public accountability and corporate responsibility of private firms. Listed below are several key existing and potential mechanisms for codifying corporate behaviours.

1. *United Nations Code of Conduct*: Beginning in the mid-1970s, the United Nations began negotiating a code of conduct on transnational corporations that prohibited bribery of public officials, required corporate disclosure of potential dangers of products and production processes, banned the export of goods or factories deemed unsafe in one country and several other measures. The Reagan administration played a prominent role in politicizing the negotiations; by the early 1990s, the negotiations deteriorated into gridlock. The process should

be revived and its scope broadened to include many of the standards and principles enumerated above.

2. *Maquiladora Code of Conduct*: A binational coalition of religious, environmental, labour, Latino and women's organizations are pressing US corporations on the US–Mexico border to adopt a set of standards in their plants that will ensure a safe environment on both sides of the border, safe working conditions, an end to sexual and physical harassment and a livable wage for workers.

3. *Individual Corporate Codes*: In recent years, Levi Strauss, Sears and a few other firms have begun to respond to union and public pressure by adopting their own corporate codes of conduct, committing the companies and their subcontractors to certain labour practices. These codes should be standardized and expanded to all firms that operate internationally, with each industry adopting appropriate standards.

4. *Fair Trade Marketing*: Alternative trade organizations in Europe and the United States have for years been promoting international trade with an emphasis on establishing a fair relationship between poor producers and consumers in the developed world. These organizations have spearheaded efforts in the European Community to adopt a new 'green seal' programme that will alert consumers to products that meet environmental standards at all stages of the production, packaging and disposal process. This could serve as a model for a North American system, with the addition of respect for workers' rights and labour standards as part of the 'seal' process.

5. *Foreign Environmental Practices Act*: Several groups on the US–Mexico border have proposed a US law that would require US–based corporations working in Mexico and other countries to follow US environmental standards, except when the standards of the host country are more stringent.

Sustainable Alternatives

In addition to addressing inequalities and setting new international rules, each country can take several proactive steps to promote more sustainable development of the continent. Such steps – left out of the NAFTA package – are outlined below.

Abiding by international human rights law All three nations should adopt the norms and procedures used by the United Nations and the Organization of American States and establish effective mechanisms to defend human rights.

High wage, high skill development Unless each country encourages high-wage, high-skill development that expands North American markets, workers in all three countries will continue to suffer the consequences of corporate strategies to reduce costs by lowering wages.

Alternative energy and natural resource policies Each country should adopt policies to speed the transition from fossil fuels and nuclear power to energy efficiency and clean renewables, a shift that will create jobs and improve the economy as it protects public health and the climate.

Sustainable agriculture In order for trade and agriculture policy to contribute to regenerating rural communities, all three nations should be encouraged to expand successful supply management systems and to negotiate international commodity agreements where possible, and any new agreement should help enforce the ban on exporting goods at prices below the cost of production. In addition, each nation, as well as sub-federal jurisdictions, should have the power to determine the level of health risk each is willing to tolerate in its food system.

The UN Commission on Sustainable Development Trade and development agreement negotiators should seek counsel and advice from the UN Commission on Sustainable Development to ensure that future agreements respect and encourage sustainable and equitable development.

The US–Mexico Border

The US–Mexico border, with some 2,000 foreign factories employing half a million workers on the Mexican side, harbours some of the worst environmental and labour conditions on the continent. As a result, there is an urgent need for action along the border. Dozens of citizens' groups on both sides of the border are taking the lead in developing innovative proposals for improvement. The following are some salient parts of proposed alternatives.

Immigration Perhaps the most glaring yet deliberate omission in NAFTA is the lack of attention to immigration issues. The human rights of immigrants, which are constitutionally guaranteed in each of the three nations, must be safeguarded and new rules to protect migrant rights and economic wellbeing should be instituted. As a first step, we call for the creation of a bilateral commission on violence at the US–Mexican border. With the participation of non-governmental organizations, the commission would investigate the excessive use of force by border control agents from both countries.

Polluter repairs principle Corporations should pay for and clean up the environmental damage for which they are directly responsible, and they should pay their fair share of taxes.

North American Commission on Health and the Environment The Border Ecology Project and the Proyecto Fronterizo de Educacion Ambiental suggest the expansion of the proposed North American Commission on the Environment to address public and occupational health issues.

The right to know The Texas Center for Policy Studies, working with other groups, has proposed legislation that would require US companies on the border to file with the Environmental Protection Agency toxic emission data comparable to that required under federal 'right to know' legislation.

The initiatives outlined above are offered both to clarify the deficiencies and problems of NAFTA, and to contribute to the framework for new trinational negotiations that can replace the proposed NAFTA package with a just and sustainable development initiative for North America.

18

Alternatives to the World Trading System

Reinaldo Goncalves and Luis Carlos Delorme Prado Goncalves

At the July 1944 meetings in Bretton Woods, New Hampshire, US and British leaders designed the World Bank and the IMF to govern relations in two of the three main arenas of the world economy: production and finance. Designs for an institution to govern relations in the third arena – trade – were left to a world conference in Havana in 1947, from which emerged blueprints for an International Trade Organization. Like the World Bank and IMF, the ITO responded to the widely shared desire to avoid the horrors of economic breakdown of the Great Depression years.

The Havana Charter of the ITO had clear objectives: to foster economic development and full employment. In this regard, trade policies and agreements were seen as instruments to achieve economic development through reductions of tariffs and non-tariff barriers, greater market access and the creation of dispute resolution mechanisms. Moreover, the ITO would deal with the need for new inter-governmental commodity agreements, preferential trade arrangements for developing nations, measures against restrictive business practices by transnational corporations and international cooperation for economic development and reconstruction. The ITO, as designed in the Havana Charter, was a development-oriented trade institution.

Despite the fact that fifty-three countries signed the Havana Charter to establish the ITO in March 1948, the US Congress refused to ratify the charter. Instead, the US government led a successful effort to get other nations to sign on to one small section of the ITO, an agreement that offered rules for the reduction of tariff barriers. This agreement, known as the General Agreement on Tariffs and Trade, has governed trade relations since 1948. The agreement is flawed, incomplete and heavily favours the powerful trading nations of the North. In the most recent round of GATT talks, the United States has bullied other nations into expanding GATT powers through the creation of a World Trade Organization.

The sections that follow describe the deficiencies of GATT and the proposed WTO. It suggests a new framework for world trade based on some of the old principles of the ITO, but updated to embrace a broader people-centred, environmentally sound and socially equitable agenda.

GATT: The Bastard Descendant of the ITO

The development of a post-Bretton Woods trading system is a complex issue that precludes a full analysis here, but the following points may be made. First, a free trade economic order has never been established since Bretton Woods. Second, the liberal economic order that has been created through multilateral trade negotiations has been slanted towards the interests of the powerful trading nations that have refused to accept more liberal rules on industries in which they are not competitive. Third, the GATT, as the sole forum for multilateral trade negotiations under the Bretton Woods economic order, has never been able to defend the interests of the Southern countries and, therefore, has legitimated the protectionist actions of the Northern countries.

GATT was the first of a number of agreements that were to be negotiated under the auspices of the ITO, and it was meant to be a temporary arrangement, intended only to serve until the ITO was implemented. When it became clear that the Havana Charter would not be ratified, GATT became by default the basis on which negotiations on tariff reductions were conducted. Thus, the GATT is not technically an organization of which countries become members but an agreement with contracting parties.

All GATT members are expected to participate in conferences where parties negotiate tariff reductions. These are known as the rounds of multilateral trade negotiations. There have been eight rounds: Geneva, 1947; Annecy (France), 1949; Torquay (UK), 1950–1; the Dillon Round (Geneva), 1960–2; the Kennedy Round (Geneva), 1964; the Tokyo Round, 1974–9; and the Uruguay Round, 1986–93.

The two main principles of the GATT – non-discrimination and reciprocity of concessions – were a heritage of the US tariff bargaining process. If one is to presume that the trading partners are, at the outset, in an equal position, then these principles make sense; in the real world, which is made up of countries with unequal economic power and unequal shares of world trade, these principles cause problems, actually contributing to locking in the status quo.

First, negotiations begin bilaterally, by requests and not by offers; only the largest exporter of a product to one market is entitled to request tariff reductions from the importing country. Then, on the basis of the non-discrimination principle, the tariff reduction process will spread to other exporters to that market.

Second, according to the principle of reciprocity, tariff reductions should be exchanged for an equivalent concession from a trading partner. An equivalent concession is understood to be a tariff reduction that affects an equivalent volume of imports.

These mechanisms prevent Southern countries from assuming a strong role in the negotiation process. The large trading countries always determine the priorities and the limits of the negotiations. This happens because they are larger world suppliers, and thus the main beneficiaries of the principal supplier rule. They can also offer concessions on large absolute trade flows that can be a very small share of their overall import trade. On the other hand, a Southern country can offer a lot in relative terms, but, because it means very little to the Northern countries, the former carry very little bargaining power.

GATT and the South: Shortcomings and Inequalities

In the beginning of the 1960s, Southern countries were dissatisfied with the absence of developmental considerations in GATT and put pressure on the United Nations to call a conference on trade and development. Their demands led to the creation of a permanent UN Conference on Trade and Development (UNCTAD), and a new chapter in GATT that became Part IV (Trade and Development) of the General Agreement. The main innovation of Part IV was Article XXXVI which established that Northern countries should not expect reciprocity for commitments in trade negotiations to remove tariff and non-tariff barriers to trade of Southern contracting parties.

In reality, most of the accomplishments of the Kennedy Round (the first negotiations in GATT after the incorporation of Part IV) were in areas where Southern countries had smaller export interests. Thus, in practical terms, the negotiations prevented any real improvement of the GATT considerations on trade and development issues.

Moreover, the GATT principles were applied in an unequal fashion. Double standards were the rule when the interests to be defended were those of Northern countries. Despite an increasingly favourable overall trade balance in agricultural products, for example, the United

States imposed quotas on imports of products such as sugar, cheese and beef. When acceding to GATT, countries had to commit themselves to using tariffs for protection, not quotas. Nevertheless, the United States was able to obtain in 1955 a waiver exempting its quotas from GATT coverage.

When Southern countries became competitive in textiles, however, Northern countries found ways to exclude these products from the GATT rules. During the last few decades, trade in textiles and apparel products has evolved from trade relations encumbered only by high tariffs, to a system of regulations that includes both high tariffs and restrictive bilateral import quotas through a Multifibre Agreement. This resurgence of protectionist policies against imports from Southern countries was introduced in the GATT agenda by the United States in 1959 after a surge of imports from low-wage countries.

Northern countries have successfully pressured for the regulation of other labour-intensive markets as well in order to annul the Southern advantage. Every time that Southern countries became competitive in an industrial sector, non-tariff barriers were created to prevent them from benefiting from their lower labour costs. This happened first in agricultural products, then textiles and apparel, shoes, and, later, in steel.

Hence, the postwar trading system was never completely committed to free trade. In fact, behind the liberal arguments, there was a strong defence of Northern national interests, while the marginalization of Southern countries in the world trade system widened the gap between them and the Northern countries.

The World Trade Organization: Upgrading Inequality

As we approach the twenty-first century, GATT powers to act on behalf of Northern interests are being strengthened. The Final Act of the Uruguay Round of GATT on 15 December 1993 included an agreement for establishing a World Trade Organization. This organization will be responsible for all the concluding agreements of the Uruguay Round and will have 117 members (the current number of contracting parties of GATT). The basic feature of the WTO is that all countries that signed the Final Act are obliged to join all the agreements of the Uruguay Round, including the agreements on the new themes (services, trade-related aspects of intellectual property rights and trade-related investment measures). Hence, the WTO will deal with a far wider range of issues than GATT.

Does the establishment of the WTO go back to the origins of the Bretton Woods system, when the Havana Charter was endorsed by the main trading nations? Or, is the new WTO just an improvement and upgrading of the existing GATT structure? Or, does the WTO give rise to a more powerful instrument of inequality in the world trade system?

Like GATT, the World Trade Organization is clearly a trade-oriented institution. Even though there is some rhetoric about sustainable development and environment in the WTO text, the WTO focus and goal is trade liberalization. Indeed, international trade is treated as an end in itself, insofar as the fundamental objective is the removal of trade barriers. It is by no means true to suggest that the WTO aims at a generalized removal of obstacles to the free play of market forces in the world economy – managed international trade is still a basic feature of the world economy. As discussed in the previous sections, this has been one of the main shortcomings of the GATT system. In this regard, the WTO is not significantly different from GATT – a multilateral institutional framework oriented to the regulation of international trade flows.

There are other reasons for concern about the new World Trade Organization. The WTO will become a very powerful institution inasmuch as it has a mandate on services, foreign direct investment, intellectual property, in addition to trade in goods. Of foremost importance is the extent to which the WTO will override both national laws and international arrangements. In this regard, the WTO will be significantly more powerful than GATT.

The WTO is likely to become a powerful economic instrument of foreign policy for the stronger countries. This has been, indeed, the destiny of the remaining Bretton Woods institutions – the IMF and the World Bank. Moreover, the WTO represents the multilateralization and legitimization of the guidelines of an aggressive US trade policy based on threats to restrict market access and threats of cross-sectoral retaliation. At the multilateral level, the WTO will be a complementary instrument of forced market-opening initiatives of Northern countries at the bilateral level.

In fact, the WTO is neither a new institution going back to the origins of the Bretton Woods system (a development-oriented trade organization like the ITO, as designed in the Havana Charter), nor a simple upgrading of GATT. While it is true that the WTO embodies the institutional improvements of GATT brought about by the Uruguay Round, it is also true that it will enhance the shortcomings of GATT as a multilateral institution. The geopolitical imperatives will continue to have a key influence on decisions at the WTO, and the consensus-building exercises will maintain the evident bias in favour of the stronger countries. The well-known lack of transparency of the decision-making process in GATT is kept in the procedures of the WTO, as is the lack of public accountability.

From the Competitiveness Agenda to a People-centred International Trade Agenda

To match idealism with pragmatism is the real challenge facing societies. The current reality – the existence of an international economic system based on the mercantile principle, whereby everything (and everyone) is a commodity and, therefore, has a market and a price – is the quintessential obstacle. The ideal is to achieve an environmentally sound, economically rational and socially equitable development on a world scale.

In the aftermath of the Bretton Woods meeting, there was an important movement in the Southern world to change the focus from a 'market-centred international trade' to a 'development-centred international trade'. The Havana Charter, the proposal to establish the International Trade Organization, the centre versus periphery debate and the import-substituting industrialization policies were all parts of this overall movement.

Trade is not an end in itself. Indeed, there are different types of international trade that should not abide by the 'commodity principle' or be subjected to the implacable mechanism of 'market forces' (in particular, ethically condemnable trade, economically perverse trade, environmentally detrimental trade and socially unfair trade). A first and fundamental element of this new agenda would be to strictly regulate certain types of unacceptable international trade, like the ones mentioned above, at a supranational level.

Beyond this fundamental regulation, new rules and institutions must be built to shift the focus to a 'people-centred international trade' agenda. Such an agenda could begin by making use of the years of thought and energy put into proposals found in the Havana Charter, GATT, UNCTAD and the recent demands of non-governmental organizations. In all of these documents, there has been a positive agenda dealing with processes, structures and institutions related to changes in international trade covering the following issues: mechanisms to regulate undesirable international trade (such as that mentioned above); greater market access and preferential treatment for Southern countries; financial resources for development and structural adjustment; technology transfer to Southern countries; control of restrictive business practices; mechanisms to promote a fair international trade; and greater transparency, public accountability and democratization of negotiations and decision-making in multilateral organizations.

Re-imagining the World Trading System: The Power Dimension

All types of unacceptable international trade bring about profit and income opportunities – some of them, extraordinary. To design realistic strategies one has to keep in mind that some of the types of unacceptable trade mentioned above are actually promoted by national governments. Moreover, the survival of some of the weakest social groups of different societies may depend on these unacceptable forms of international trade. The most evident examples are the international trade networks of weapons and drugs. Whereas the former is formal (based on strict governmental regulations), the latter involves an informal network. By implication, the establishment of a new institutional framework to deal with these issues faces the opposition of governments and specific social groups in both Northern and Southern countries.

Also at issue is the extent to which people want to change their consumption patterns and lifestyles. The most basic change is, however, related to the redistribution of power, wealth and income – in both Northern and Southern countries. To the extent that governments tend to represent the interests of the most powerful social groups in each society, national governments are not immediate allies for an agenda of change. Yet national governments are the sole representatives of nations, and only governments can sign and enter into international agreements.

The role of national governments has become particularly important since the last decade, largely due to the increasing influence of the so-called 'competitiveness agenda'. With a clear liberal bias, government policy and structural and institutional reforms have been determined primarily by the objective of greater international competitiveness. The generalized dispute for larger shares of world trade has significantly affected social, environmental and economic policies in most countries. The basic outcome of this increasingly powerful international role is that fierce competition in the international arena has strengthened the arguments in favour of trade-centred strategies for development to the detriment of people-centred ones.

The democratic state should represent all social forces in a given society. However, governments seldom represent effectively the interests of the weakest groups in society. In consequence, a new multilateral trade organization should be open to the demands of local groups, community representatives, local or provincial governments and non-governmental organizations. Public accountability and public participation should be key elements of a new people-centred multilateral trade organization.

What would this new institutional configuration look like? Structurally, it would have a general council, an executive board and specialized commissions. Membership would be given to individual states and an equivalent number of representatives from non-governmental organizations. States would hold permanent membership, whereas the non-governmental members would rotate (to avoid co-optation) every five years. Non-governmental members would have one vote in the general council of the organization.

The guidelines and the decisions of the general council would be carried out by an executive board of twenty, of which ten would be governmental representatives (five from the North, five from the South), and ten non-governmental representatives. Again, each member of the executive board would have one vote. The specialized commission would be responsible for the operational side of the organization. The new organization would also have a director-general appointed by the executive board.

In the near future, however, international trade relations will remain in the realm of *realpolitik* and under the dominant influence of international economic groups. The convergence of an overwhelming desire for security of nation states with an all-consuming desire for profits by multinational corporations is the pillar of the present international world order (or, rather, disorder). Nor can the fact be ignored that in this struggle those who want deep changes are faced with powerful opponents, such as governments, local economic groups and consumers who benefit from the current international economic system.

However, a growing number of individuals and social groups are becoming aware of the need to strive for an environmentally sound, economically rational and socially equitable development – on a world scale. It is a matter of self-interest and survival. Here, one can talk not only about the 'have-nots' but also about the 'haves' in both Northern and Southern countries. A 'people-centred strategy' for international trade would incorporate these ideals, and would also be based on fundamental human values such as dignity, freedom, solidarity, peace and justice.

Undoubtedly, the WTO is not the appropriate multilateral arrangement for facing the challenge of shifting from a trade-centred institution to institutional arrangements associated with people-oriented strategies. Perhaps, the WTO will be more effective than GATT as regulator of international trade and as a dispute settlement institution. However, it is likely that the WTO will also become a more efficient instrument of economic foreign policy for Northern countries.

As the plight of the thirty-six million people unemployed in the North and the misery of hundreds of millions of people in the South grows worse, the world economic system will have to confront the fact that it is no longer creating employment for tens of millions of people and, therefore, is no longer creating consumers for the international goods it is producing. The lifestyles of millions are deteriorating in both Northern and Southern countries, where the 'wretched of the Earth' continue to be abandoned by their governments. The 'competitiveness agenda' – which subordinates fundamental human objectives to growing shares in the international market – is one of the main determinants in these phenomena. The challenge is to replace this agenda with a new agenda of people-centred international trade.

19

Accountability and the World Trade Organization

Myriam Vander Stichele

Through the [World Trade Organization], the Uruguay Round will change the way the world economy is shaped.

Peter Sutherland, Director General of GATT,
Davos, 28 January 1994

Since the end of the Cold War, trade has played a more central role in international politics as nations have placed increased emphasis on 'competition', 'economic security', liberalization and 'conquering markets'. As economic conflict grows, international trade institutions will have an important role to play. They will not, however, be able to contribute to increasing wellbeing if they are not made more accountable. After fifty years of Bretton Woods, it is clear that the top-down approach in the original design of the Bretton Woods institutions needs to be replaced by a bottom-up approach that is centred on accountability.

The Third Pillar of Bretton Woods

In discussions about the Bretton Woods institutions, one often forgets that the original design of the postwar international economic system was comprised of four institutions. The World Bank and the IMF were to be complemented by an International Trade Organization and a soft aid programme linked more directly with the UN. Each of the four institutions was to coordinate different aspects of macro-economic policy, such as balance of payments between countries, exchange rates, monetary, finance and trade policy. This coordination was considered to be the basis for avoiding the conditions which brought about the Great Depression and World War Two, namely, each country transferring its economic difficulties to other countries via protectionism and devaluations of currency.

This system of international macroeconomic coordination was incomplete from the beginning. The 'third pillar' of Bretton Woods, the ITO, was not created because the US Congress, and consequently other countries, failed to ratify it. (The soft aid programme became the International Development Association in 1960 and was linked to the World Bank.) One part of the ITO was created in 1948 as the General Agreement on Tariffs and Trade to deal with commercial policy and reduction of tariffs and trade barriers in order to avoid a new round of protectionism. GATT was set up on the provisional basis and as a contract with legal rights and obligations between the signatory governments.

In the following decades, a number of different proposals emerged in the United Nations community and from academics to revive the ITO, or create some other comprehensive trade body, expand GATT or change its provisional status. These were not implemented; instead, other UN organizations dealing with social aspects of the ITO agenda were created.

During the Uruguay Round of GATT, European and other countries proposed to give GATT a permanent structure which could also cover new sectors of the world economy. The proposals put GATT on an equal footing with the IMF and the World Bank and limited unilateral trade actions, especially by the United States. The design of the new World Trade Organization that was created in the Uruguay Round is a far cry from the original ITO, but it does stress cooperation of the WTO with the World Bank and the IMF in order to achieve greater global policy coherence.

The Need for Accountability

The new GATT round and the WTO are but the most recent manifestations of a global movement towards trade liberalization that includes the World Bank's structural adjustment programmes and the North American Free Trade Agreement. In all of these programmes, the impact of international trade on all aspects of the economy and society – including employment, food security, the environment, development, cultural diversity and civil society – has become more apparent. The new trade liberalization agreements are submitting more and more productive sectors to international rules by requiring certain minimum norms in domestic policies. The corporate contention that trade liberalizations will only have positive effects has been challenged. Indeed, more and more citizens' groups understand the importance of making trade policies more accountable in order to shift international trade from an end in itself to a means for better wellbeing.

More than 100 countries are part of the GATT and will be members of the WTO in 1995. These institutions currently lack the checks and balances and accountability vital to more democratic international decision-making.

The structure of these trade organizations is inadequate in part because the legislative and executive powers are not separated. Government representatives and ministers negotiate the new rules and are responsible for their implementation; parliaments or congressional representatives are hardly involved. There are no guarantees for equity, accountability or transparency in the GATT and the future WTO. Current decision-making structures are based on economic and bargaining power; the country which can offer the most market opportunities can bargain for the most benefits, while poorer countries are often left out of the negotiations because their trade has little global economic weight.

The instruments of the GATT and WTO are also deficient in that they do not advance basic objectives such as sustainable development, food security, poverty alleviation, employment and social equity, and international regulation of restrictive trade practises by global corporations. This constitutes a 'democratic deficit' not only between rich and poor countries but also between country representatives and the public.

This chapter suggests new ways to promote accountability of trade policies at the international level under the WTO.

Accountability of the WTO

The ITO was designed to deal in an integrated manner with the many ways in which trade affects commercial policy, employment, development, investment, practises by transnational corporations, commodities and even transfer of technology. It would have been an active organization in the management of the world economy. The ITO was also to have other important functions such as independent analysis, consensus-building, coordination of activities with other international organizations, technical assistance and training.

In marked contrast to the careful deliberations that went into the ITO, the creation of the WTO in the Uruguay Round followed little preparation. There were no formal negotiations and hardly any national parliamentary debate.

Predictably, the WTO is a far cry from the ITO proposal. Its link with the UN and especially ECOSOC – and therefore with the socio-economic basis for world peace – is totally left out; no structural link is made between the non-trade areas the ITO was supposed to deal with. The WTO is based on the GATT and Uruguay Round practises and agreements, with their strong bias towards free trade and protection of Northern interests.

The WTO is an umbrella organization for administering and following up all the agreements that were agreed to before and during the Uruguay Round in the area of goods (including textiles), agriculture, services, intellectual property rights and investment. The highest level for decision-making and carrying out the functions of the WTO is a ministerial conference which will meet at least once every two years. In between its meetings, different councils and committees will execute the functions of the WTO.

The WTO will be more than an executive 'umbrella' body. It will be of crucial importance because future discussions, negotiations and agreements on trade and related issues are likely to take place in the WTO. Issues that have already been proclaimed to be subject to future negotiations in the WTO include: the interaction of environmental and trade policies; international competition rules (which could cover subsidies, cartels, merger policy and public monopolies); workers' rights; and investment. The Uruguay Round agreements also provide for continuous negotiation on agriculture, services and trade related intellectual property rights. The creation of the WTO has clearly reinforced the tendency by the rich countries to take all economic decision-making out of the UN and to abandon the idea of the ITO.

The proposals that follow suggest ways to increase the accountability of the WTO through changes in the way it relates to parliamentarians, citizens' groups, other UN bodies and the World Bank and IMF.

Relationship with Parliamentarians

The negotiations of the Uruguay Round demonstrated clearly how little most parliamentarians and members of Congress have been involved in the establishment of the mandate for the negotiations of their governments, in the monitoring of the negotiations and in the assessment of the impact of the Uruguay Round agreements. Parliamentarians were only allowed to participate during the few ministerial meetings as observers. The few parliamentarians who took the effort to look into the talks complained about the lack of information, involvement and accountability.

In the WTO, no rules or structures are provided to ensure that the parliamentarians have a democratic say in the decisions or that the decisions within the WTO are accountable. As a first step, the WTO could set up a parliamentary body linked to it. Precedents for such a body include NATO, which has a 'North Atlantic Assembly' with two plenary sessions a year and committees and seminars in between. Likewise, the Joint Assembly of the Lomé Convention (between the European Union and the former European colonies) has shown how such a parliamentary body can establish a useful dialogue.

The purpose of a parliamentary body in the WTO would be to bring parliamentarians from all the member states together to discuss issues and problems related to the WTO and decisions by the ministerial conference. The body would issue opinions on rules, decisions and dispute settlements of the WTO which the ministers and councils would have to take into account. A workable structure would be an assembly of one to three parliamentarians per member country (depending on its size) that would meet once a year and at a time that would make influence on the ministerial conference possible.

Relations with NGOs and Civil Society

The WTO foresees that the general council, which meets in between the ministerial conferences, 'may make appropriate arrangements for consultation and cooperation with non-governmental organizations concerned with matters related to those of the WTO'. No further details were provided for at the official level before the signature of the Uruguay Round.

The GATT has had no rules or procedures on how to deal with NGOs and lobbies, let alone with civil society. In practice, business lobbies have been allowed to participate in the governmental delegations to GATT. Relations with NGOs were on an ad hoc or personal basis and the GATT secretariat chose the NGOs it wanted to consult with. GATT officials often met with business but inevitably found excuses for not attending NGO meetings.

A first step towards new dialogue and relations should be a code of conduct for non-governmental groups including businesses, NGOs and lobbies. It should establish rules for lobbies and organizations that want to monitor or participate in WTO proceedings. The code should define how NGOs can participate in the country delegations. It should state the obligations of lobbies to register and to disclose basic information about their organization or business. The code should also set obligations for WTO officials towards lobbies in terms of how to meet, what WTO information to give and how to transfer the demands and information from the lobbies to decision-makers at the WTO.

A second arrangement should be to set out the modalities of giving observer status to NGOs and lobbies concerning the decision-making process, the implementation and the dispute resolution mechanisms of the WTO. The UN procedures to deal with NGOs should be taken as an example. Public interest groups should be given special facilities.

In order to provide more openness on which better accountability can be based, the WTO should contain an institutional recognition of the right of access to information. This could take the form of a special information service set up by the WTO secretariat to deal with parliamentarians, NGOs, corporate interest groups and civil society. This service could be supplemented by an independent ombudsman. A special and sufficiently large budget should be allocated for these services. The basic function of this information service should be to provide all interested non-governmental individuals and organizations with the information they request in the form of publications, documents, speakers and interviews.

This service should also automatically provide basic documents and publications to parliamentarians and research institutions, and provide easily accessible information to the press and interested NGOs and businesses. The information service should also be active in the reverse information flow, to bring assessments of different sectors of society in different countries about a decision that will be or has been taken under the WTO. These different analyses should then be published and provided to all member governments of the WTO, the ministerial conference and, if applicable, to the dispute-resolution panel.

The information service should also investigate public complaints and bring them to the attention of the decision-makers and the dispute panels. One proposal calls for a new council that would ensure that the interests of all persons – governmental and non-governmental – affected by a dispute panel's decision would be taken into account in the opinion of the panel.

Relationship with UN and Other International Intergovernmental Organizations

The WTO general council is instructed to 'make appropriate arrangements for effective cooperation with other intergovernmental organizations that have responsibilities related to those of the WTO'. No more details are given. Hence, there are no structural links with other UN bodies as was provided for in the ITO. In order to balance national and corporate interests which governments mainly represent, and avoid domination by the powerful countries, active checks and balances should come from outside the WTO system. An 'external point of reference' should preferably be based within the UN, such as the International Court of Justice, the General Assembly or specialized UN agencies.

The tasks of the 'external point of reference' would be to settle disputes about interpretation of the WTO statutes, resolve conflicts between the WTO agreements and other international treaties, and investigate complaints from states and non-governmental bodies that are not being taken up by the WTO.

The UN Conference on Trade and Development should implement its original mandate of assessing the functioning of the global trading system. It should evaluate the WTO system and its impact on global trade, on economic, social and environmental issues, and on national economies and development. Proposals for corrections of the WTO system could be proposed and discussed in UNCTAD.

As the international trade agenda becomes more complex, it involves the fields of investment, technology, debt, money and finance, as well as such aspects of economic and social policies that are situated outside traditional trade parameters. Thus coordination of activities between the WTO and other trade organizations performing different functions on trade related matters is of utmost importance.

All UN agencies should increase their capacity to analyse the trade-related aspects of their sector and bring their analysis to the attention of the WTO's committees, councils and ministerial conference as well as to registered lobby groups of the WTO through publications, seminars and meetings with press and parliamentarians. UN and other intergovernmental agencies should be able to participate in the working sessions of the WTO related to their field. WTO officials should have the capacity to participate in working sessions of other intergovernmental organizations.

Coordination of the WTO with the World Bank and IMF

GATT proponents, including the organization's director general, claim that the WTO is (as was the ITO) the third pillar of Bretton Woods. They hide the fact that the ITO's conceived function was totally different. Accordingly, the GATT director general assumed a high profile as future chief of the WTO at the 1993 annual meeting of the World Bank and the IMF. Yet, the UN secretary general was not allowed to address these meetings. Legally and technically, however, the IMF and World Bank are specialized agencies of the UN and their guidance by the UN General Assembly and UN Economic and Social Council is still embodied in their respective charters.

Northern governments eroded further the role of the UN to coordinate the global economy by giving the WTO the function 'to cooperate, as appropriate' with the IMF and World Bank and its affiliated agencies 'with a view to achieving greater coherence in global economic policy-making'. This is one of the several functions the WTO took over from the ITO.

More economic policy coherence and cooperation at the international level would be beneficial in the current era of globalization and growing interdependence between trade, investment, finance and money. A number of UN institutions, especially UNCTAD, are well-situated to facilitate such cooperation.

However, the Northern-dominated Bretton Woods institutions and the WTO are increasingly taking over the global macroeconomic policy dialogue because they have the power to change things. This is a dangerous trend for many people in the South and for NGOs. Indeed, the cooperation between the two Bretton Woods institutions and the WTO will only reinforce the implementation of the liberal economic model of globalization that each of them embrace, with all the negative consequences for the environment, workers and communities. The power of each institution is heightened by their adherence to cross-conditionality. (Cross-conditionality refers to when one of the three institutions wants a country to implement its economic policy reforms or trade liberalization, and receives backing from the other two institutions which make support or concessions to that same country dependent on implementing the same measures. For instance, when the trade policy review mechanism of the WTO indicates the sector(s) where a country's liberalization is deemed insufficient, the structural adjustment programmes of the World Bank and the IMF could easily target these sectors for more liberalization.) Increased cross-conditionality will further reduce the flexibility which developing countries have enjoyed in their trade and investment policies under the multilateral trading system.

Cross-conditionality could be used in a positive way. For instance, World Bank and IMF programmes could be designed in such a way so that no more trade liberalization is required than what was agreed upon during the Uruguay Round and all succeeding trade negotiations. They could also decree that no more debt repayment is required than is possible from the export earnings under the existing trading rules and system.

In order to weaken the grip of the Bank, Fund and WTO, far greater input into their operations should come from the specialized UN agencies, and from international representatives of NGO groups and business. Input from the national level should come from finance, development, trade, labour and international affairs ministers in coordination with other national ministries. A special parliamentary committee should be created in each country to deal with international economic policy coherence. This input could be given in the form of publicly accessible advice, analysis and reports of monitoring before and after decisions are taken. It could bring into these agencies a greater emphasis on the objectives of food security, poverty eradication and ecologically sound development. Councils on trade and food security, trade and related social issues (employment, poverty alleviation, migration) and trade and sustainable development could be created. They would allow more flexibility and selectivity in the implementation of the international trade and finance rules for poor countries and groups who are negatively affected.

Only when parliaments, citizens' groups, other non-governmental actors, and UN agencies demand input into – and accountability from – the World Bank, the IMF and the new WTO, will these institutions begin to serve the ends of a more just world economic order.

Index